boys *in the* trees

boys *in the* trees

A MEMOIR

CARLY SIMON

FLATIRON
BOOKS
NEW YORK

BOYS IN THE TREES. Copyright © 2015 by Carly Simon. All rights reserved. Printed in the United States of America. For information, address Flatiron Books, 175 Fifth Avenue, New York, N.Y. 10010.

All song lyrics reprinted by permission of Carly Simon

Photographic credits:

Pages 50, 59, 60, 71, 72, 83, 102, 133, 134, 157, 158, 185, 186, 201, 202, 209, 210, 217, 220, 231, 245, 246, 262, 275, 276, 317, 341, and 356: copyright © Peter Simon
Page 261: copyright © Tom Hanley
Page 301: copyright © Bruce Weber
Page 302: copyright © Jim Shea
Page 318: copyright © Norman Seef
Page 371: copyright © Richard Koehler

All other photographs courtesy of Carly Simon

www.flatironbooks.com

The Library of Congress has cataloged the hardcover edition as follows:

Simon, Carly.
    Boys in the trees : a memoir / Carly Simon. — First edition.
        p. cm.
    ISBN 978-1-250-09589-3 (hardcover)
    ISBN 978-1-250-09590-9 (e-book)
    1. Simon, Carly. 2. Singers—United States—Biography. I. Title.
    ML420.S56296A3 2015
    782.42164092—dc23
    [B]   201503819

ISBN 978-1-250-09591-6 (trade paperback)

Our books may be purchased in bulk for promotional, educational, or business use. Please contact your local bookseller or the Macmillan Corporate and Premium Sales Department at (800) 221-7945, extension 5442, or by e-mail at MacmillanSpecialMarkets@macmillan.com.

Designed by James Sinclair

First Flatiron Books Paperback Edition: October 2016

10   9   8   7   6   5   4   3   2   1

Dedicated to the first Orpheus, Richard L. Simon, my father, my beloved hero, understood too late for our peace to come during his lifetime.

CONTENTS

BOOK ONE

BOOK TWO

BOOK THREE

BOOK ONE

Uncle Peter "Snake Hips" Dean.

My Father, 1918, at twenty-one.

My mother, 1930.

Chibie (pronounced Sheebie), who would never allow a picture of her taken. Sorry, Chib.

CHAPTER ONE

133 west eleventh street

This day may have been *the* day, the very day when my identity was born. Before the incident occurred, I didn't think about who I was. After, I would spend the rest of my life testing myself to see if I had been right.

The whole family was gathered after dinner to make the acquaintance of a possible nurse for Peter, my brother, just born five months before. Lucy and Joey, my two older sisters, and I were all under the age of eight. We lived in the top floor of a six-story town house on Eleventh Street.

"Quick, girls, it's almost eight, the plane got in an hour ago. Get dressed and wear shoes and socks and brush your hair." Mommy was holding a cigarette between her lips. She tried to get a brush through the tangles of my feathery hair, and finally grabbed a barrette, attempting to get my hair to go somewhere it stubbornly wouldn't go. She left it in a web of blond knots and went on to an easier task: brushing Lucy's hair.

Andrea Simon still had to neaten up her chignon, don her black calf heels, and apply a new layer of lipstick. She always wore bright red.

From at least three rooms away I could hear Daddy playing the piano: a strong, beautiful classical piece he'd been working on. It sounded just like a record.

Daddy had been in the hospital for five weeks after Peter was born. He had had a "nervous collapse." I would not learn about psychology until later, when the names and labels and diagnoses would collect and sprawl before me.

"Quick, girls." Mommy hurried us along. "Don't forget your manners," she might have repeated several times so it would stick.

"I wish he'd play something from *Carousel* or *South Pacific*," Mommy thought aloud. "It would make Mrs. Gaspard feel more comfortable, I should think. Rachmaninoff isn't for this kind of meeting," as if any of her three young daughters would know. She really did mean it, though, because she issued one final direction to us and then walked very fast into the living room to tell Daddy, I presume, to stop playing what he was playing and play something more "fun." We girls followed her and could hear them having a minor argument, and then Daddy started playing "The Man I Love," from *Strike Up the Band*, by George Gershwin. Gershwin had sent him a copy. My father was at the center of the publishing world in 1948, and he had gotten to know Gershwin while the company was doing a book on him. Daddy had started the company, Simon & Schuster, in 1924, with Max Schuster, and by 1948 things were only getting better.

"And he'll be big and strong, the man I love," Joey sang at the top of her voice. Daddy looked up approvingly at his eldest daughter. Mommy had gone for a minute to neaten her hair, and no one noticed that I was not only barefoot but I also had not changed out of my nightgown. It was almost as pretty as a dress, though. The best thing was that Daddy was back! Back to his old self! He was back at the top of his game.

The doorbell rang, and Mother, coming refreshed from her and Daddy's bedroom, said in a singsong voice, "Coming." She opened the big, heavy front door, and a woman entered slowly and with the grace of a ballerina. She was tall and had an attractively square head surrounded by light red, very wispy hair. I was nervous that maybe she would be very strict. But she was so tall and regal, us kids all came to the same conclusion: the potential nurse was auditioning for the job the way an actress would for a part in a play.

Daddy stopped playing and came out in front of the piano and introduced himself to Helen Gaspard. It was the kind of exchange Daddy was famous for: witty and charming. Helen seemed quite taken with him, as was everyone. With his height, standing straight at six foot five, his narrow and piercing blue eyes, and his full lips, he looked like a man back on the track. A man who could do almost anything.

Mother spoke to Helen as if she were sauntering down the gangplank of the *Mayflower*, a slowly enunciated, plummy Philadelphia accent. The accent was real—she had been born there—but it had also been consciously honed by watching Katharine Hepburn movies. Helen, however, was from *Canada*, and Mother's pretentions were lost on her.

The entrance and placement of the Simon daughters must have looked choreographed: first Joey, tall and gangly but ultra-sophisticated, with perfect constellations of freckles like Daddy's crossing her straight and perfectly proportioned nose. Her eyes, like Daddy's, were narrow and blue, and her mouth was ingénue-perfect. She wore a white cotton blouse and a gray cardigan carefully tossed over her shoulders in just the right careless manner— a touch maybe inspired by some late-night Lana Turner melodrama. Her decorous full plaid skirt came to the middle of her slightly knock-kneed legs, and her white high socks fit neatly in black patent leather Mary Janes.

Lucy, five years old, was as demure as Bashful the dwarf. Her nose and freckles were almost identical to Joey's, but Lucy's eyes were like those of an Eskimo princess who had gazed too long into the icy waters of the North, causing a permanent squint to form. Lucy wore a rose-colored velvet dress with a white lace collar and, like Joey, patent leather Mary Janes. "Sweet" was written all over her, as she half hid behind her regal and slightly aloof older sister.

At almost three, I was the baby girl, a waif, blond sprouting in competing directions from my scalp. My nose was wider at the bridge than both my sisters', a source of embarrassment for my father, who, I would later find out, favored the Nordic look in the women he loved. My nose wasn't the only way I disappointed him. After two daughters, he'd been counting on a son, a male successor to be named Carl. When I was born, he and Mommy simply added a *y* to the word, like an accusing chromosome: *Carly*.

My mother made introductions, oldest to youngest. "This is Joey . . ."

Making perfect eye contact, Joey took three steps forward to shake Helen's hand. "And this is our darling Lucy," my mother went on. Lucy approached shyly, before hurrying back to her starting position and Joey's protective hand. At last it was my turn.

"Carly, sweetheart, this is Helen. Can you say hello?"

I still remember that moment, that night, when I tapped into a new, unfamiliar part of my personality: I wanted to be noticed.

My uncle Peter had recently taken me to see the old 1927 film *The Jazz Singer*, starring Al Jolson. At that second, the only image that came to my mind was of a man in blackface, folded down on one knee, arms outstretched. Barely thinking, I jumped onto the nearby coffee table. With all eyes on me as I bent down onto one knee, my toes curled under to position my weight and steady my balance, I extended both arms, waving my hands and calling out, with as much volume as possible, a single cheery, brassy:

"HI!"

The town house at 133 West Eleventh Street, between Sixth Avenue and Seventh Avenue South in Greenwich Village, was my first home, the building where I, during the winter season, spent my first six years. There were six floors in all, with two apartments on each, and my parents had combined the two highest units to create a rambling penthouse. The style, if any, was eclectic, the rooms furnished in Simon-family Victoriana, books mashed and sprawling from cases and shelves barely able to contain them. Everything crowded together; nothing fit or matched. The children's rooms were divided by plywood partitions that didn't quite reach the ceiling, with single beds, off a hallway lined on both sides with little slots housing our shoes, sneakers, and boots. Dresses and coats drooped from little hangers off a pole. It wasn't a matter of money, although my parents did like to think of themselves as being thrifty.

As the owner of 133 West Eleventh, Daddy populated our building with family members, extended relatives, friends of friends, people who worked for us, and even his colleagues, creating a close-knit boardinghouse of sorts. Among the residents was my mother's mother, Chibie, who lived in a third-floor apartment with our Irish-born cook and nanny, Allie, and one floor below were my father's sister Aunty Betty and Uncle Arthur and their two daughters, Jeanie and Mary (Jeanie was my best friend). Below them lived my father's younger brother Uncle Henry and his wife, Roz, and close by, too, was Daddy's lawyer and friend, René Wormser, who would later play a part in my father's professional unraveling. Old friends of Chibie, assorted nurses and caretakers, as well as the building's superintendent, Mr. Porter, filled out the other apartments. Some paid rent; Daddy took care of the rest. The residents of 133 moved up and down, from floor to floor, thanks to Jimmy, our elevator man, who opened and closed the iron doors with an accordion flourish. When I was little, Jimmy would always ask me, "Which floor, little lady?" That exchange never got tired.

It was Chibie, above all, who fascinated me. Who was Chibie? Where had she come from? No one knew for sure, and Chibie's origins were complicated. One story went that she was the illegitimate daughter of King Alphonso XIII of Spain and a Moorish slave he had gotten pregnant. When Chibie's mother visited the king, infant in hand, he promptly dismissed them. Eventually, Chibie was handed off to another slave girl planning passage from Valencia to Cuba, who concealed the infant under her clothes. Arriving in Havana, Chibie was handed over to the Del Rio family, Asuncione and Raymond, who, after rechristening her Alma, dispatched her to a convent in England where she was raised by nuns until the age of sixteen.

While her dramatic origins were never fully verified, I was able to confirm that until her mid-teens, Chibie lived in England, and that when she left the convent, she could read in eight languages. She was brainy, brilliant, and an utter original. She had dark olive skin and spent the rest of her life bleaching it in order to "pass" in a Caucasian world. Chibie entered into an arranged marriage with a German-speaking Swiss man named Frederick Heinemann. Three children, two boys and a girl, followed—Dutch, Peter, and my mother, Andrea. Mr. Heinemann's alcoholism and physical abuse led to brutal fights and his eventual abandonment of the family.

There was another story, too: that when my own mother was sixteen and dating an older man named Steve, who played football for the New York Giants, Steve was enchanted by the then-thirty-four-year-old Chibie. For the next four years, Steve lived with Chibie, my mother, Uncle Peter, and

Uncle Dutch in their hot, cramped, downtown apartment beneath the El train until my mother finally left home. True? Not true? It's hard to know. Certainly a lot of it is verified by my mother's diary.

Chibie herself was adept at covering her tracks and her heritage, repeatedly telling my sisters in a theatrical English accent, "When I die you shall find *nothing*! But *nothing*!"

I spent my early childhood in the company of Chibie and Allie, our nanny and cook, who always made time for me. I'd show up at their apartment on the third floor with a satchel filled with shiny jewels raided from my mother's jewelry box—her tourmaline engagement ring, her pearls, and her Jensen necklaces—and gave them with a flourish to Allie, who had many fewer bracelets, necklaces, and earrings than my mother did. I knew instinctively that there was a socioeconomic gap between Allie and our family. Still, as my friend, why shouldn't Allie have the same jewelry as Mommy? My Robin Hood–like jewelry-filching became so habitual that a routine of sorts developed: I would pirate the jewelry to Allie, who would then drag it all back upstairs to my parents' apartment, and by dinnertime, my mother would be back wearing her pearls and rings, no fingers pointed, no harm done.

But my two favorite adults, the ones who made me laugh the most, were Uncle Peter and Uncle Dutch, who lived in the basement apartment. Uncle Peter was my first crush. During the summers in Stamford, Connecticut, I was his Robin Hood, too, sneaking across the lawn at night and dropping off desserts from my parents' elegant dinner table at the doorstep of his little coffee-drip cabin. Uncle Peter loved me as much as I loved him. He told me jokes. He spoke in funny voices. He made scrunchy faces behind everyone's backs. He did a dance I can only liken to an eggbeater churning, his torso twirling, rubber-boned, as he made strange, ecstatic, spasming hand, leg, and facial movements. He also taught me how to play the ukulele, on which I learned the precursors to my first guitar chords.

Growing up, I assumed every family in the world sang, harmonized, and played the piano together. Half of the residents of 133 West Eleventh Street were musical, including Mr. Porter, the super who sang "Silent Night" all year round. My mother had a light, gentle soprano familiar to me from the Brahms lullabies she almost whispered as she was putting us to sleep.

It was Uncle Henry, my father's younger brother, who came up with the idea to start an orchestra and chorus, holding rehearsals every Wednesday night in his neat, overly beige apartment. Like the rest of the refined, upper-middle-class, Upper West Simons—Daddy and his five siblings were all named after British monarchs—Uncle Henry had developed his highbrow taste in prep school, in his case, the Ethical Culture School in Manhattan. Our orchestra, at least as Uncle Henry imagined it, would devote itself exclusively to church hymns and liturgical pieces. At first, everybody was excited to play together, though Uncle Peter and Uncle Dutch would have been much happier playing show tunes, blues, and jazz. Dutch played a mean mouth bass, and Peter could play anything that Louis Armstrong played, the difference being that instead of a cornet or trumpet, all the sounds came razzing, tooting, and spilling directly from Uncle Peter's mouth.

I soon grew to dread those Wednesday night chorus rehearsals—I hated classical music, hated hymns, hated the seriousness of it all—and was relieved when Joey, Lucy, and I were kicked out of the chorus for mugging too much. (In fact, we deliberately sang out of tune in hopes of being expelled.) Uncle Henry *often* complained about the uneven tonality of the three Simon sisters, our seeming inability to hold a tune due to our "kidding around" and the bad habit we had of laughing "like predatory goons" behind our hands.

To me, the best part of those rehearsals was when they ended and I migrated downstairs to the basement apartment, where Uncle Peter picked up the ukulele and together we sang "Yes Sir, That's My Baby," with Peter harmonizing and me singing melody. Over time I would collect different sounds in my head, ways of hearing notes together—a fourth here, a dominant seventh there, though back then certainly nothing had a name!—and harmonizing would come almost as easily to me as singing melody.

Daddy's family was well-roundedly musical. His youngest brother, George, was a drummer who helped found *Downbeat* magazine. Another brother, Alfie, was the program director for a music radio station, WQXR. Henry was a classical music lover and conductor, as well as a Shakespearean scholar. Daddy, though, was the most talented of them all, a nonprofessional pianist who played as well as the professionals.

Whether Daddy ever dreamed of being recognized for his musicianship is something I'd guess yes to. He began studying the piano seriously at age six, and every night spent three or four hours playing Liszt, Brahms, Chopin,

Mozart, Rachmaninoff, Beethoven. Mommy used to say that though Daddy's playing didn't have the technical perfection of Rubinstein or Horowitz, he played with more emotion and originality, subtlety and abandon. He seemed to relish the position of his hands on the keys, and to this day I can still picture the dramatic curve and sweep of his wrists and fingers. Before Daddy founded his publishing company, his first job out of college was working as a salesman for Steinway & Sons. In time, the piano would become his only refuge from the hurt and damage of his life, but in those days, Mommy told us only that Daddy could have been a concert pianist if he'd wanted, and that his playing was so nuanced and moving that George Gershwin and Vladimir Horowitz had told him they would rather sit it out than follow his playing. Although his playing was sensitive, there was no question he could be imposing. Mommy was proud. It reflected well on her.

As the youngest of the three Simon girls, I remember how many times Daddy made me leave the dinner table as punishment. I also remember kissing him hello and good night, but never getting much affection in return. "Darling, remember to kiss Carly, too," I heard my mother say more than once at bedtime, as if without her reminder and gentle diplomacy, he might have forgotten all about me. During the day, with Daddy at work, I turned to my two slapstick-loving uncles, Peter and Dutch. They were my private version of the Marx Brothers, making up songs the three of us sang together, teaching me risqué language, and taking me on double-decker bus jaunts up Fifth Avenue, at an age when my childhood, and my family, seemed as though they would last forever.

In those days, when Mommy was still in love with Daddy, our two houses, the building in Greenwich Village and our summer place in Stamford, Connecticut, were a medley of sounds and images: the tinkling of ice in cocktail glasses, the tiny gold violins and birdcages of the women's charm bracelets, slingshot repartee, muffled downstairs laughter, glasses tipped against lips, dips and martinis, shrimp suspended in tomato aspic—bell peals and light flashes that made up the percussion section of the orchestra that was my growing up. In his role as the Simon half of Simon & Schuster, Daddy surrounded himself with his own Bloomsbury group of the beautiful, the clever, the neurotic, the talented, and the sporty, among them some of the best-known artists, writers, musicians, athletes, painters, and cartoonists of the time, including Benny Goodman, Bennett Cerf, Vladimir Horowitz, Jackie Robinson, Arthur Schwartz, Richard Rodgers, James Thurber, Oscar Hammerstein, Peter Arno, Charles Addams, and Sloan Wilson— an author my father had discovered and nurtured, who wrote the 1955 bestseller *The Man in the Gray Flannel Suit*—as well as whatever artist-in-residence happened to be staying on our third floor in Stamford that summer, whether it was a Hungarian émigré pianist just passing through or an exchange student from Mississippi. By the end of the 1950s, Albert Einstein and Eleanor Roosevelt had both come for lunch, and Daddy had also struck up a letter-writing correspondence with President Eisenhower on the topic of nuclear disarmament. Daddy and Ike had become bridge and golfing buddies, with Ike eventually becoming a Simon & Schuster author. Asked once why he had so many famous friends, Daddy replied, "They're more interesting!" He was not ashamed of feeling that.

My parents entertained all year round, in Manhattan or at the Georgian mansion in Connecticut. On nights they went out on the town, Mommy would sweep into my room to kiss me good night. Her smile was warm and dazzling. Her mink stole cuddled her shoulders, her hair swept upward in front, in a French style held in place by tortoiseshell combs. At five foot four, she was buxom and tiny, especially in contrast to my six-foot-five father—Mommy and Daddy had tiny and tall all wrapped up—and so beautiful that when she picked me up from school, I'd sometimes pretend I'd left my homework in my locker—*I'll be there in just a second!*—so I could show her off a minute longer to my friends and their mothers. Mommy never wore any makeup other than the reddest possible lipstick, which she pooled lightly and dabbed with one fingertip onto her Hepburn cheekbones, and always that pompadour, the French up-do. In fact, if Joey, Lucy, or I happened to catch her in the bathroom after a bath or shower, with her hair flat and damp, Mommy would cover our eyes to make sure we never imagined her that way ever again. Among Daddy's soaring social set, Mommy must have often felt out of place—she had first met Daddy while working as a low-paid Simon & Schuster switchboard operator—though her personality was bright, generous, animated, interested, tailor-made for the glamour and drumbeat wit that surrounded her. She often didn't feel up to the conversation that tried to involve her.

Physically and personally, Daddy dwarfed her, as he did practically everyone. Handsome, glamorous, wryly funny, he was a passionate lover of people, conversation, art, and culture, all wreathed in a constant corona of cigarette smoke. Dick Simon had charisma, everyone said—he made everyone around him better. His business partner, Max Schuster, was quiet and dogged, but Daddy, everyone agreed, had "twirl"—a certain kind of sexy flourish. He gave spur-of-the-moment parties—to celebrate a book's publication date, a sale to a book club, someone's birthday, or just for the sake of Why-the-Hell-Don't-We-Throw-a-Party-Tonight? Daddy was also famously absentminded, elsewhere in his head, setting down and losing manuscripts, papers, and letters so frequently it was said that every Simon & Schuster employee had memorized the phone numbers of all the city's major lost-and-found offices.

Daddy and his old Columbia College classmate had founded their company in 1924 out of a one-room office, their first publication a crossword-puzzle book with a pencil attached to it (Daddy's stroke of marketing genius). The book was a runaway bestseller, the first of a series that's still sold today, creating the foundation of what would eventually become a publishing empire. From the mid-1920s on, Daddy and Max published books that went on to sell millions of copies, everything from Dale Carnegie's *How to Win Friends and Influence People*, to *Bambi*, to the Little Golden Books—*Dr. Dan the Bandage Man* (sold with an actual Band-Aid inside the cover), and others—to groundbreaking works of history and politics like Will and Ariel Durant's eleven-volume *The Story of Civilization*.

When I was a little girl, I thought my father was a hero, a king. Although I noted the lack of attention he paid to me, it made me think less of me, not him. On my visits to Simon & Schuster's offices in Rockefeller Center, I naturally assumed the enormous bronze-cast statue of Atlas sitting in front of his building was Daddy, supporting the celestial spheres on his shoulders. Inside the lobby, I'd board the mirrored, gilt-edged elevator to the twenty-eighth floor, where Louise, Daddy's executive secretary, would greet me with a smile before escorting me down the hall to Daddy's office, offering me a ginger ale with a cherry as well as any snacks I wanted. Midtown Manhattan was a grown-up, chaotic world, and my father the most formidable man inside it, just as he set the elegant tone of the cocktail parties and dinners Mommy and he hosted in New York, Stamford, or, for two or three weeks every August, Martha's Vineyard.

If Mommy seemed to idolize my father back then, Daddy, in turn, showed her a lot of affection, as well as adoring my two older sisters, Joey and Lucy. Early on I convinced myself that Lucy and Joey were Daddy's darlings, leaving me . . . who or what exactly? The little girl who'd introduced herself to the new nanny with a big, barreling *Hi*? Growing up, Joey and Lucy were both beautiful, a pair of queens-in-waiting to my father's dashing chessboard king. By the time they were in their late teens, they were going places, too. Joey was set on becoming a famous opera singer, and Lucy planned to study nursing (to which Chibie, I remember, responded, "Uggh").

Me, I wanted to be a baseball player, a pitcher, the first-ever girl to break into the major leagues. Growing up, I was a tomboy, with irregular-length hair, Dodgers baseball cap, jeans rolled up just below the knees, punching my baseball mitt, trying to break it in. Outside of my baseball fantasies, I had no idea where I was going, and for reasons I didn't quite understand, my relationship with Daddy was always remote, uneasy. One Father's Day in kindergarten, I vividly recall holding one hand in Daddy's and the other in Uncle Peter's. I preferred the feel and texture of Uncle Peter's hand. Why? I don't know. I knew only that Daddy had smooth, dry, unfamiliar skin, as if he belonged to a different family, or tribe. It was Peter, after all, who had taught me to play baseball and tennis, and, best of all, music. If for some reason Daddy loved Joey and Lucy the best, then Uncle Peter was mine, and I was his, too. I doted on Peter whenever the opportunity arose. I handed him clean white towels as he came off the tennis court in the summer, as well as milk shakes made of fresh strawberries and vanilla ice cream, with freshly picked four-leaf clovers on top. I never felt the same impulse with Daddy. I felt a strange detachment whenever we were together, though more and more I knew that I was mirroring back what he felt for me. My inability to get and keep Daddy's attention, and the suspicion that of his four children I was the one he cared for least, was a problem I'd spend my life questioning and compensating for. Not an unfamiliar scenario.

From the outside, Mommy and Daddy's marriage was iridescent, like a pearl under radiant light, especially on nights when they put on a show for an audience of dinner guests. Alone, once the guests left, they were never quite as shimmering. Professionally and personally, Daddy would rise, and by the mid-1950s, when I was only ten, begin his slow-motion fall. The rising part, when Daddy was a publishing entrepreneur, innovator, and magnate at ease with high society and the New York City intelligentsia, is mostly a legend to me, hard to square with the pained, remote, brittle father I remember much later, whose company and wife had both been wrested from him, and who roamed the floors of our house as if he were already a half-vanished man.

"Hi."

Jeanie and me communicating with Mr. Hicks, Meany, and the reasonable one: Ha Ha Ginsberg.

CHAPTER TWO

_____

summer in the trees

There was a certain summer—I think it was 1951—when I spent a lot of time in the fruit trees in the orchard near our play barn in Stamford, just beyond a sprawling copper beech tree. The orchard was randomly dotted with apple trees, mostly Cortlands, McIntoshes, and a few more exotic, hard-to-name varieties. Nearby, too, was a pair of cherry trees, large ones, whose trunks were thicker, their barks darker, grayer, and tougher on your skin. Cherry trees were harder to scale than apple trees—they took twistier turns—though once you reached the top, the rewards were thrilling: spotting the first sweet, dark purple cherry, twisting off its stem, chomping around the pit, savoring the meat, and then—the best part—fingering the small wet stone like a bead and hurling it gleefully at a human target below. Then, with hardly a breath in between, biting into another, sometimes not as ripe as the first, and after a sour sample bite, hurling it with disdain at the ground, or at the sister or brother or cousin you'd missed the first time around. By the end of the summer, I'd become adept at the art and science of pit-marksmanship.

The Stamford property was enormous, around a hundred acres in all, anchored by the main house with its tall columns, pediments, eaves, dormers, balustrades, and French doors. We all referred to the place as Stamford— as if we owned the entire city—though the heart of the property was the pool house, known as Stoneybroke, a word Daddy had carved with a broken twig on the steps while the cement was still wet, a declaration of how much more the pool house had cost than he anticipated. The house was only a forty-five-minute drive north in Daddy's old woody, or my mother's Cadillac convertible, from the big brick colonial house in Riverdale, just north of Manhattan, that my parents had bought once Joey began middle school and we left 133 West Eleventh Street behind for good.

Helen Gaspard had been with our family for a few years, and with Helen acting as the resident scriptwriter and theater director, Joey, Lucy, and I spent that summer memorizing lines for the plays that we performed for the adults. We practiced dialogue while dangling from the trees, shouting down lines to one another, crook to crook, branch to branch, chewing on apples and cherries as we waited our turn, sipping from milk bottles we'd poured out and refilled with orange juice. As the only boy in this overhanging female tribe, my baby brother Peter tore around under the branches in light blue overalls, singsonging and babbling, toddler-yelling up to us to toss him down a cherry.

As always, my two first cousins, Jeanie and Mary Seligman, lived with us that summer. As the youngest, Jeanie and I always had lesser parts in our family plays. My sister Joey, the ringleader, flattered us into taking inconsequential roles. Jeanie and I were still young enough to believe, as spear-carriers all over the world are told, that although we had only two lines, our dialogue was crucial to the success of the performance. In the play *The Monkey's Paw*, for example, my entire role consisted of knocking three times on a barn door. It didn't matter. Joey had led me to think I was the star of the show, and during curtain calls, the audience, in on the joke, rose to applaud me as though I were Sarah Bernhardt.

When I wasn't busy practicing my lines, I sprawled alongside Jeanie on the grassy circle beneath the apple trees, engaging in make-believe conversations among the imaginary friends we invented, including Mr. Hicks, Meany, and Bypress Fongton. The latter two made their home atop the pool house weather vane, whereas Mr. Hicks, lacking a permanent home, roamed between the orchard and the deep end of the pool, stirring up conflicts and making trouble for another of Jeanie's imaginary friends, Ha Ha Ginsberg, a character who over time got to be so famous for unknown reasons that her name later showed up in a *New Yorker* story. When her father gave her this news, Jeanie, I remember, called upstairs, "Ha Ha, guess what, you were in *The New Yorker!*"

Our made-up characters were us, and we were them; they gave us life, and in return we gave them desires and destinies. They fended off moths and bees, stumbled on forbidden gardens, judged singing, dancing, and somersaulting contests, peered in family drawers, and reigned over the acres of fruit trees extending to the giant copper beech, the sycamores, the maples, and the elms. We were the children of the orchard—the future actors of the Connecticut night. Fongton, Meany, and Ha Ha rang the bells of mischief as they choreographed their flight between the trees and the stars and back again, taking good care of us as we did our nighttime dreaming.

That was also the summer I began turning in on myself. I had always been an anxious child, jittery, insecure. I was scared to be alone, scared of the dark, scared of the arrival in winter of Jack Frost. Going to sleep at night had always been an ordeal. Around 8 or 9 p.m., my mother or Allie would flock close by me at the bathroom sink as I brushed my teeth and faced the nightly torment of what to do about my hair. I was born not with hair but, rather, feathers, so fluffy and hard to brush that I often slept with braids, closed within plain red rubber bands. Joey and Lucy had grown weary of the nightly drama surrounding my hair—the twisting, the turning, the yelling. A year later, Joey even set up a mock salon in my parents' bathroom, and with Lucy as her accomplice, set about scissoring away all my hair with a pair of enormous chicken shears. Joey managed to get only the left half chopped off before I broke down in tears and fled outdoors. It took six months of uneven pigtails for my hair to grow back.

Getting to bed was one problem, insomnia another. From early on, I would make up strange games in my head to force myself to fall back asleep. One of my most fun fantasies had as its setting a naval warship on a black, cold, rough sea. On board, life was pure hardship, and it was my fate to share a bunk with a bunch of other sailors—"me maties," as I called them. I was a deckhand, though not nearly as lowly as the others. Me maties snored and sweated, exhaled coughs, chokes, wheezes, and smoker's breath, had dirty feet and teeth, hairy legs and armpits. As the boat lurched and tipped, they flopped and fell from side to side, threatening to hurl one another off the bow or gunwale—*Drown, you dirty swab . . . no more vittles for you . . . you want your Froghog? That's all yer worth.*

As I put in my time on board, scrubbing the toilets and decks, I would permit myself another inch of space on my actual bed—an edge of blanket, a corner of the pillow. *Good swab!* called out the boat's admiral, who regularly showed up to inspect things, and every time I heard those approving words, I pulled in a few more inches of bedding.

When the admiral had finished his inspection rounds, more and more of the bed, and the pillow, would be mine again, and safe. "Thank you, Lord," I'd say, before God-blessing Mommy and Daddy and Lucy and Joey and Peter and Allie. I'd also include Chibie, Uncle Peter, and Uncle Dutch. Then I'd tug my blanket up to cover my poor, salty, shivering body, imagining a celebration and an imaginary back rub given to me by the admiral, a dead ringer for Clark Gable as Rhett Butler.

Daddy also made an effort. Having been told by Mommy that some "Silly Putty therapy" might help me get to sleep, he would come into my bedroom at night and take a seat on the edge of my bed. "Just imagine you are a wad of Silly Putty, all cold and tightly bound together," Daddy would say in a low, soothing voice. "The Silly Putty comes into your warm bed, and as if by magic, it is you! It is your body. Because it is you and you are it." He went on like this for a while, closing with, "Now your eyes are getting heavy and want to stay closed, Carly, darling girl, you are so sleepy, just like the Silly Putty, so sleepy . . ." As Daddy left the room, sometimes I heard the striking of a match outside in the hallway, the sound of his cigarette burning to life. He was just trying to help, but more often than not, having been told by Mommy that cigarettes weren't good for his health, I'd end up worrying about him instead.

That summer, Joey, Lucy, and I were all cast members in Helen's production of Louisa May Alcott's *Little Women*. A stage was created at the front of the big red play barn, with three white sheets forming a curtain separating the stage from the Ping-Pong table and scattered chairs for the audience. Jeanie, playing the part of Hannah, the maid, had only one line to say to us Little Women: *Will you have hash or fish balls, girrrls?* I, on the other hand, was playing Amy, my largest speaking part by far in any family play to date: twenty-five lines. The kind of recognition I had dreamed about. It was the coffee table and "Hi" coming to life.

Rehearsals got under way, and costumes were found, assembled, and sewn from scratch. This was real theater, and we tackled it with insouciance. Memorizing our lines had been crazy, effortless fun for the past few weeks, but now Helen called us all onto the stage, no scripts allowed.

We gathered in the barn, barefoot, our wet bathing suits dripping onto the wood, and began our scene. Joey, playing Jo, the main character, said with attitude and precision, "Christmas won't be Christmas without any presents," to which Lucy, playing Beth, replied, "It's so dreadful to be poor," followed by me, as Amy, the baby of all the Little Women, saying, "I don't think it's fair that some children get so many presents while others get nothing at all."

As I started to say the line, my throat went into spasm. It was as if a snake, which had been coiled and asleep around my esophagus, had suddenly reared up, strangling the words. "I don't think it's—" and as the next word, "fair," came out, the snake cut off its entrance, suctioned its oxygen. My brain and tongue sprang up, fell back, tried again, fell back again, then, at last, the word tumbled out, ravaged, in need of oxygen.

That was the unhappy, astonishing birth of my stammer, or at least my first conscious awareness of it. If they noticed at all, my sisters and cousins said nothing about the jerking, guttural noises coming from my mouth. Whatever it was, they probably took it to be some temporary, puzzling thing. Surely it would fade and recede, like the scratches, bruises, and sunburns that were part of summer life.

It didn't, though. As rehearsals went on and my stammer started holding things up, my sisters' reaction became unsympathetic. "Stop stuttering," Joey said calmly at one point, as if stopping were as easy as taking off my shoes. Helen said nothing. No doubt she had already consulted with my mother, who, knowing Mommy, had already contacted a leading psychiatrist or speech therapist to find out if stammering was developmentally normal for a little girl. I wasn't dropped from the play, even though my speech problems were now creating long silences in the script where no silences had existed before.

A week before our first, and I believe only, performance of *Little Women*, I remember climbing my favorite cherry tree, past my usual safe crook, higher than I was supposed to go. My arms and legs found a brittle branch, beyond which no more branches or fruit grew. Beyond me was pure sky. I was half hoping I would lose my balance and fall, breaking both my legs. Or, even more dramatically, that I would shatter every bone in my body and end up in a full body cast, unable to play Amy, or anyone, especially myself. My body cast would show the world I had a visible handicap I couldn't help, which would be easier than the bottled, twisted one in the back of my mouth that was somehow my fault. My main concern was: Do I have any control over this? Once you stutter, and notice that you do, you stutter a lot more.

On opening night, before the curtain rose, I heard whisperings backstage: *What if Carly stutters? Should we just cut her line? Should someone finish her line for her?* My stutter may have been new, but nothing humiliates stutterers more than to have their words or sentences finished for them. We don't want to be noticed. Overhearing the backstage murmurings, I heard only one thing: I had an unspeakable aberration that from now on had to be covered over, shushed, camouflaged, lived out in secret. Mercifully, that night a calf had been cast in *Little Women* to play—well—a calf, and when Jeanie led it onstage by a rope tied around its sweet little head, the calf proceeded to urinate on the makeshift stage curtain as it let out a particularly vocal little cow *Moooooo*. The audience laughter completely drowned out my opening line, "I don't think it's fair that some children get so many presents while others get nothing at all." I don't remember how the rest of the show went, but afterward I ran back into my bedroom and cried until my mother appeared. She didn't know what to say, but she cradled and soothed me.

If up until that point words and life were easy, and limitless, my stammer made me aware that life could also be tough. There was very little it would not affect about me. All of my future phobias borrowed energy and nerve endings from this thing that, at the time, I understood so little about. Lines were deepening between neurons creating pathways which were like a trench, growing deeper and deeper, more associated with embarrassment and low self-esteem. I waited for the stammer to arrive and almost always it did. I had no idea that over the next decade, all through my grammar and high school years living in Riverdale and then for two years at college, I would face the daily struggle to speak naturally or unself-consciously. I usually failed. During my time in lower school, various classmates would tease me mercilessly, either to my face or behind my back, not just for my stammer, but for the facial contortions and grimaces that accompanied it. Inside, I felt assaulted, broken, consumed with self-hatred.

After school, I would come home and crawl into my mother's arms and cry for hours. Friends of hers had given her advice about possible stuttering cures. One, which involved filling your mouth with marbles and talking, we never tried. But beginning with *Little Women*, my stammer created a bond between Mommy and me. She was the only one who understood the shame I felt, that was beginning to define me. Almost every day, I huddled in her lap, practicing my words, as she rocked and relaxed me. She also placed a hot-water bottle on my morning stomachaches—"your worry lump," Mommy called the aching spot—which sometimes made it so hard to swallow I almost gagged. Sometimes, though, a word would roll off my tongue, pushing past my throat guards, undetected, a prison break of sorts. "See, darling, you can do it!" my mother would say, and I felt that my victory was hers. But just as soon as her excitement for me passed, my fearfulness would begin all over again. I had accomplished something. Would I be able to do it again?

My stammer followed no laws or patterns, and it still doesn't. Some days I could easily say a word beginning with a vowel, like *August* or *owl*, but hit a wall with *comb* or *garden*. Other days I could manage an *s*-word like *store* or *Sunday*, but a *t*-word, like *train* or *toothpaste*, defeated me. The next day, without warning, it was reversed, the *t*-words easy, the *s*-words petrified. *H* was always hard. If the phone rang, I couldn't even say "Hello," and so, like a lot of stutterers, I came up with accents, tricks, or techniques to tackle problem words in sidelong ways. One trick involved expelling all my breath as the phone rang and picking up the receiver pushing out a breathless ". . . ello?" Other days, feeling as though I were cupping a strong, queenly *S* in my throat, I answered the phone with assurance, and delivered a majestic "Simon residence." No doubt this must have sounded ridiculous, but it gave me a small feeling of pride. Still, I spent every night worrying about the next day, and the range of excuses I could make: I had to blow my nose; I needed to go to the bathroom; a sudden bout of hiccups had come on. My worst fear was that my stammer would ruin my "timing," and therefore ruin any anecdote I might be telling, or if I were answering a quiz or a problem, everyone would think I didn't even *know* the answer in the first place.

When I was around seven years old, I started writing a diary, with most of the entries about what I'd eaten that night for dinner. As the years went on, I started making up my own code language to deal with my stutter at school. I wrote once, "Please—I pray that when I have to read aloud in class I won't famul." *Famul:* a word I'd invented that meant "stutter," designed to obscure its actual meaning in case a stranger happened upon the worn leather-backed journal I'd taken to hiding under my mattress, a word helpfully defined in a back-of-the-diary glossary. Locked inside my own apartness, I couldn't imagine that others might head straight for the glossary, easily deciphering what I meant. What mattered only was that hiding was now my game, discovery my shame.

When I was a teenager, my boyfriend, Nick Delbanco, told me he loved my stammer. It was late at night, and Nick and I were seated in the front seat of his Impala convertible beside a lake in Larchmont, New York. Nick was a sophomore at Harvard, and I was in eleventh grade at Riverdale Country School for Girls. That night wasn't the first time I'd met Nick's parents, and I felt at ease with them. Though trial and error had somewhat improved my speech over the years, Nick's mother had definitely noticed that something was amiss. Had she noticed it before?

Achieving this ease with your boyfriend's parents is hard enough, even without trying to hide your stutter. This particular evening was intimate and questions were aimed at me. I hesitated a lot, trying to hide my facial contortions. I could not have known that on this night Barbara Delbanco, a fiercely intelligent, dark-haired German woman who had raised a trio of brilliant little boys, would be scrutinizing me from the line of my stockings to the silences surrounding my words. That night, Mrs. Delbanco was unerringly focused on me. Though none of the three Delbanco boys ever disappointed their parents—all would eventually become eminent in their fields as a physician, a scholar, and in Nick's case a prolific writer—Nick was, to my mind, his mother's Buddha baby, the handsome, brilliant son who could do no wrong.

At dinner that night, I used all my stammer shortcuts and tricks: word swaps, glancing away during a facial contortion, letting Nick answer questions intended for me. Once or twice I spewed out the worst of what I had to offer: eyes flashing up into my head as I struggled over a word, locked mouth, tensed lips. Those few moments didn't escape Mrs. Delbanco's notice. At one point I joined Nick's brother Andy upstairs—he was showing me a new game he'd just bought—and when I got back downstairs, I was so embarrassed by my performance that night that I told everyone I had to go home and write a paper, neatly cutting short the evening with an excuse that made me sound scholarly and responsible at the same time. "Of course, of course, Carly," Mrs. Delbanco said. "We loved seeing you."

Nick walked me out into the limpid Larchmont night, and he and I drove to the lake. Nick cut the engine, got out of the car to take down the top, and retook his seat beside me. "What's wrong?" he asked.

I was slumped beside him in the passenger seat. "Nothing. Just tired." Then, "What an experience."

Nick was silent. "You know," he said, "when you were upstairs in Andy's room, my mother said she thought she detected a stammer in your speech pattern. I told her she was right. I'd just gotten used to it in you. She said she had, too, but it appeared to be more challenging this evening."

Tears started spilling down onto my cheeks. "I know, I do stammer. I'm so embarrassed. I'm so sorry—"

Nick wouldn't let me finish. "Stop," he said. "I know you do. I knew that about you the first time we met."

The thought horrified me. He knew, but he hadn't said anything? "Well, why didn't you tell me that?" I said.

"Because I loved it, that's why."

I couldn't even get the word *stammers* out without stammering. "But . . . but . . . b—"

"It's sexy. It's part of you. I don't love you in *spite* of your stammer, I love you because of it." In the long pause, after I straightened up, drying my wet face with my sleeve, Nick reached for me and just held me there, tightly. "Carly, it's sexy," he repeated. "It's also *charming*."

Charming: what an alien idea. I had spent the last ten years doing everything I could to conceal my handicap. Now, in just a moment's time, my stammer was charming and, even better, sexy. Nick Delbanco, a confident, worldly, literate Harvard boy, had loved away my stutter's stigma. Just like that, I was exotic, different, and in a positive way, too, and it had only taken ten years!

These days, I stammer when I'm tired, when I'm nervous, or, more rarely, for no good reason at all. I still can't tell a joke that requires "timing." Whenever I read aloud, I sound halting and unconvincing, and all at once I'm brought back to the old red barn of my childhood, *Little Women,* and the stop-start fickleness of my own throat. I sometimes think about and savor the night in Larchmont when a boy I adored told me he found my stammer charming. But acceptance has helped me speak around it. When my children were young, I made up stories for them at night, in the dark, and they seemed to love them, no matter how I sounded.

Besides the orchard, my refuges during that summer of *Little Women* and the debut of my stammer were tennis and swimming. Every day I spent hours in the pool, with my little bathing cap on, trying to perfect my swan dives and jackknifes. Swimming, and the freedom I felt in the water, was maybe what I hoped my speech might someday become: smooth, fluid, without any boundaries. But the moment I remembered that I stuttered, my stutter would reappear. Still, something else happened that summer that changed things for me. My family was at the dinner table one night, and I was trying to say "Pass the butter." For some reason I forgot to change *pass* to *ass* or "send the butter over." My stammer became frantic, and as usual, Joey or Lucy helpfully finished my sentence for me, a gesture that made me all the more aware of my speech handicap.

Then Mommy tossed me an idea that would change my life. "Carly, darling—try singing it."

Not surprisingly, I couldn't, not at first. It felt too strange, the transition too daunting. I sat back in my chair instead, exhausted. Joey and Lucy tried to encourage me by singing "Pass the butter" to whatever melody they could think of, but that only made me feel more on the spot. My little brother Peter laughed at me, which actually made me feel relaxed.

"Try tapping your foot," Mommy said, and I did, halfheartedly at first, then speeding up the tempo. She went on: "Try saying 'Pass the butter,' but as if you were singing it. Make believe it's a note."

I began hitting my thigh with a steady 4/4 beat. I had an instinctive ability to say the words on the offbeat, on a syncopation of the 4/4. The result even made it swing. From there, it was an easy step to add a little melody—C, B flat, E flat—at which point the whole table, including Sula, our cook, joined in, a heavenly choir jamming to "Pass the Butter." We used the table and the tableware for percussion. It became a mode we naturally lapsed into when stuttering wasn't even the catalyst.

It was a release, though one with the slightest, most cutting edge of shame about it. At last I had a technique that worked, but I also thought, Oh my God, I'm someone who *needs* a technique. Still, I've never forgotten that moment. It was a turning point. I had a way, suddenly, of handling my stammer, at least when I was at home. Naturally, at school or at a friend's house or inside a department store, I couldn't sing what I wanted to say, but did that really matter? A melody now existed inside my head. It helped me. Not completely—there were years to go, unnumbered *D*'s and *T*'s and *S*'s to face down—but I'd just been handed a crucial new piece of ammunition. I could sing it instead. Maybe I would be a singer!

"Pass the butter."

"Twinkle, twinkle, little star."

CHAPTER THREE

———————————

frunzhoffa

When I was about eleven, it became clear that my stutter was getting worse and even affecting my grades at school, since I did everything possible to avoid talking in class. Mommy set up an appointment for me with an experimental music therapist. She may have had other worries about me, too, based on something I'd told Joey and Lucy, who, in turn, had told Mommy. In retrospect, I think Mommy was handing that "something" over to a professional so she wouldn't have to deal with it.

Dr. Frunzhoffa was a German speech therapist with a mustache and straight gray hair parted in the middle. It was Dr. Frunzhoffa's idea to use the melody and pulse of "Twinkle, Twinkle, Little Star" to help me deal with my speech impediment. At one point during our appointment, he put on a record and asked me to dance with him. The two of us stood there, a few inches apart, clasping hands, like Fred Astaire and Ginger Rogers. His heavy, scratching shoes emphasized his lack of grace as he carried out his mission of distracting me so I would answer his questions.

Then he finally asked it (or rather sang it): "Ginger Rogers, Fred Astaire," he crooned. "Has a man ever *touched* you down there?" Another lyric followed. "Has a man had his way with you? Tell me, tell me if it's true?" I sang: "Daddy loves me, Mommy too, they live hap'ly in the zoo."

"You're a smart one, Carly," Dr. Frunzhoffa encouraged me in his German accent, "so you can make up ze next line. It doesn't matter if it doesn't rhyme. Vot matters is ze truth."

We started all over again with the Fred and Ginger line: "Ginger Rogers, Fred Astaire . . . Has a man touched you down there?" To which I responded, "I stood so tall and he did stare / then he sat me on his chair." Hah! I was invested in keeping the secret I was holding, believing myself clever enough to outmaneuver my therapist. Across from me, Dr. Frunzhoffa's eyebrows were raised in ecstasy. He must have thought he'd made a brilliant discovery, piercing all my secrets as I circled around them, already learning how to compartmentalize my emotions. No doubt Frunzhoffa was reeling over his certainty that he'd discovered some new form of treatment that would rival psychoanalysis: *Music unblocks the unconscious!* "Zat's it, Carly!" he exclaimed. "Now let's stay with ze same melody! Did he touch you in ze chair?" and as Dr. Frunzhoffa made a half turn around the room, I answered him almost immediately: "Yes, he touched me right down there."

"Are you quite sure he touched you dere?"

"Quite sure, quite sure, in the chair!"

What Dr. Frunzhoffa would never know was that I would protect my secret attachment at all costs. *Love:* forever more light and lovely than lurid and sad, even in the face of a late-night shower stall and a boy named Billy.

When Mommy first brought me to see Dr. Frunzhoffa, the nights with Billy inside the pool house and the swimming pool had been going on for several summers in a row. The trouble I was in hung in the air like the single note of a violin, a note that got imperceptibly higher every second. Still, a week after my appointment with Dr. Frunzhoffa, it seemed Billy and I were safe and in the clear. I was protecting our relationship and in fact would continue taking whatever Billy wanted to give me.

I was around seven when my "interludes" with Billy started. Like a lot of kids, I'd first discovered sex alone, and by accident. I was five, lying on my narrow five-year-old-kid's bed. My hand slipped underneath my torso and landed three inches or so below my belly button, and I began moving my body back and forth, very gently, against my own hand.

Nor were naked bodies unfamiliar to me. Spending Augusts on the Vineyard from the age of five on, I'd been exposed all my life to Windy Gates, a nude beach in Chilmark with high dunes, where the more "artistic" grownups hung out alongside children, pets, picnic baskets, and books. The scene there was both innocent and feral. Preadolescent girls and boys ran and leapt like bronzed wildlife down the powdery dunes, all bones and sinew, hair stiff from the salty waves, their most sensitive naked parts on sunlit parade. Bodies, beautiful, homely, and everything in between, bounced, jiggled, sprang, and strutted from the waves. Everyone was there, wearing nothing at all, from Joey and Lucy and their friends to my parents and *their* friends, with their cucumber sandwiches and martini shakers.

You would never see me naked at Windy Gates. The idea of letting my own towel fall, and exposing myself with everyone else, felt like an unimaginable torment. I felt ashamed of something, likely something having nothing to do with my nudity. Still, when my family returned to Stamford from the Vineyard, leaving behind the warm brown bodies of Windy Gates, I was vulnerable, maybe, to some of what I'd been seeing and sensing.

From my perspective now, it's disturbing to look back on what happened to a young girl with a much older boy. The thing is, even though I instinctively knew I couldn't tell anybody, it didn't feel shameful at the time but, instead, thrillingly clandestine, and full of naughty fun.

Billy was the teenage son of family friends who were visiting Stamford from Chicago, where his father was a lawyer. They were renting a house in the neighboring town of Westport that summer. One thing about Billy was clear. He made no secret about how much in love he was with my sister Lucy. In fact, the first time I saw Billy, he was spying on Lucy through a window as she made her way to the swimming pool, wearing her sexy black bathing suit.

That summer, on our first walk up the hill to the house after dinner at the pool house, Billy asked me whether Lucy was "developed." I must have looked as confused as I felt because he added, "I mean, does she have hair down there?" I told him that I didn't know, but the subject was never far from my mind that summer. Every time Lucy was nearby, Billy mooned over her as if a goddess had favored him with her presence, a rank of deity I could never come close to matching.

A few evenings later, Billy and I found ourselves in the living room after everyone was asleep, talking. Billy told me about a Swedish movie he'd seen recently. He described the two actors, and when he went on to say they were both naked, and touching each other, I couldn't help myself: what he was saying excited me. Billy was a little beer-drunk, maybe, when he proceeded to tell me how good looking I was. The way I felt didn't show on my face, but at the same time I found I couldn't keep still. I felt physically aroused. Then Billy suggested the two of us go swimming.

We walked to the tennis house in silence. It was dark, maybe ten at night, and the air had a hot, saturated feel to it, as if it were about to rain. Inside the tennis house, Billy and I began changing into our bathing suits, Billy in the men's room, me in the ladies'.

Earlier that night, Billy had asked me if I'd ever skinny-dipped, and I said no. Now he went for the kill. "Carly," he said, the sound echoing like a signal from a boat in distress, "have you got a quarter?"

"I don't have a quarter," I said, my voice sliding across the tennis house's cement floors and pinewood interior. I slipped on my favorite plaid shirt over my bathing suit. Then, in an attempt to please him, I began poking around in ashtrays and in the pockets of the robes hanging off hooks, where my fingers found a dime. Would a dime be good enough? I called out.

"If you want," Billy said, as if he were doing me a favor, and then he proposed a bargain: if I brought him my dime, he would give me a quarter in return. I felt even more excited, grown-up, and my heart stepped up its beat.

That night, the only light came from the cocked lights trained on the pool, which cast spooky shadows.

"Come in, and bring the dime," Billy said again from behind the men's room door.

Which I did, moving stealthily, sensitive to any and all shadows that moved. I felt scared, less about being attacked by someone or something lunging from the shadow than by the thought that some punishing, responsible adult would barge in on the two of us. I continued to feel physically aroused in a new, unfamiliar way. I couldn't stop thinking about the sexy Swedish movie Billy had told me about that night, and I entered the men's room with a mix of confidence, terror, and excitement.

Billy was standing in the center of the room, bare-chested, a skimpy white towel around his waist. At sixteen, he towered over me, and must have weighed twice as much as I did, too. He was handsome, with olive skin and sandy, straight hair like corn silk, almost down to his eyes. Instead of saying hi, or even greeting me, he said only, "Give me your dime and I'll let you pull the towel off my waist."

I didn't understand. Billy persisted. He knew that I wanted to see him without his towel, he said. I began to say something, but felt my stammer rise up and clamp the back of my throat. I was trying to buy some time. I started to say something again, and then I simply decided to relax. My arms felt light and funny, my knees boneless. What would it be like, I wondered, to go skinny-dipping with a boy? My crush on him, or whatever it was, was growing bigger by the second.

Billy repeated his invitation. In fact, he now dared me to pull down his towel. "Either you can do it now, or we can go down to the pool," he said, implying he was offering me an opportunity that few other girls would dream of declining.

That first time, at least, I didn't fall for it. Instead, the two of us made our way down the cement steps toward the swimming pool. It had turned into a soft, beautiful night. It wasn't going to rain, after all.

At the pool, Billy began badgering me again about skinny-dipping. First I would take off his towel, and then I'd strip off my own bathing suit, and the two of us could jump into the pool together. *It's easy, Carly.* It wasn't a proposal, or even a request, more like an order. I was starting to think this was a semi-dangerous idea. Billy stood beside me, half lit by the pool's dim floodlights. He'd let his towel slip slightly from his rear end, the front of him still holding it up, as if it was dangling off the end of a pole.

I wasn't thinking, and had no idea what would happen next, when I moved forward and quickly pulled off his towel, accidentally scratching his skin with my fingernails and making him cry out, "Jeeeesus!" Nor did I sneak a glance at what the towel had been covering. At the same time, I knew I had just crossed a line, one that I wasn't ready for.

In a second, Billy had jumped into the pool, naked, and was asking me— no, again ordering me—to take off my bathing suit and join him. I made up the excuse that I was freezing and had to get into the shower, and I took off across the lawn back toward Stoneybroke and the women's changing room.

I kept my bathing suit on as I stood under the hot water in the ladies' room shower, feeling like a character in a scary movie. I was waiting to see if Billy would follow me in, half praying he wouldn't, half hoping he would. Two minutes later, Billy was standing in the shower stall next to me, naked. I stared down at the tiles on the floor of the shower, doing everything I could not to look at him. Billy told me not to be scared—that it was perfectly okay if I didn't want to remove my bathing suit, the bigger point being that Joey and Lucy both "did this," though he wasn't clear what "this" was. Then Billy took the soap and began lathering his own naked body. Up and down. Side to side.

Joey and Lucy did this? Did what? I was positive Billy was lying. Even though the shower water was hot, I was shivering. Billy, though, didn't seem nervous in the least, nor, surprisingly, did he appear at all happy. No, the expression on his face was something else entirely: strange, focused, private. There was a look of determination. I can't say I knew what he was feeling, but it was clear that he was the male, I was the female; he was the one strutting, and I was the one holding back. By now I wasn't shivering anymore; I was shaking. Was it fear? Was it desire? I couldn't tell the two of them apart. Billy reached down and kissed me on the cheek, doused his hand under the shower needles, and dripped hot water on my face, guiding it down in little drips from my forehead.

"Okay," he said softly. "You'll be more comfortable on your knees."

I obeyed what seemed like the right next command.

"Okay, Carly Darling, look up at me." Billy called me "Carly Darling" a lot, as if mimicking one of my parents, who called me that. I did as he asked, gazing up at his face, though a moment later, by moving my chin lower, Billy made it perfectly clear he hadn't meant me to look up at his face. "Take it in your hand," he said.

How? Like a baseball bat? Like a dinner fork? Like the stem of a flower? I felt the first rise of anger. I wanted to be the one in charge, not Billy. Still, I did as he asked, kneeling on the wet tile and lifting my eyes upward. Then, as fast as possible, I touched him. My shakes dissolved. I couldn't have given a name to what I was feeling; it was way too complicated. There were opposites at work, but there was no doubt about it: I was also turned on. But that was it for the night. I pivoted and ran back to the night-lights of the main house.

After that night, wherever Billy and I happened to find ourselves alone, we misbehaved. A bathroom here, a closet there. A beach, a random patch of grass. During Sunday lunches, Billy would try to pull me into his mood in an upstairs bathroom, as the potatoes were being passed downstairs. By the time I saw Dr. Frunzhoffa, I'd become so benumbed to Billy's behavior—which mostly involved him touching himself, with me never undressed; Billy's only interest, it seems, was in being observed by another person—my numbness itself almost deserved a verse of Frunzhoffa's Fred-and-Ginger ballad. Meanwhile, the whole time I was secretly tortured by the fact that Billy was lusting after my sister Lucy and had no qualms about telling me so. On his part I must have represented some covert compromise, I who was too young to know any better, and too infatuated to bust him, even to Dr. Frunzhoffa.

My "interludes" with Billy lasted, but with less frequency, for six years, into my teens. Until that time, he was my captor and I was his slave. *Love:* that was what I felt for him, or so I convinced myself. During those years, I waited on his every word, gesture, glance, and mood. Being in pursuit of such a low, sneaky, treacherous catch caused me to retreat even farther down inside myself, if that was even possible. It wasn't just that I didn't want to get Billy into trouble, more that I didn't want anyone to stop me, or bring to light how ashamed and conflicted I felt about what the two of us were doing.

When I told Joey and Lucy about Billy, they both accused me of making it up. At the same time, they told my mother, who expelled Billy for an entire month of one summer, which in retrospect feels like a strangely mild response. The biggest secret and vanity of the Simon family was to insist that nothing was wrong when, in fact, so much was wrong, and neither one of my parents ever owned up to it. Today, when I hold my preadolescent diary, small and old and blue, with its cover graphic of a little girl holding a mass of flowers, I have in my hands the tenderest possible proof of my own innocent, flailing, unparented judgment, all of it expelled and encrypted inside that diary whenever it took place. After finishing each entry, I would secure the cover with its tiny key, keeping my fascinated public at bay for another day. If someone had been interested or persistent enough to dig, my diary, with its secrets both exposed and concealed, would have called out: *Someone, please read this and save me.*

I was falling in love with Billy. Lucy was in love with her boyfriend, Marty, Joey was in love with her current paramour, and Mommy, well, Mommy . . . I didn't know yet, but she seemed to be waiting. Just waiting.

That, right there, is such a crucial point in my emotional life. I was already doing things that grown-ups, who shouldn't be doing what they were doing, were doing anyway in an overly sexual atmosphere, where the night was a series of dark corners inhabited by couples swinging branch to branch, lost in music and rapture. The night was a wild cat, stalking from garden to garden. One big copper beech tree in the center of this Garden of Paradise may have been keeping its secrets. It was a part of the thoroughfare on which Daddy would walk at night, like the ghost of Hamlet's father on the ramparts. How many were in those bushes, in those shadows, that if my father had known about, would have taken his life then and there? But he walked, looking straight ahead and never at the shadows.

Me graduating from sixth grade.

Ronny and Mommy, 1955.

---

CHAPTER FOUR

carly, meet ronny

In the mid-1950s, around the same time Billy was quietly stealing a part of me, I started losing my parents. Mommy and Daddy were still there, of course, but in altered forms. Love, as I'd defined it up until that point, took on darker, more secretive meanings and shadowy forms. Our house became a place of intrigue, and implications, and late-night taboos.

Until that time, and in spite of what was going on with Billy, I'd been happily suspended in a Little Golden Books world, with their sunny, skinny spines and images of family normalcy—Daddy coming home from work; Mommy turning around from the stove, where she was placing the top crust onto the apple pie; Laurie the dog wagging her tail. I didn't understand how beneath what looked to the world like an enviable marriage, each one of my parents must have felt so alone, to the extent that in 1954, my mother began a relationship with a much younger man.

Granted, I knew nothing at the time. In fact, not until 1960. But the relationship hung so heavily in the air that I intuitively knew something was happening, knew that my parents weren't in love, knew that what my sisters had told me was true: that when Mommy and Daddy kissed, it was nothing more than a show. And then I repelled that notion and forgot it. A few times as I was growing up, probably in thrall to a romantic movie I'd just seen, I would ask Daddy to bend Mommy down as if in a swoon and kiss her with "passion." When they obliged me, the meeting of their lips came off as awkwardly as two antiques clanking together in the back of a moving truck. In retrospect, I knew there was a reason that I was always watching Mommy and Daddy for signs, hints, clues of what was really going on in their marriage, trying to read between the lines, and yet rejecting everything that didn't fit in with my storybook fantasy.

Why was Mommy so interested in this man, and why did she move him into our house? What did they have in common? I could only guess. Mommy grew up poor in a row of red-brick-porched houses in a lower-middle-class part of Philadelphia's Germantown neighborhood. Cockroaches were underfoot, utilities and rent bills went unpaid. Mommy always seemed proud of her hand-to-mouth background. Even as Mrs. Simon, she was never a snobby, prissy, uptown brat, never had matching table linen, silver spoons, or china with no nicks. Throughout her marriage, Mommy had done everything she could to impress Daddy and the social circles in which they moved. Lacking easy wit, she had tried to appear a woman of words, not realizing that brilliant men rarely seek out brilliant women. Maybe she had enough finesse, of acted-out glamour, of "putting it on," flinging her hair back, applying red lipstick, coming up with the "just so" word or story in between the dessert course and the after-dinner brandies. Maybe she felt bored, unappreciated, undesired. What she didn't know was that the secret love she was about to embark on inside her husband's own house would impair Daddy's health and probably even hasten his early death. Or maybe she suspected but had just stopped caring.

Mommy had always feared for my little brother Peter's manhood in an all-female household. Daddy was worldly and sophisticated and driven— no one really expected him to be the lawn-mowing, basketball-dribbling, baseball-batting type of father, too. Which is why one day, Mommy tacked up an ad on a bulletin board in the hallway of Columbia University's

Teachers College. Wanted: A young, athletic male companion who had the time and patience to oversee the only boy, aged six, in a household of girls, and who could shuttle the boy back and forth to assorted playing fields and sports events. More or less.

I was eight years old and making myself a peanut-butter-and-banana sandwich the afternoon Ronny first appeared in our kitchen in Riverdale, the official reason being that he was a perfect candidate for the Peter-babysitting job. Ronny was maybe an inch or two shorter than Daddy and densely muscled, his physique that of a big, healthy football player, with a light rubbery ring of hard flesh around his waist. It was a kind of alien mid-western bulk I'd never seen before, one where I could almost imagine what lay underneath: steaks and potato salad, mingling with Ronny's own gristle and fascia. It took only a few weeks for my mother to begin likening him to her idol, Gary Cooper, by which I think she meant Ronny was more a body man than a word man.

As Ronny stood beside her, I picked up subtle changes in my mother. Her eyelids fluttered and her lips puckered: "Ron will be staying with us upstairs, in the back bedroom," Mommy said, adding that he was from Pittsburgh and studying to be a teacher. Mommy was forty-two at the time, Ronny only nineteen.

The first time I laid eyes on Ronny, I felt an immediate, electric dislike, followed by an inexplicable disgust. The world felt suddenly unstable, as though it had gone from solid to liquid, but rather than confront what was going on—and really, I had no clue at the time—I focused on something else: Ronny's sandaled bare left foot, specifically his toe. I just couldn't ignore it. The explanation was simple—Ronny had an ingrown toenail—but all I could think of was that his nail was alive, an aquatic horror-movie creature pushing and burrowing further inside his body. I turned away, but it was too late: Ronny's toe had already registered in my brain. Already there was a wrongness about him, building connections inside me on a cellular level. Or maybe I was already responding to the invisible currents between him and my mother.

In the weeks and days before we packed up to go to Stamford that sum-mer, Ronny was officially hired by the Simon family. It made perfect sense for Peter to have a male babysitter. Along with writing and putting on plays,

Helen Gaspard, now the nanny for our whole family, had taught us girls to sew, make up plays for our dolls, and put on stage makeup. In contrast, Peter and his friends collected baseball cards, played with wooden soldiers and train sets, and shook down the adults for spare change in exchange for elaborate card tricks. Ronny seemed custom-made for the job.

He was awkward and uncomfortable around the adults, but no matter—Ronny was also custom-made for Mommy. The connection between them was instantaneous, and they must have found private solace in their shared vulnerability. An orphan, Ronny certainly must have told Mommy his backstory—how he'd watched the airplane that held his mother and father explode as it took off from the airport in Pittsburgh, crashing to the earth, leaving him parentless and alone. No doubt Mommy could match him sorrow by sorrow, as she told him about sitting in her drunken father's lap or sleeping out on the fire escape in summers, with the intermittent swish of the passing train the only thing that cooled her off on hot black nights. Had Mommy never felt good enough, appreciated enough, loved enough, until Ronny came along?

Whenever I heard Mommy and Ronny in conversation, their words flew around like big, beautiful, dumb birds. Clearly it came as a relief to Mommy not to have to pit herself against Daddy's fast-witted authors and friends. Having felt pressured to be publicly funny, like our occasional dinner guests S. J. Perelman, Dorothy Parker, and George S. Kaufman, Mommy was now free to wallow and laze in the relief of easy agreements and dozing silences, *ahhh*s and *oooh*s and other cries of delighted seagulls on the wings of easy flight.

The appearance of Ronny in our lives signaled the end of my family's before, the beginning of our after. As soon as she and Ronny became attached, Mommy's apparent dedication to her husband and children began to fall away. Her lifelong mission—to be the superlative hostess of two elegant households, the cheerful, organized overseer of children, dogs, and assorted houseguests—turned cloudy and sloppy. She seemed to lose interest. In our private relationship, she drifted away too. Without warning, the closeness between us was bashed in the heart. There was something new and unfamiliar between us. Our tenderness, which I'd always taken for granted, seemed suddenly forced. When we hugged, I felt self-conscious for the first time ever about our bodies making contact, as if hugging her was some old, remembered ritual, both of us just going through the motions. It wasn't just that I was getting older and gaining on her in height, but more that her hugs seemed to lack their familiar warmth. Did Mommy know, or suspect, that I was picking up a new current of sexuality in her? I knew only that I no longer made a beeline for her lap whenever I was afraid to go to school. Later on, I would realize that it was Ronny who had stolen her away, but back then all I knew was that if Daddy had never been mine, Mommy wasn't mine anymore, either.

With no alternative than to put up with what was taking place in secret in his own house, Daddy withdrew into his work, his misery, and himself. His relationship with Ronny was always glancing, odd. Whenever the two of them crossed paths on the stairs, their eyes never met. Nonetheless, Ronny regularly sat down for family lunches and dinners. He was a mostly silent presence. When Daddy was around he acted in an intentionally servile way—clearing the table, taking out the garbage—but if Daddy wasn't there, he acted like just another person at the dinner table. As for my little brother, whose physical and academic advancement Ronny was supposed to be overseeing, Peter's role from that point on was to serve as a beard for Mommy. They stole off to Coney Island at midday, attended nonexistent school picnics, and drove up to Stamford in midwinter to check on pipes that were running perfectly well and basement leaks that were causing no imminent threats. Naturally, Mommy began spending far more observable time with Peter.

No longer able to confide in Mommy, and with my stutter preventing me from talking easily, I began confessing everything to my diary, making up a new slew of code words to prevent anyone else from knowing what was really going on in my life at school, or with Billy. *Stammer* evolved from *famul* into *stanform*, the word close enough to Stamford, the town, that any diligent trespasser would get confused. Ronny was *Disk*, and then *Hark*, the name of a mysterious character I'd taken from my favorite James Thurber book, *The Thirteen Clocks*.

In page after page, I penciled out my dislike and resentment of

Ronny—"an intruder," I called him. I wrote that he smelled, adding, "I won't even tell you how much I hate him." Once I wrote in code about the night Joey, Lucy, and I caught Ronny spying on us as we were in our bathroom. Posing as if for a French Impressionist painter, the three of us were combing out our long hair and rubbing our naked bodies with oils and lotions when Joey suddenly whispered, "Sshhh!" and tiptoed to the bathroom door where she found Ronny hunched, with one eye peering through the doorjamb crack. Thinking quickly, Joey went out the other bathroom door to Lucy's room and circled around, coming towards Ronny from the other direction. Ronny pretended he'd been practicing a random football move, grunting out an unpersuasive "Hike!" as he sprinted down the hallway without looking back. This was really quite amusing, and we didn't know what to make of it. Then there was this diary entry: "Oh God, please make them happy, and please God, try to make Mommy love Daddy as much as he loves her. Most of all, please make Daddy be happy. Make Hark go."

None of my wishes came true. Still, it came as a huge relief to me when a year or so after he moved into our house, Ronny was drafted into the army in the fall of 1955, and stationed in Germany. By that point I had started to act out around Ronny, to the point where I told him to his face that I hated him, and invited my more tomboyish friends over to the house to gang up on him and punch him—often in the crotch—though looking back, my behavior was less play than misguided sexual attraction mixed with confused revulsion.

When Ronny left for Europe, not to return at least until the following summer, our house seemed to exhale. Life resumed a mood of normalcy I could barely remember. Despite harder and harder days in the office, once again Daddy had Mommy to talk to when he came home from work at night. The smells of Daddy's favorite dishes wafted in at night, and Mommy seemed more attentive, sitting in the evenings and listening to him play the piano— and I may be mistaken, but I believe there was some smiling at each other.

Which is why a degree of mystery surrounded Mommy's decision to take a trip to Europe in late October that same year. She would travel by herself, without Daddy. Of course, in retrospect, her trip had everything to do with Ronny. I was ten when Mommy left for England by boat a few days before Halloween. Ten days later, Daddy suffered his first heart attack. Even when she was told that her husband had been rushed to the hospital, Mommy didn't come home. Instead, Aunty Jo, a warm, zaftig Swiss woman who had taken care of Daddy and his siblings when they were growing up, picked up the slack, moving into the house for nearly two months to oversee Daddy's physical and psychological care. (She explained that he'd had a "muscle spasm," like the ones people sometimes get in their eyebrows, or eyelids.) Daddy went back and forth from home to the hospital several times, suffering from one tiny ministroke after another, the ambulance racing and blinking up our street in Riverdale in the middle of the night. Every day Joey, Lucy, and I confronted the fear that Daddy might die, and then what would happen? Every time the phone rang, my heart shook. Aunty Jo always made it a point to reassure us that Daddy was slowly getting better, and that he was going to be all right, but none of us ever quite believed her. How could she know for sure? Why wasn't Mommy coming home to be by his side?

During her nearly two-month stay in Europe, I grew to hate some part of my mother, her absence a dark stain that lingered long after she returned home in mid-December and proceeded, as if nothing at all had happened, to deck the house with boughs of holly for Christmas. By then, with Daddy going back and forth to the hospital, I'd begun a new, nightly ritual of knocking on wood exactly five hundred times before I fell asleep—a compulsive superstition that would keep Daddy from dying, or so I convinced myself.

Later, I found the letters that Mommy and Ronny wrote to each other in the months before she went to Europe to visit him, and the love between them was obvious. It was also clear that Mommy had no wish to flaunt their relationship in public. As ever, Andrea Simon, wife of the cofounder of Simon & Schuster, was eager to avoid notoriety or scandal, for everything to be as dignified as possible. Mommy wrote to Ronny that she had no intention of hurting my father, or "starting tongues wagging," and that she would "be very happy to give Dick a divorce if he wants one." Regarding Daddy, Mommy wrote, "I have seen very little of him, but that's just as well. Mostly he's more of a nuisance than a help," adding that she was actively encouraging my father to ignite a romance with tennis champion Don Budge's wife, Deirdre (possibly because it would make her feel less guilty about what she was doing with Ronny, or maybe because she'd have more obvious grounds for divorce). She and Ronny were both decent, honorable people, Mommy wrote in another letter, going so far as to liken the two of them to Romeo and Juliet—"They too had a miserable time of it, darling," adding that even if he, Ronny, wasn't in her life, she would feel the exact same way. "Money," she concluded, "never justifies misery and loneliness, with which I have lived many years."

Ronny loved her back. "Darling," he wrote Mommy at one point, "[it has been] twelve days since I have said 'goodbye' to my beautiful and darling one. And you were beautiful that night, darling, as you had been every single moment I have been and I had been—or have ever been or had ever been with you. You are radiantly beautiful. In forty years you will not have changed and I bet I will love you more with a terrible passion and I'm sure the old man that I will be, you will be young and beautiful."

Once Mommy returned home from Europe, Daddy, officially the third man in his marriage, did everything he could to show his forgiveness, and to be a better husband. By 1956, once he'd recovered from his heart attack, Daddy felt well enough to travel to Europe himself on business, and his letters home to my mother at that time were filled with sentiments like "I love you, my Cosa." Then there was this passage:

"I suggest . . . that both you and I forget completely any gripes that we may ever have had about one another. We have both been living 'with our own blessedness of strife' (Wordsworth) and it's about time to cut that dead-end kind of relationship. Given my physical condition, I am not allowed to do the kinds of things that would make me the most wonderful husband in the world. But soon I'll be able to do those things. The way to begin, is to begin . . . Lovingly yours, Dick."

It wasn't until I read those letters later on that I became swept up in my mother's other, more secret-filled life; saw her, for the first time, from the perspective of my own life and years; realized, as if I needed to be reminded, that what happens in a marriage can never be understood by anyone but the people inside it.

Still, by Christmas 1955, my ten-year-old self was mostly relieved: Ronny was gone, out of the country, out of our lives. He wouldn't be coming back for an eternity, and even when he did my parents would have fallen back in love again, Daddy would be well, and Mommy would be everybody's Mommy again, especially mine. My parents were intact, golden, or so I wanted to believe.

My mother and father; then, left to right: Joey, me, Peter, and Lucy, 1952.

Adolescence springs upon me.

CHAPTER FIVE

splinter-happy steps

I could hear the buoys as clearly as if they came through the radio next to my ear. It was thrilling to come back to the Vineyard. The return was more and more thrilling each time. Those years that spanned the late forties and most of the fifties we rented or borrowed a house on the North Shore, a short walk away from the village and beach of Menemsha. The whole family (not always Joey) went up together. Lucy and I shared a bedroom and clothes and books of chord sheets for folk songs.

In the summer of 1956, Martha's Vineyard was still, as we used to say, in "the olden days." There were dune buggies and woodies and Jeeps, and filling up water buckets at the local well. For the most part there was electricity, but still, not everywhere. There were Lillian Hellman and Dashiell Hammett, Bill and Rose Styron, John and Barbara Hersey, Kingman Brewster, Katharine Cornell, James Cagney, Thomas Hart Benton (and his beautiful daughter Jessie, who was my idol), Yip Harburg, Roger and Evelyn Baldwin, Paul McGhee, Felix Frankfurter, and a whole slew of impressive radical thinkers and educators ready and waiting with their run-down porches and their gin and tonics to welcome you to the island and maybe turn you into a "Commie." Mostly they lived below the radar.

The Vineyard is famously lovely, compared often to sections of Scotland and Ireland. Plots of land are casually separated by stone walls, like a sentence that doesn't take the turn you think it will take, but takes another way around. Sagging barns on ponds look over fields and marshland. The island gets a bit flatter on its south side, as the interior ponds and streams advance to the ocean. Turn around and then a path or an inlet leads you to a dock and a pint-size rowboat with a single oar. Scruffy fishing vessels nearly disappear under the large coils of rope used for hauling pails and other traps that bring lobsters in from the deep.

My parents went there almost every summer between 1938 and the late fifties, when my father was less able to travel for a variety of health and business reasons. In the early, halcyon days, my mother was still in love with my father. And during the summer of 1956, the sound that the buoys made against the dock was still the "Daddy and Mommy are in love" sound.

She still idolized him, as far as I could see. Mother was proud of her husband and his aristocratic and romantic sway. She still gave forth a natural and appreciative throaty laugh in response to his famously dry humor. His narrow but shining blue eyes, when they focused on you, were almost too much to take. His tan against his white shirt rolled to the elbow, showing only his Bulova watch, and his smile from the land of the leaders, seemed to keep her happy. Mommy loved to entertain Vineyard style. Just lobsters or clams, corn on the cob, baked potatoes steamed in seaweed in a trash can out on the lawn or the beach, and simple wine. Simple neighbors (or fancy ones acting simple) came for a sunset dinner. They laughed and sang songs and wobbled their way home under the stars.

"Dickie, can I make you a gin and tonic?" Mommy called into the bedroom of the Leventhals' Menemsha house, which we were borrowing for two weeks. The one that had that long flight of splinter-happy steps leading down to the beach on the North Shore.

"Oh, that would be perfect!" (Oh good, time for cocktails. We would send down to Seward's soon to get dips and carrots and to Larsen's to get some shrimp.)

Needing to make a local call, Daddy then called out, "What's 'Information'?"

"Just call the operator and ask her to get you whoever you want." (That was the old Vineyard way.)

Daddy dialed 0.

An operator picked up, and Daddy said, "Would you put me through to the McGhees?"

The operator said, "You've reached the operator."

Daddy asked in a polite, quizzical way, "Can you tell me what Information is, please?"

And the operator sweetly answered, "Well, sir, Information is when you don't know a telephone number and you have to ask for help."

Well, times *had* changed. But just a little.

Next morning, Lucy, my brother Peter, and I made our second little peregrination via a different route to the Menemsha market (Seward's) to get *The New York Times* as well as muffins for breakfast. We went down Dutcher Dock, then up a hill, and passed the five little houses sitting prominently on a bluff overlooking Vineyard Sound. Our parents had explained to us that those houses constituted "Socialist Hill," because the heads of labor groups either met or lived in those houses during the forties. It seemed very romantic, all the stories about people who rebelled against capitalism. Max Eastman, our great friend who had originally introduced us to the island, had written about Trotsky, Lenin, and Stalin. He made them seem like romantic outlaws. I couldn't picture outlaws. What did they say? What did they wear? I ended up owning one of those five houses up on the hill many years later, in the eighties. For ten years I spent time there living with ghosts of the Bolsheviks as I cooked clam chowder.

That radiant day walking over Socialist Hill and admiring the tender little waves as they lapped on the shore of Menemsha Beach, Lucy, Peter, and I were aware that we were trespassing as we picked a few sprigs of this and that. Mostly, though, we followed the path, and as we approached Seward's, I could see a reflection of myself in a car window that was parked in front of the market. I wore a white, off-the-shoulder elastic top that left my tummy bare. My hair was medium length, half blond, half brown, half short, half long, and therefore, in the end, a tousled, compromised mess, though just in the last three days I'd gotten a tan. Certain that I looked good enough to be seen, I edged in front of my siblings.

As I was rounding the store porch, I caught sight of an extremely cute boy who, from what I could tell, was a few years younger than I. He was sitting on the steps of the porch next to Davy Gude, another Vineyard boy, whose parents and mine were friends. Lucy called out a casual "Hey" to Davy. The two of them, Lucy and Davy, had once been the subjects of a series of photographs taken by Daddy, holding hands as they ran through fields of daisies. As far back as kindergarten, Lucy, poised and charming, had already been claimed by the class's youngest male deity, in this case Davy Gude, who was devastatingly good-looking even as a four-year-old boy.

Davy said "Hey" back, favoring Lucy with his curvy, one-sided smile, lifting his head up from the guitar he was balancing on one knee. As he sang his song, "Didn't Old John Cross the Water," he demonstrated a chord, or a picking technique, to his younger friend, virtually covering an entire octave as he sang the word *Galilee*. He then introduced the other boy: "This is Jamie." Jamie could have been Davy's younger brother. We were all tall and lanky, but even sitting down, Jamie was the lankiest. Both boys had a stringy, androgynous allure, a bony teenage elegance, early out of the gate.

Telling everyone I had to get the mail, I disappeared into Seward's, swinging my hips as I opened the door. This was a brand-new trick, and I had to sneak a peek over my shoulder to see if either of the two young gods, Davy or Jamie, had followed my stride with their gaze.

No such luck.

Inside the store, I bought what I needed to get for Mom, and then gave Bill (Seward) a dime for a vanilla ice cream Popsicle, deciding that Lucy could have half. As I left, the screen door slammed with a sound that traveled on the breeze right into the center of Davy's note. He sang the word *roll* perfectly in pitch with the squeak of the door. Jamie was playing the guitar now. I pulled down just a little on my white elastic top, which had ridden up my left shoulder. All of them, including my little brother, who didn't know the song, were singing a chorus of "Roll On, Columbia, Roll On," as I sat down on the step next to Jamie and removed the paper from the Popsicle. I started to eat it. Jamie turned his head to the left and there I was, sitting right beside him. He was playing the chords to the song perfectly while indicating to me, by pointing his long chin in the direction of my ice cream, that a bite might be a good thing, but . . . he didn't even look at me. He just took a nice bite right off the top. Then another one. He had consumed half of the pop when he began singing with Davy again, never looking at me once. He just had great ice cream aim.

"Jamie." That's what everybody called him. His whole name was James Taylor. On the Vineyard the next summer, Daddy and I went to a "sing" at the Chilmark Community Center. Davy was going to be singing with Jessie Benton (Thomas Hart Benton's brilliant daughter). I sang along with them on "Dr. Freud, how I wish that you were differently employed." The whole audience was sitting on the floor, and almost everyone sang with them on the chorus. Jamie Taylor was there, sitting not too far away. His brother was with him, whose name I learned was Alex. Alex was very blond and a little chubby, in contrast to Jamie's dark lankiness. Daddy was just staring at Jessie Benton. "She's a knockout," he said. He was right.

I was feeling sick about Billy. These gods of music, these gorgeous tan boys who were singing and smiling, were my age. As I thought about Billy, I almost had to leave the community center. It was such a terrible feeling. But I forgot about it soon, and I learned to think of it as something completely "other." Maybe it had never happened. Wouldn't that be wonderful? I kept thinking I saw Jamie on his bike everywhere. I found out the Taylors lived on South Road right near Stonewall Pond, where the ocean almost connects to Menemsha Pond. Up-island.

Before that summer was over, my diary revealed that I wanted nothing more than for Davy Gude to fall in love with me, but that wasn't going to happen. The real, live, beautiful couple that summer was Davy and Jessie. But Davy did lots of good things for me. At his house one afternoon, he brought out his second guitar. He taught Lucy and me a new strumming technique for "Winkin', Blinkin' and Nod," Lucy's song that she had written based on a Eugene Field poem, but which Davy was going to record for a record label!!! Lucy and I began to sing that wonderful song at my parents' parties, and eventually *we* recorded it. It was our "starting point," our "break."

In addition to learning a lot of music, listening to it, and listening to other people play and sing, I came across a book at the house we had rented that summer about the Greek gods. I spent an hour reading about Orpheus and Eurydice. I savored every tragic detail: how Orpheus, the magical musician and poet, falls deeply in love with Eurydice. As he strums his lyre and sings to her, they fall more and more in love, and eventually they marry. Bitten by a snake, Eurydice dies in Orpheus's arms and descends to the Underworld. Desperate to bring her back, Orpheus follows her, begging the Lord of the Underworld for his assistance. Overwhelmed, as everyone is, by the beauty and the magic of Orpheus's singing and playing, Pluto agrees to allow Eurydice to return to the surface of the earth, but with one condition: during their ascent, Orpheus is forbidden even to glance at her. Not once, not even for a second. If he does look, Eurydice will disappear forever.

Orpheus agrees, but as the two of them are making their way out of the Underworld and Orpheus catches a glimpse of the first welcoming light, he loses his faith. Unsure that Eurydice is really still there, he looks behind him, and the moment he does, she, the woman he loves more than anything in the world and knows he will love forever, vanishes slowly backward into the hazy, twilit nothingness of the Underworld. "The story isn't real, it's a myth," I remember Daddy trying to reassure me. Was it? I thought. Is it? Why did I feel so connected to its power at such an early age?

For me, the wind-and-water-swept romantic, the myth of Orpheus and Eurydice was all about everlasting love, about a beautiful musical god so in love with a woman that he couldn't stand not to look back at her. It was about the cool, cleansing air of music, whether it was exhalations of relief and anger I heard coming from my father at the piano while I was in my bed at night, or the sounds of Davy Gude's guitar as I gazed at the lost, mystical, beautiful expression on his face. Music brought me closer to the idea of God. Music gave me the energy to revise, revive myself; renew, rebirth myself. It was a palliative, a relief. I have always known it would rescue me, as it had bandaged Daddy, bypassed my stammer, brought my families together. Both of them: my family of origin, and the children I would eventually give birth to. There was always an Orpheus in my orbit.

Orpheus was a boy who could quiet the wind, charm the rocks, silence the trees, the stones, the fish, the animals, who could divert the course of rivers and even take up arms against the Underworld, his lyre eventually transported to heaven by the Muses to take its permanent place among the stars. A boy who sang the sun up to red-orange, who played the guitar with such delicacy it made every girl swoon and every boy want to be him, in whatever form it took, Orpheus was a teacher. Whatever he knew the rest of us would borrow, add on to as we would. Eventually I would come up with my own sound, my own voice. I hoped and prayed, and still do, that Orpheus will always find me when I dip into my own private underworlds, and that when my soul loses direction—as it has so many times since my discovery—I will be able to find it again. That I will remember:

Orpheus, it could have been,
You could have held me again
You said your songs had all gone
That the road back up was too long
But it was there for us, it was there for us
I loved you all along, Orpheus
Out of despair and believing I was gone
You gave up on my love
You gave up on us,
But it was there for us
It was there for us
I loved you all along, Orpheus.
  —"Orpheus," 1983

The Vineyard beach at a time when you could count the footsteps in the sand.

Joey: the only person who could get the brush through the knots.

CHAPTER SIX

the dinner party

It was July 28, 1956, and my parents were hosting a dinner party in honor of the esteemed English publisher Victor Gollancz. Peter, too young, always got a pass, but as usual, Joey, Lucy, and I were expected to make a formal appearance—never forgetting Mommy's whispered instructions: no jeans, no bare feet, no sneakers, no nail polish, no hair in curlers (of course!), no hats, no tight dresses, and if we insisted on wearing makeup, only a little, since Daddy had recently yelled at Joey for overdoing it. In fact, he had called her a trollop. She cried very long and hard, which told me what *trollop* might mean.

Joey and I shared a front bedroom. Our second-floor bathroom had a balcony overlooking the front lawn, affording us stealthy glimpses of the guests as they drove in and around the circular driveway, a procession of Cadillacs, woodies, and Bel Airs. Occasionally, one of us would be lucky enough to spy a private moment—a kiss, or a front-seat argument, before the couple in question carefully reattached their dinner-party masks, that sneak spyglass-peek of lust or vitriol all the more thrilling for having been seen from our hidden aerie. A man's body came into view. It was Dickie Bauerfeld, the boy who trimmed dead branches and picked fruit from the fruit trees. It was late in the day for him to be there. We all had crushes on him. Or at least his shoulders. Sometimes we'd stare at him for five minutes straight, but even so I hardly ever saw his face.

That night began innocently, with no hint whatsoever of the surprise that would come at its climax, causing my diary to overflow with page upon page of coded entries over the next few months. I took a shower before Joey, having won the coin toss. That year, my hair was shoulder-length, and after removing the knots with a broad-tooth comb, I set about copying Lucy's and Joey's method of creating pin curls around the base, plus a few extra in the bangs, my quixotic hope being to create a dip à la Rita Hayworth.

For twenty minutes, I sat under the hair dryer reading an *Archie* comic book, the machine so noisy that I couldn't hear Joey pounding on the door. From experience I knew that my own hair would likely either unravel or frizz up fast, but *Seventeen* magazine had taught me a few insider's tricks. I removed the pin curls and let them dance damply and loosely on my head before combing them into what I hoped would resemble Rita's hairdo. I then found a scarf to keep everything in place while it dried. Hair. Hair was everything. Finally, I heard the pounding and let Joey in. She was all red with anger. I said I was sorry and we exchanged places.

Next, I applied makeup before the bedroom mirror. Joey and Lucy had taught me well. First came Persian Melon lipstick, followed by a midcoat of Pink Innocence, and at last, the crucial finale: a lip blender, Nude Spring Dance. My salty, damp, oily skin tended to make the acne I was trying so hard to cover over look like a miniature volcano about to erupt, so I added Clearasil over my breakouts, reapplying it every few minutes, as it had a tendency to melt. Next, remembering a scene from *Gone with the Wind*, I had the brilliant idea of putting powder over those spots. I called out to Joey, asking her if she had some talcum powder, but she was still peeved at me for taking so long in the bathroom and didn't answer.

I put on "Moonglow," my favorite song that year, the beguiling string parts humming and crackling through the speakers of my portable record player, turning up the volume as loud as it would go and dancing as Joey continued to ignore my pleas for talc. I moved my hips and watched myself in the mirror thinking that this is what Davy and Jamie might have seen if they'd followed me with their gaze.

Earlier that day, I'd decided to wear the blue sleeveless dress that Lucy had passed down to me. Not wanting to disturb the turban holding in the pin curls, I put it on feet first, pulling it up carefully, negotiating the arm holes, angling it onto my body, coercing it into a strange, unfamiliar shape. After two summers clinging to Lucy's body, it would forever hold her particular camber. I was hoping that my bust would be almost as curvy, sexy, and grown-up as Lucy's, but when I stood up straight, instead of a bust there were two puckers that looked as if I'd been punched twice from the inside, by a baby's fists.

When Joey finally opened the bathroom door, holding the talc, she found me with my back to her, stiff-shouldered, still trying to maneuver Lucy's dress around my gangling, resistant shape. I couldn't help but gaze at Joey's chest, from which protruded an infuriatingly grown-up pair of what were then politely called "bosoms," or more alluringly, "breasts." Looming from inside Joey's white slip, floating just above the waterline, they were Hallelujah breasts, breasts that belonged to the climax of Beethoven's Ninth Symphony, and I couldn't have been more fascinated, nor hated her more.

From behind the bedroom door, we both heard my mother's voice rushing us, calling from the bottom of the stairs. The two of us exchanged a fast, nervous glance. "I know a trick," Joey said suddenly, and in her voice was now a distinct tone of compassion. Opening up her sock drawer, she took out a pair of white cotton tennis socks, balling them up in her hand and rolling them out as flat as she could. Once they were in position on my chest, Joey rezipped my dress and we both surveyed the results: two points of uneven, lumpy, linen shapes, jutting out into the room, again like babies' fists punching from within.

Joey tried hard not to laugh, even though by now I was crying, convinced nothing in my life would ever work again. But Joey knew another ruse. Tearing off a piece of tissue, she spread it so it leveled the lumps in the socks, pushing and mashing the sock-tissue mix more deeply against my chest. Still, a dead giveaway. We heard Mommy's voice again, this time warning and insistent. Defeated, I removed the two sad little white socks. Joey draped a scarf around my shoulders, which I'd have to keep close. Then the two of us walked like ladies downstairs.

Among the crew of regulars that evening were Don and Deirdre Budge, Benny and Alice Goodman, Jackie and Rachel Robinson, Bennett and Phyllis Cerf, and Daddy's new author Sloan Wilson. I was relieved to see Uncle Peter there, too, and silently prayed I could sit beside him. As usual, Joey was the first to enter the living room, absorbing a royal cascade of *oooh*s and *ahhh*s as her natural birthright. All the men except for Daddy rose to their feet, while the women at the table hesitated, stealing glances at the other females for clues on how to react. On how to respond when a much younger woman takes all the attention in the room. As dinner music, Daddy had put a record on the turntable. Gershwin's "Rhapsody in Blue." If heaven was preparing a dramatic dénouement, it landed on its mark perfectly. The horns seductively swelled and reached their peak, just as Lucy took everyone's breath away, simply by entering the room.

She appeared in the hall doorway inside a golden hazy ray of the dying afternoon sun and took a lone step forward, shy, sweet, nervous, corruptible. She wore a sleeveless rose-brown dress that buttoned all the way up from the shapely middle of her legs to where her waist pulled in tight. In her hair was a dusting of polyanthus, and in possible defiance of Mommy, her feet were bare. In all our days together, Lucy was never as beautiful as she looked that night and, for the first time, I saw her through the guests' eyes—the eyes of a larger audience—and, not least, in questioning contrast to myself.

Daddy had risen to his feet for Lucy's entry, too, his eyebrows cocked slightly upward in approval. No one saw it but me. It was as if Daddy had just seen an angel descend to earth, and what's more, realized that he was that angel's father, a certified angel-maker. At that moment I knew one thing for sure, one thing that had been true for as long as I could remember: Lucy was Daddy's Darling, the ingénue to the star, Joey, who was loath to—and never would—relinquish her power. I was long past wishing I were Daddy's favorite—I didn't want him, in fact, and was officially out of the running, which was okay with me, as I had Uncle Peter to love. Tonight, as always, Uncle Peter would step in as my parent substitute. My entrance was flawlessly unnoticed. I slipped between the guests, otherwise preoccupied, neither shadow nor star. Uncle Peter saw me and whispered, "Don't worry, we'll get through this together."

At dinner, I sat between Jackie Robinson and Don Budge, at one point the top-ranked tennis player in the world. As for the Robinsons, our family had a long history with them. Jackie and his wife had lived with us during the construction of their own house a few miles away in Stamford. Daddy, Jackie, and I used to drive to Ebbets Field to watch the Brooklyn Dodgers' home games. In the dugout I would sit on Pee Wee Reese's lap, and was once even informally named the Dodgers mascot, with the team stitching together a special jacket for me with DODGERS printed on the back and CARLY on the front. I was *very* proud of Jackie, and my knowing him was a *very* big deal. His son Jackie Junior was my brother Peter's best friend. Jackie even taught me to bat lefty, though it never took. I loved him. He always had the cutest look around the side of his mouth, as if he were thinking about what he was about to say before he said it.

Across from me at the cramped, cozy table, Mommy looked glamorous and lovely. Her gardenia matched the white stripe in her stiff black-and-white cotton dress, the two colors zigzagging diagonally across her bodice in dramatic contrast to her red lipstick. She could have been a dancer. She danced as she passed the hors d'oeuvres and her eyes danced as she lived most of her divinely choreographed life. Who wouldn't have envied Andrea Simon and her marriage to one of the reigning kings and innovators of the publishing world? Even though Daddy had suffered his first heart attack a year before, he was still making round trips to Europe, returning to the office with new books and new strategies to publish them. That year alone, he had published books by the great French photographer Henri Cartier-Bresson, William Whyte (who wrote *The Organization Man*), and our dinner guest Sloan Wilson.

At age eleven, it was embarrassing to admit I still wasn't sure what a publisher even did. I imagined paper dipped into vats where colors and dyes ran and swirled together, alongside piles of parchment paper in need of sanding so they could become smooth enough to allow tiny, monklike people wearing hats adorned with pompoms to write on them. Eventually, miles of Scotch tape and string would bind together the finished books. Even though it was absurd to think I ever believed that, it was as comfortable, and comforting, to me as the ridiculous notion that Mommy and Daddy were in love with each other. Notions could be absurd and still stand, after all.

The conversation at dinner that night was typically wide-ranging, from how the Dodgers were doing to the recent sinking of the *Andrea Doria*. An ocean liner sinking: I could now add drowning to my long list of other fears, which included spiders, earthquakes, shark attacks, and getting through sentences. Benny Goodman, who had just finished recording the Mozart Clarinet Quintet with the Boston Symphony Orchestra, dominated the conversation. Even if Benny had interested me as a musician—and at the time I was preoccupied with Frank Sinatra and Elvis—he was far better known to Joey, Lucy, and me as a suspected kleptomaniac, a sneak-stealer and pocketer of one of our family's pens. He was never indicted, mind you, only suspected.

Today, I can't help but think back on Jackie Robinson and Benny Goodman at the same table that night: Jackie, the athlete who'd broken the baseball color line in 1947, and Benny, the musician who ten years earlier, during an era of segregation, was the first bandleader to integrate jazz by hiring the pianist Teddy Wilson and the guitarist Charlie Christian to play in his bands. A counterattack in the eternal war in American race relations was brewing, and later on I felt proud to have been part of such an "advanced" era, especially as it was just another Saturday night in my parents' house.

The publisher Victor Gollancz, who made more noises than words, said to Rachel Robinson, "So, you are a singer, yes?" Daddy laughed, cracked his knuckles, and warmly defused any confusion. In England, all beautiful black women in the U.S. were assumed to be either Ella Fitzgerald or Sarah Vaughan. Benny was going on at length about melody, and his surprise at how well classical music and his own sound dovetailed, before the conversation moved on to Billie Holiday and how, in general, artists gravitated toward self-destructiveness. At one point Jackie asked Daddy about George Gershwin, and both Daddy and Benny chimed in. Daddy regaled the table with a story of the time in 1928 when he met Gershwin in his suite at the Bristol Hotel in Paris. "George had a ten-foot grand piano that just stood there, for him alone," Daddy said. "Can you imagine? Then George said, 'Do you mind if I play just a little something?'"

"What kind of ridiculous question is that?" Daddy asked George. "Are you kidding me?" In response, Gershwin took a seat at the piano and played Daddy some of *An American in Paris*, which he described to Daddy as a "tone poem." "George was using the honking of Paris taxis as horns in his huge orchestra, as well as all kinds of other sonically suitable traffic sounds," Daddy added.

Uncle Peter had been waiting patiently for his turn, and now he glanced over at Mommy. "Don't you remember when you sang 'Summertime' for George and Ira?" he said, adding to Daddy, "And you accompanied her?" Mommy covered her mouth with her cloth napkin. Of course she remembered; it was the most embarrassing moment of her life. "There we were," Mommy said, "George and Ira, sitting in front of Dick"—meaning Daddy—"as I sang 'Summertime,' since they had never heard it sung in a woman's voice before. But then, what did he do? Your father?" Deliberately, with both eyebrows raised, Mommy's eyes found Joey, Lucy, and me. "Your daddy stopped me halfway through the song and said, 'No, Andrea, that's not quite right, it goes like this—'" Mommy hesitated. "And then he sang the melody himself. Your daddy actually interrupted me to correct a note! I was so mortified, I was about to run out of the room when George stopped me and commented sweetly that my version might have been the better of the two melodies after all!"

The table exploded with laughter, my mother leading the way, and once it had subsided, Mommy asked me whether I'd perform the tune I'd been singing all morning, the one that had gotten so stuck in my head from the recent movie starring Bill Haley, *Rock Around the Clock*. Singing for the table was nothing out of the ordinary; our entire house was an opera, with all of us singing and harmonizing day and night. Wrapping my shawl tightly and self-consciously around my top, I thought, Oh, to be Joey and Lucy, who would have sung a song in seconds, without even thinking about it. To my relief, Joey started off:

One, two, three o'clock, four o'clock rock,
Five, six, seven o'clock, eight o'clock rock
Nine, ten, eleven o'clock, twelve o'clock rock
We're gonna rock around the clock tonight

And a few moments later everyone at the table joined in, whether they knew the song or not, with Uncle Peter even kicking in the saxophone sound he liked making with his mouth, Satchmo style. Benny Goodman roared at Uncle Peter's performance.

Just then, our three dogs, Porgy, Bess, and Laurie, started barking, clambering out from under the dining room table and racing toward the kitchen. Had a doorbell rung and no one heard it? Was there somebody out there? Poised for any excuse to leave, I told the table I'd be right back, and tore off after the dogs through the pantry and into the kitchen.

There was someone at the back door, knocking softly.

The three women working in the kitchen that night—Sula, Bea, and Lena—puzzled aloud as to who it could be: Who would show up at the back door so late at night? They suspended putting the coffee cups on the trays. Excited, the dogs scrambled together, a mass of fur and tongues. It was then I heard Lena's exclamation, hushed, shocked: "Well, well, my word. It can't be. We weren't expecting you. Not yet."

A tall, good-looking man wearing a tan army uniform stood on the doorstep, his brimmed hat slanted at an angle, shadowing his face. Ronny. When he gazed straight at me, in that instant, I forgot to breathe. Without even saying hello, I slid past everyone—the three women, the three dogs—into the back pantry, where the big freezer was, bolting on tiptoe up the narrow back stairs to the servants' quarters. I stood there, extremely still, shaking.

What should I do? Should I stroll back downstairs into the dining room and announce, as any grown-up hostess would, that Ronny had dropped by unexpectedly, and could we pull up an extra chair at the dining table? Ronny, in fact, was the last person in the world I ever wanted to see again. I had thought maybe I wouldn't. From the dining room, I could make out the charged, adult hum of raised voices and laughter. Ronny was still chattering with Lena and Sula in the kitchen, and as I stood there on the steps, all I could do was hope and pray that this whole thing was a giant mix-up that could be reversed with the touch of a button, that Ronny would simply retrace his steps to a car that would scoot him back to the airport that would in turn bring him back to the war. The wonderful, wonderful war that had removed him. A ragged memory of the ingrown toenail in his foot flashed in my mind, and repulsed me. I wondered if that nail was still there. Perhaps the war had removed it. . . .

It didn't happen that way. Three days later, Ronny had moved back into our house and into our lives. My feelings for Ronny hadn't changed, but this time around I told my diary I would keep them to myself. Looking back, it was almost as if I'd realized how handsome he'd become, that I couldn't put a name to what I was feeling, but I knew, too, how dangerous that feeling was to my own composure. "He really is a sweet boy," I wrote at one point, "and not bad looking at all." I knew, in that way a child knows, that Ronny and Mommy had simply picked up where they had left off. I was also uncomfortably aware of feeling jealous, since Ronny was paying more attention to Lucy and Joey than he was to me.

Ever since Ronny had infiltrated our house, I had no idea what to do with my feelings: Feeling unloved. Feeling I was plainer and less desirable, somehow, than my two bird-of-paradise sisters. Feeling jealous of the attention Lucy and Joey got from Daddy, and from boy after boy, too. Upset, even, by the idea of Mommy looking sideways, with a flirtatious smile, at Ronny. The secrets, subversions, and dark spirits inside the Simon household were extremely real. Billy. My mother. Ronny. I sought some kind of freedom in music, in the promise of transcendence and the idea that the purity and the innocence of a mythical god could somehow deliver me from darkness. Music to dance to, music to sing, music to play with Uncle Peter, music to listen to my father play. I remembered reading about Orpheus. I started wanting to find him. To meet him.

Three Simon girls on the lawn in Stamford, Connecticut. It was so easy.

"Darling, don't let us Simons bother you, this is just
something we always do."

CHAPTER SEVEN

moonglow

I never got to witness the arrival of Ronny into the dining room. I don't think Mommy was expecting him that night; why did he come in the back door? Maybe he *did* disappear again out through the screen door and falling into his own dark history. But only three days later, he was back in his civilian clothes and incorporated back into the household. He was too tall and handsome and bulky and muscular to fade into the woodwork. I didn't know where he would be sleeping. Soon enough I found out that he was on the third floor of the house, where Mommy had also taken up residence. "Daddy's snoring is really bad now," she'd said.

As you ascended the flight of stairs to the third floor, there were two rooms on either side of the landing. The one to the left was the guest room: the grandest room of the house. It was decorated in pale greens, not unlike Joey's and my room, which was directly below it. It had two Early American twin beds that were neither single nor double. They were that indeterminate size for which you can no longer find mattresses to fit. Consequently, the mattresses on those beds felt as if they had been there since the Revolutionary War. There was a sitting area that faced toward the front of the house, and it was furnished with my father's mother's Victorian couch and chairs. They had been upholstered in a print with apple red as its primary color. The mahogany wood surrounding the tufted loveliness was sculpted into the usual cherubs and palm leaves.

The bathroom to that kingly suite was was all violet-, lavender-, and rose-colored tiles.

On the other side of the landing as you arrived on the third floor was a cedar closet: a nice big one that had a heavy door that we imagined you could have hidden slaves behind when the Confederate Army came. It smelled of camphor and was filled with hatboxes and old suitcases from the twenties and thirties. Both sides of the large closet were taken up with rows of hanging clothes. Hand-me-downs, we called them. When we were little, Jeanie and I loved to go up to the cedar closet and play with our dolls there. Lots of fantasies could be enacted and clothes tried on from the poles that were within our reach. To the right of the closet was another door. It led to the room that Mommy had slept in before Ronny had gone off to war.

Shortly after Ronny returned, there are some significant entries in my diary:

July 30th:
This evening Daddy got sick and had pains in his chest and arms. The doctor came and said he was all right. I'm rather relieved.

Aug 3rd:
I got home from the Wilsons and Ronny was there. Tonight I got such an inferiority complex from Lucy cause Ronny kept looking at her and not me.

Aug 4th:
Ronny is kind of rejecting me. He seems not to think anything of me and to not think I'm pretty, but to think Lucy and Joey are beautiful and fair.

Aug 5th:
Mommy seems to say things that aren't true. Tonight she said "I wish I looked like you" and of course she only said that to make me

feel good. She just isn't sincere. She must have told Ronny I had an inferiority complex because he looked at me on purpose. Tonight we all sang songs and played records. Daddy joined in too. It was so much fun.

Aug 6th:
Daddy didn't feel well and didn't go to the office.

In early September, Mother came down to the tennis court where I was practicing alone, hitting balls against the backboard; she was hiding something in back of her. It turned out to be my friend Nora, whom I hadn't seen all summer. She was a good friend from school, although not really in the clan of girls I was best friends with. Nora was a little older and lived in Westchester. In retrospect, I'm pretty sure Mother arranged the visit with Nora's father for her own purposes. She didn't want distractions from her time with Ronny. Daddy was back at the office full time, and Peter was preoccupied with Jackie Jr. and his friend Michael Crosby and being taken care of by the babysitter of one of the other kids.

Lucy was off with Marty and Joey was in New York. I believe Mother wanted those days between nine and six pretty much to herself and Ronny. It must have been chaotic, this juggling by my mother.

I was surprised but pretty happy to see Nora. She had gone to camp over the summer and had a boyfriend. I think she may have been the first in our class to really have an actual boyfriend. Nora had turned a corner that I hadn't yet turned. We watched a lot of TV. I could tell Nora had outgrown dolls. And since Joey was away, she slept in Joey's bed. We pushed the two beds together, sprawling on them to play cards. The next day Mommy and Ronny went to Jones Beach. Nora and I were allowed to stay behind with Lena as long as she was on duty in the house. We were feeling the thrill of having the house to ourselves. There were things to be discovered. We snuck up to the third floor and went into the room to the right of the landing, where Ronny had left his unpacked suitcases from his long trip away. We tiptoed around. We opened his bureau drawers and ignored the mundane things like shirts and pants, but when we opened the top drawer and saw what Nora identified as a jockstrap, she pulled it out and tried to determine the size of what would fit inside it. I was repulsed but excited. I said that we'd better put it back. Nora wanted to keep looking. It was then I noticed the dresser was pulled a little away from the wall.

Was there a plug back there? Nora was an intrepid explorer. She pulled the not-so-very-heavy bureau farther away from the wall, and we saw what looked like a very small door in the wall.

If we hadn't discovered that door, maybe my life would have unfolded in a different order. If a piece of paper blows against your leg in the street and you pause just long enough to reach for it, and a car smacks into you while it's backing up, everything instantly changes. That's what this was like. What we discovered was profound. My first thoughts had to do with feeling exposed: Nora was seeing this. What if there were family treasures hidden there with certain notes or instructions? Or very, very private things? Then I imagined fairy tale small people who might fit through this door, for it was fit for a gnome or a troll, an elf or a witch. Rumpelstiltskin or one of his cohorts could turn the darkness that we faced into gold. Darkness to gold. Yes. I had to think fearlessly. Nora didn't know the geography of the house, therefore it wasn't a surprise to her. She was just waiting for me to explain my shock. I told her that it was the first time I had ever seen this little door. I guessed that it could have been a closet that I never knew was there. Maybe it was a closet for Ronny to put his guns in. It could fit guns. We peered into the closet as if anything was possible. There was no light coming from anywhere, and the space turned left at a forty-five-degree angle, leading to—Where? My mother's bathroom?

It was then I heard a sound, which I guessed was a human being or an animal about to attack us. Nora was staying safely behind me. I looked back at her for a comfort that wasn't going to be given. The room was darker, or was it my imagination? It wasn't that late in the afternoon. Maybe three or four. But it felt as if it were much later. I looked out the window above the double bed, and the sky looked dark, too. The trees were blowing, and so I knew a storm was coming.

"Maybe we should close the door and push the bureau back against the wall." Scary movies filled my mind.

"You've never seen this door before?"

Then, all of a sudden, someone was very close.

"What are you girls doing?" It was Ronny. He wasn't angry, but he didn't seem like himself.

"What are you doing up here?" he asked again.

"I just noticed the bureau was stuck out from the wall and wanted to push it back." I didn't breathe and I didn't look at him, though I could feel him. Ronny was very tan. Even tanner than when he had gotten back from the war. I knew he and Mommy had been at Jones Beach. They went there a lot, sometimes with Peter, the Beach Beard. Ronny looked like Rock Hudson, darker than the dark room, and if you want to be polite and scary at the same time, ask him how he did it.

There was a thunder strike. I looked down at my feet, and without any excuses, I moved toward the stairs. Nora followed me out of the room. The two of us were like secret agents whose cover has just been compromised. We deliberately didn't run down the stairs, but held on to the banister tightly, hurrying down the steep steps. Nora was right behind me, and soon we were in my room flopping on the bed, exhaling as if we had been holding our breath since Ronny first caught us. I couldn't believe we had said nothing at all. No excuses, no little screams.

It was now raining. I didn't know what to say. We couldn't go out. I felt constrained to my room, as if some revelation was going on beyond my range of hearing. I imagined Mommy would soon barge into my room in her German-tank mode. When she wasn't sure of herself, she used her eyes, which were narrow and went light instead of darker when she squinted. They could terrify me. But she didn't come in.

We settled down, and I suggested we write letters, since I had four or five to answer. I had some extra postcards of the fishing boats that lined the Menemsha harbor from our time on the Vineyard. We started to write, but neither of us could get it out of our minds that there might be some punishment coming. I also thought of the little door, the dark hole of the nightmare. What was all that about? Did I expect an explanation, or would I be preempted by an explosion from the grown-ups? Instead, an hour passed, and the rain came and got harder and disappeared completely, and then came back again.

Around six thirty, Mother, trying to arrange her attitude, came in my room. I could read the discomfort on her face. I was already into the letter I was writing to my friend Jessie, telling her how annoyed I was that Nora was there, using a code name for Nora, of course. Another little lie. I wanted to erase the whole impression of what had happened in the last four hours. Then my mother said, "Dinner in five minutes! Mac and cheese!" as if everything was normal.

Nora and I changed out of our Bermuda shorts and put on skirts with matching tops. She wore a red-and-white plaid short-sleeved shirt, and probably a bra under that. The dress rules were flexible on nights when it was just family. This was an in-between night. Nora was a guest, but not one who required formality. She took a lipstick out of her suitcase, which was inside its own little pouch. She opened it up and it was fire-engine red, like her shirt. She went to the mirror over the dresser and carefully applied it to her ridiculously Cupid's-bow-shaped lips. I say ridiculously because I had never seen lips like that in person, only in movie magazines. I too put on lipstick, and we both—though we could have spent hours on the details of our burgeoning beauty—quickly fixed our hair. I put mine into a ponytail. Nora turned upside down from the waist and brushed her long, shiny, chestnut brown hair, which had the unique ability to shape itself into a perfect wedge when she turned upright. We generated the kind of energy that adolescent girls have a premium on.

Mommy, Ronny, Nora, and I sat around the dining room table, which was not set. It was what Mother called "buffet." The cooks had made dinner before they left, but there were no place settings, just a stack of plates for us to help ourselves. Those were the most fun and casual of times. Music was always playing from the living room. That night *Carousel* was on. I hadn't seen the Broadway play yet, but all bodies in the house (as Mommy called us) were going around singing and harmonizing to "What's the Use of Wond'rin'?" and "You'll Never Walk Alone." Ronny was singing in his most self-conscious baritone: *Walk on through the wind, walk on through the rain, though your dreams be tossed and blown, walk on, walk on, with hope in your heart* . . . He stopped just before the climax of the highest part—well, not really stopped, but carefully dipped down to a harmony a third below. Then I joined in on the repeat: "You'll never walk . . . alone." Mommy clapped, and in walked Peter and Jackie with yo-yos and freshly dirty hands. Nora and I served ourselves. The volume of the music was often a contest of wills. Daddy liked it very soft. Mommy liked it quite loud. If it was Elvis or Sinatra, I liked it loud.

Mommy said, "Your dad is staying in the city tonight." I could have told her that just by the volume of the music. And the fact that Ronny was singing at the top of his quite well-trained but thoroughly irritating voice. There was competition coming from the storm outside as well. It was the kind of sonic hysteria that contemporary rock 'n' roll bands hope to achieve. So, dinner was quite noisy, with half of us singing while we were eating. Nora looked at me sideways. She was hearing me sing for the first time. I was pretty good at singing, but it was more for the love of the act. It was so freeing and fun to sing when I was beyond stuttering. Nora thought maybe she should sing, but my mother laughed and put her hand on Nora's head and said, "Darling, don't let us Simons bother you, this is just something we always do."

Later that night, we watched a TV movie about someone with a drinking problem, probably with Jack Lemmon or Susan Hayward. When it was over we went upstairs and played "Magical Hand" with Peter and Jackie. It's a game where we scared the hell out of the boys by entering their darkened room just a jot, holding a flashlight over our hand positioned to look like a claw. They'd scream, we'd scream, and we'd enter their room and tickle their bellies until they laughed with a combination of terror and merriment. Then we'd go out of the door, turn off the flashlight, and wait for them to be really quiet to begin again. We wore them out, and after an hour of fun and games, we closed the door to Peter's room. It was just across the hall from Joey's and my room. What Mommy and Ronny were doing was anybody's guess. I think there was a soundtrack of something playing. Probably *Guys and Dolls* or *Kiss Me, Kate*. Between the pulses of rain, I could hear the music swelling and dropping from above, on the third floor.

The storm was rearranging itself between the twigs and among the branches. Acorns were snapping against the screens and the glass-paned windows and the sides of the house. It was the Indian summer dance of the sycamores, oaks, maples, and the big tall elm right outside the window by my bed. I hoped Daddy was all right. It was unusual for him not to come home. Probably because of the storm. I put "Moonglow" on the turntable of my portable phonograph and as I got undressed into my nightie, Nora was in the bathroom with the door closed. I turned on the music and danced in front of the full-length mirror, appreciating how pretty I looked. I rocked. I turned up the volume so the music could be heard over the storm outside. I rocked some more and put the 78 on again. The toilet flushed and Nora came out of the bathroom. She was wearing a loose, shimmery white pair of shorty pajamas. She saw me in front of the mirror, so I toned my dancing down so it looked less like a performance and more casual, just as Mommy had said about singing at dinner, *it's just something we do here.*

Nora was stunning, and something in her was a little too sinful to know what to do with. She said, "Look at this, watch *me* dance. Eric and I danced at the cookout on the beach the last night of camp. We did this fox-trot to the slow dances, but the rumba and samba and the lindy to the faster ones. He picked me up like this." Nora was smaller than I, but she raised me just slightly off the floor. "Then he let me fall, but his arms were there to catch me and we did this dip. It was so neat. I love him and I'll bet we're going to go all the way pretty soon." I was horrified but didn't let it show. Even I had my limits!

She started to get into the right rhythm of the song and she pulled away from me, doing a dance she might have learned from Rita Hayworth in *The Lady from Shanghai.* Then she took the scarf that was on the end of the bed and waved it through the air and around my head as though it was a feather. She had been so quiet, and now she had come to life. I followed her lead in what I supposed was a reenactment of her dances with Eric. She was looking directly at me and smiling with a reassuring look I'd never experienced with any boy I had ever danced with. It was heady, and as the song was coming to an end, I imitated Kim Novak's move with her hips and arms in *Picnic.* Oh, wasn't it fun to be a movie star? I put my palms together and crisscrossed them, brushing them up and down as the strings soared. My arms partly extended and my neck leaned back, allowing my head to move seductively. Nora watched me and tried to copy me. She and I led each other and, as in a perfect dance, communicated viscerally.

The light went out on a large thunderclap, and the lightning was so close to the thunder that it must have struck the house or maybe the elm, the tallest tree on the property. The music that seemed to have brought the storm on slowed and then stopped, and there was only howling. The storm said: *Come dance with me*. Nora and I bumped into each other, but not by chance. We fell back on the bed. Her hand moved explicitly under my nightie, and she startlingly, with the finesse of an animal but the beauty of a young goddess, put her hand right at the heart of my desire. A hot white wind blew. It came tapping through the andromeda against the side of the house. And then the breathtaking whipping sound of the elm made me open my thighs. Somewhere a door slammed, one of the outside doors, stopping us for a minute, but we were both so otherworldly hot, and anyone coming in the room to check on us would have seen, by candle or flashlight, just a tangle of white sheets and two young girls hiding in each other's arms from the thunder and lightning. Nora said, "This is how he does it to me."

The blackness around me held my shyness at bay, and Nora was over my body, kissing my breasts. The hissing of smaller, higher winds into the larger gusts reassured us of our privacy, and we moved to the unpredictable sound-and-light show.

"You touch me now," Nora whispered.

I knew this was the future. This was the way I would writhe in the future. But for now I passed my hand over her thighs and felt for her. I was boiling for all the future times, not quite able to be in the moment. She hula-hooped her hips in a circle as I touched her. Then another gust of wind as the elm right out my window shook and whipped like someone being spanked. She asked me not to stop. Her hard breathing became a cry of an animal. I was worried that she was hurting, but more worried that Mommy would hear us and come running through the closed but unlocked door. Nora still didn't know how excited I was. She was the one needing and asking. I was only complying with her requests.

Now the rain slanted so heavily against the glass of the window right next to the bed that I was sure something would break. "This is just what Eric does. Please do it some more." I smelled the sweetness of her. There was nothing like it ever before. She reached with her head down the length of my torso and her hair was thick with sweat. We got into an awkward position with each other, but I imagined we were like two smaller branches of the elm, twisting and tossing and making room so that they could move against each other without breaking.

I heard footsteps running down the hall right outside the room. Nora and I quickly disentangled our bodies as Peter opened the door.

"Are you scared?" He was so thrilled. "It's a *hurricane!*"

Did I want to be Euridice or Orpheus or Al Jolson?

"Go chase the wild and nighttime streets, sang Daddy."

---

CHAPTER EIGHT

the twenty-ninth floor

At night in bed I heard God whisper lullabies
While Daddy next door whistled whiskey tunes
And sometimes when I wanted, they would harmonize
There was nothing those two couldn't do
Embrace me you child, you're a child of mine
And I'm leaving everything I am to you
Go chase the wild and nighttime streets, sang Daddy
And God sang, Pray the devil doesn't get to you

—"Embrace Me, You Child," 1972

S ome things you pick up early, but there are no words for them yet. They're simply fragments of a puzzle created by other people doing things, thinking things, deciding things, forgetting things, and not least, lying about things.

My whole life I'd never been able to put a name to the feelings I'd had for my father. I had spent my childhood craving his love and never getting it. As time went on, I drew away from him, losing myself in a sky full of many different kinds of clouds. I'd never been good at any of the things I believed mattered to Daddy. I had no innate talents to speak of. I couldn't play the piano, and I wasn't as pretty as my sisters. I couldn't help but think back on the night he scrawled in my autograph book, *Roses are red / Violets are pink / I love you with your darling fat nose / I've just had a drink.* In Daddy's eyes—despite my mother telling me not to take what he wrote seriously—I wasn't even good at my nose.

There was more. I wasn't funny in front of him. I stammered and stuttered, and then I cried about it afterward. At school I learned slowly, and aside from swimming, I wasn't good at sports. Once, when I was three or four, and Daddy was recovering from the nervous breakdown after Peter was born—an expression in vogue at the time, which I believed meant a person got so nervous he fell down the stairs—Mommy asked if I would mind putting on my tutu and going upstairs to dance for him. It didn't work. Nothing seemed to work. As ever, the tall man in the house whose long legs I had inherited never seemed to want to have much to do with me. Instead, he looked past me. He seemed to be seeking something he'd lost, Mommy maybe, or even his old self.

No: my only halfway decent talent was for loving people—Daddy, Mommy, Joey, Lucy, Chibie, Allie, Uncle Peter, Uncle Dutch, my dogs, and, no matter how damaging and wrong our interludes were, Billy.

I'd study the people around me for clues. Clues to figure out whom to emulate, how to dress, how to speak, how to act, how to dance. I'd grown up feeling unworthy and underloved. I wanted nothing more than to feel secure in myself—to feel that I was really good at something. Instead, I was shy, scared, wounded, frozen, a scratchy bundle of nerves, a walking pile of needs and conflicts. But my desire to hide met its match in an equally strong desire to be noticed, to be on top, to be wanted, connected, asked, begged, loved, admired.

Depression ran in the Simon family, and of his five siblings, Daddy was probably the one hit the hardest. He'd had his first depressive episode when he was a child, and over the years he'd managed to keep his demons at bay, but by the late 1940s, his mood swings and bad health had caught up with him. Like some time-bent sailor, he did what he could to steer a course through his own sadness, but the wheel escaped him and the waves began filling the boat, and by then he had lost the will, or ability, to bail water.

Daddy was no longer the man he had once been—the brilliant, innovative publisher, the jovial participant in bridge, golf, and tennis matches, the host of glittering late-night dinner parties. Instead, following any number of heart attacks and ministrokes, Daddy had grown seriously ill, and despondent, the changes in him obvious to everybody and terrifying to me. But it still didn't occur to me it could be in me too.

He seemed to recede. It was as if a sheet of glass now stood between him and the rest of the world. His illness disoriented him. Night turned into day turned into night again. He would pad around the house in his bathrobe, occasionally groaning, "Oh, how I suffer," or "I hope you children won't end up like me." He would kiss me good night sometimes with the muffled words "Good morning." Once, when I was doing my homework after school, Daddy appeared in my doorway in his by-now-familiar dressing gown. What was I doing up so late? he asked. On the way out, he turned off the overhead light to save electricity, not realizing I couldn't do my homework in the dark.

By the late 1950s, Joey, Lucy, Peter, and I had become inured to this new Daddy, and knowing his odd behavior would embarrass my friends, I stopped inviting them over to the house. Fearing Daddy could disappear any second, I became frightened to love him, creating, once again, a perfect circuit of mutual rejection. Rather than sitting down and talking, we watched baseball games together on television, him beside me in his dressing gown, sighing, absently cracking his knuckles, his breath smelling of stale cigarette smoke. But instead of welcoming his attention, I was almost scared of him, as if I were breathing in a mixture of measles, pirates, and imminent death, all blended into one musky, terrifying presence named "Daddy."

After dinner, as usual, he would retreat to his piano. Once music had been his joy, but by late '58 or '59, it was his only shelter. Joey, Lucy, and I would be upstairs in our rooms, gossiping with friends, playing with our always fascinating hair, or writing science papers, when below, like a coastal storm spinning in off the sea, the sad thundering would begin. It was Daddy, alone downstairs, hands and feet meting out his frustrations and anger in bursts and waves of Rachmaninoff, Liszt, Beethoven. Notes heard but unheard, absorbed into the floorboards and ceilings. His playing was an angry serenade to his family, to his wife and colleagues and their disloyalty, all those things that were destroying him inside and out.

At the time I had no idea what was happening with Daddy professionally, or the degree to which his morale, and his position inside his own company, was being torn out from under him. In 1944, Marshall Field III, the Chicago department store heir, had bought Simon & Schuster for $3 million, the equivalent of around $40 million today, with the understanding that upon Field's death, Dick Simon and Max Schuster had the right of first refusal to repurchase their company. When he died in 1956, both Max and the company's business manager, along with the lawyer René Wormser— who lived in our building at 133 West Eleventh Street and whom Daddy had always considered to be his best friend—urged my father to cash out.

Daddy didn't want to, but it was two against one, and in the end Max and Leon Shimkin, Simon & Schuster's accountant, prevailed. Daddy's health was an ongoing concern, Leon told him, and selling his shares would save him lots of stress. Their betrayal was further poisoned by subtle threats that unless my father signed his name to the buyout, he, Leon, might be forced to divulge publicly my mother's ongoing romance with Ronny, and what a field day the press would have with that. If René had truly been Daddy's best friend, he would have made everyone aware of the conflict of interest and recused himself, instead of advising Daddy to sell off 100 percent of his Simon & Schuster stock.

I know only that my father's life was slowly collapsing in four packs a day of cigarettes, cholesterol, a cuckolding wife, two more dollops of whipped cream than were necessary floating in his morning coffee, and double-dealing work colleagues. The arteriosclerosis had confused his wiring, cut short his attention span, and blocked his ability to recall things that had happened only an hour earlier. No wonder he was so ripe to be betrayed by his Simon & Schuster colleagues, and even by his own lawyer. Thanks to a devious decision by a bunch of pinstripe-suited double-crossers, Daddy was left out in the cold.

Whenever I asked why Daddy wasn't going into the office anymore, everyone had a different story, and I never pressed the issue. By early 1960, the official explanation was that Daddy was "semiretired." He still went to work now and again, chauffeured down the West Side Highway in a green Lincoln Town Car. Junius, his driver, would drop him off on West Fifty-second Street, wait there, then drive him home a few hours later. The names of the projects Daddy was still involved in floated through the house—*The Jump Book* by Philippe Halsman, another volume of Will and Ariel Durant's *The Story of Civilization*, a follow-up book with the great French photographer Henri Cartier-Bresson—but the truth of the matter was that his place in the company he had founded was slipping away at a frightening pace, and Daddy knew it, too, in the same way he knew that his wife was in love with an embarrassing opponent. These things together were too much for any man to take.

That summer, when I turned fifteen, was the last summer I thought of myself as a child. One day in mid-June, I accompanied Daddy into the city, dropped him off in front of the Atlas building, and spent the morning at Saks, where I was looking for a pair of low heels. Having recently been introduced to Nick Delbanco, I was concerned about the slight difference in our heights. I was five foot ten in my bare feet to Nick's five foot eight and a half, and I remembered Mommy always telling me that men prefer small women—both raiding my department of self-worth and elevating her own—which is why I was on the lookout for flats and low heels.

New shoes in hand, I made my way back to Daddy's office in the Atlas building at 630 Fifth Avenue, across from St. Patrick's Cathedral, where the pigeons flocked and hovered over pieces of popcorn, breadcrumbs, and other obscure summer treats. Once inside the lobby, I took the elevator up to the twenty-eighth floor. But Louise, my father's longtime secretary, wasn't anywhere to be found. Instead, a receptionist I'd never seen before told me that Dick Simon's office was now one flight up, on the twenty-ninth floor. "It's a shame," she added. When I asked her what she meant, she said again, "He's gone up to the twenty-ninth floor now, dear. He's got a nice big office up there."

The twenty-ninth floor was less plush and altogether less impressive than the one directly below. There was no secretary to greet me once I got off the elevator. No one offered me a ginger ale with a cherry in it. When Daddy appeared, it was obvious that the receptionist on the floor below had called him to tell him I was on my way up.

He was loping down the hall, long-legged, his tailored trouser cuffs hanging, as ever, slightly lower than his shoe tops. His chest caved in, his back hunched, he looked like a man who had been on an all-nighter at the tables in Harlem and had come out the big loser. His right hand was gripping a shopping bag—dinner, he told me, a four-pack of frozen steaks, a gift from a colleague. Would I mind carrying it for him?

I didn't want to feel the sadness I was feeling. Daddy looked so much smaller than I ever remembered, as if every fiber in him was shrinking, as if one of them could snap at any moment, placing too much strain on all the others, and he would collapse onto the floor. At that moment I felt as if it was too much responsibility for Daddy even to breathe, and that it was my duty as a daughter to do all his breathing for him. Yet I couldn't. Nobody could.

As we waited for the elevator, Daddy gave me the sweetest smile. I could see his nicotine-stained teeth peeking out dolefully like slow-down lights on the way to his next sentence. "Do me a favor, sweetie, and don't tell Mom about my being on the twenty-ninth floor."

My mouth couldn't find a comfortable position, so instead I nodded over-eagerly. I worried we would bump into various employees from the floor below. Would it be awkward? Would they want to avoid Daddy? From now on, I thought, I wouldn't be one of them; I would never, ever, avoid my father. A few seconds later, I placed my hand inside his big daddy one. He and I were now allies. On the twenty-eighth floor, the elevator doors parted. The old floor where he had been king. He had been Atlas, holding up the heavens. Daddy's eyes suddenly came to life and he looked as if he could yet be the conqueror. With those crystal blue eyes, he bore holes through the backs of the heads of the men who had so recently called him "boss." They turned their heads at awkward angles, talked nonsense, or stared at the walls—anything to avoid eye contact with Richard L. Simon.

Descending from the tropically humid Forty-second Street afternoon down the elegant marble stairway into Grand Central Terminal, I held on tightly to his arm through the triangle formed by his elbow and his shoulder. I felt less like his daughter than an aide, or a nurse. My other hand gripped the shopping bag containing the four-pack of steaks, surrounded by their frozen blue ice packs. He carried his briefcase in his left hand, his jacket slipped over one shoulder.

We boarded the Stamford local and found seats, making ourselves at home in a compartment designed for four. I stowed the shopping bag in the overhead luggage bin, and in an attempt to be ladylike, I crossed my legs under my light blue flower-print dress with the full skirt.

"Lucy, darling"—Daddy frequently called me by my sister's name, just as he often confused the names of his other children, his dogs, and his household staff—"do you know that I have a new book idea. It would revolutionize the way people see things in nature," he went on, before he suddenly changed the subject. "What's the name of that new boy you're going out with, is it Paul?"

No. Paul, I told him gently, was the boy Lucy was seeing. "I'm going out—at least sort of—with Paul's friend Nick."

Daddy was silent, and then he told me he'd heard from Mommy that I had been kissing—who was it? Was it Marty? I tried to clarify things, though I was beginning to get annoyed that no matter what I said, my father persisted in confusing me with Lucy. Mostly, though, I was worried about how confused he seemed in general. He was acting almost drunk. He said things that didn't connect with each other, skipped over parts of sentences, the expression on his face isolated from the words coming from his mouth.

"I brought home a book for you, Carly," Daddy said suddenly, "which I'll give to you when we get to Stamfie. It's called *Try Giving Yourself Away*. It's got a good message to it."

Try Giving Yourself Away: It was the first time ever Daddy had ever given me a book recommendation. "If you want me to get the message," I said coolly, "why don't you just tell me what the message is?"

Even as I said this, I couldn't bear the words coming out of my mouth. Why was I acting so snippety, so mean? Old habit? Hadn't I just pledged to myself to be on his side forever? Obviously noticing the sardonic, faintly disrespectful tone in my voice, Daddy now addressed me more directly, lest I treat anyone else that way.

"The message," he said, "is simply this: You will feel wealthy by giving. Giving to others without expecting them to give back to you is the most fully loving way a person can act."

Now I felt nothing but shame. Daddy's hand was trembling, as it had been doing for a while now. It shook when he drank his morning cup of coffee and whenever he sat down to write letters. As the train slowed to a stop in New Rochelle, he gazed out the window blankly. Whom did he have to love? I wondered. Mommy? Time and again Lucy and Joey had both assured me that Mommy's and Ronny's relationship was "platonic." I wouldn't, in fact, find out the truth until after Daddy died. At that point I still needed to believe that there was sanity and peace in our house, however fragile. *Mommy is in love with* you, *Daddy*, I wanted to say, but I couldn't look my father in the eye and say those words because I knew, the way a child knows, that Mommy hadn't been in love with Daddy for many, many years.

As the train pulled away from the New Rochelle station and picked up speed, Daddy squinted, and a few seconds later, tipped his head back against the seat, his eyes closed. Why am I being so withholding? I asked myself. Why don't I go and sit next to him? Why don't I rest my head against his chest, or wipe his forehead? What if Daddy dies here and now, right before my eyes? I automatically knocked on the wooden handle of the seat. To keep the conversation, and him, alive, I said, "I wish Ronny would leave and go live somewhere else."

One eye flashed open. "I couldn't agree with you more."

"I hate him," I added fiercely.

Both of Daddy's eyes were now open. "Well, then," he said. "Then Ronny is the one to whom you must give yourself selflessly. By that I mean being good to him, and loving him in the Christian definition of the word." Then his mouth formed a position that I recognized as his "This is bullshit" expression.

Nothing made sense. Nothing at all.

"Do you?" I tried to lighten things up, to make Daddy laugh. "Does 'Christian' mean 'platonic'?" I asked. "Did Plato have all those people living in his house?"

"Yes," Daddy said simply nodding. "I think Plato was just a fella, too."

The most outrageous things in the world can be brushed off, blocked out, wiped away. You just have to want them gone badly enough. Like the space behind the bureau in Ronny's room, like the image of Mommy crawling back and forth through that dark, airless corridor, a prisoner of love. What was Daddy doing about that? Why hadn't he insisted that Ronny leave the house?

Obviously my vision had been obscured by a combination of wishes and hopes, things I'd read about in books, things I'd seen in my friends' families and their parents' marriages, conversations with my cousin Jeanie, who wasn't just one of my closest friends but a family member. I've puzzled over the whole situation in the years since then, but the pieces never fit. The only thing I knew for sure, the only thing I believed, as Mommy had told me again and again, was this: Sex and love were synonymous. They were one and the same thing. And I was becoming less and less sure that the numbers were adding up.

Daddy rambled on for a while. He talked about the small office he now inhabited at work, and about how hard he was trying to look at the positive side of things. Just then the train curved sharply, and a colorful bead appeared on his forehead. Leaning in to wipe it off before it reached his eye, I was alarmed to see that it was blood. But where was he bleeding? Another drop of blood appeared, then another. Across the aisle, a child yelled out, "Hey, that man is bleedin' from his head!"

Alarmed, Daddy touched his forehead. We both looked up to realize it was blood from the thawing steaks. I was so relieved. Hurriedly I brought down the red-soaked shopping bag from the open shelf above Daddy's head, setting it on the seat beside me, saturated side up. Dinner, I was guessing, was spoiled. Spoiled: the operative word. The steaks. The day. The twenty-ninth floor. My father. His shirt. His world. The heavens had slipped away from his hands.

As we neared the Stamford train station, I wondered who would pick us up. Usually it was Mommy or Joey. Daddy retrieved his Italian leather manuscript bag, with me behind him holding the now-blood-drowned steak bag as delicately as if I were cradling an injured pet. It was hard to keep the juice from permeating everything. Daddy gripped the railing tightly as we took the stairs down to the parking lot, where Mommy awaited us in her convertible Cadillac, the top down. In a quietly hysterical voice, I told her I'd brought dinner home. When Mommy burst out laughing, the tension dissolved, and the bleeding steak bag ended up in the nearest Dumpster. As I climbed into the backseat, Mommy gave Daddy a dispassionate welcome-home kiss on the cheek.

Had Mommy heard anything about the outbreak of encephalitis in New

Jersey? Daddy wanted to know. No, she hadn't, but even if she had, what was she or anybody supposed to do about it? Daddy paused. "Get comfortable with the idea that there's a menace out there." He added, "Don't worry, though, they're a long way away."

Speaking loud enough to comfort me, Mommy said, "That's right, they're all the way across the Hudson. They can't get over here."

"Yes," Daddy said, "but they could always take the Holland Tunnel."

Mommy laughed, which relieved me. Daddy could still make her laugh, even if sometimes she appeared to be fighting the impulse. Was Ronny capable of saying such funny things? No: he didn't even come close. If, then, Ronny's presence signaled the demise of wit and laughter in her life, why did Mommy persist in loving him?

On the way home, we drove past poster after poster for the Broadway production of *Camelot*, with Richard Burton and Julie Andrews as King Arthur and Queen Guinevere. They were like that once, I thought.

Now, from the backseat, I thought, for the second time that day, I love you, Daddy. Nobody will ever hurt you again. He had spiraled so rapidly. Physically and mentally, he was a wreck. His wife had been carrying on an affair under his nose. His colleagues had betrayed him. He was in a weakened state, unable to act or retaliate. Recently, he and Mommy, on their way to dinner with friends in the city, had been driving past the Fifty-ninth Street exit when Daddy suffered a hallucination that he was supposed to be onstage at Carnegie Hall at eight. He became so disoriented and upset he began to cry. Was this just Mother's anecdote?

That night, long after I went to bed, the piano started up again from downstairs, right beneath my bedroom. Debussy nocturnes, Daddy's anger and loneliness, his love, all drifting together, casting up through the floorboards to my room.

A month later, at home, early in the morning of July 29, my mother and Joey woke me up around dawn. Mommy told me she had some sad news to tell me. Daddy had died the night before. Mommy's voice was sober, and she couldn't seem to decide whether or not to reach down and touch me. Standing beside her, Joey was stone-faced, and the two of us avoided eye contact. Then Mommy left the room. I went into the green-tiled bathroom, where I sat for a long time on the rim of the tub. It wasn't even 6:30 a.m. It was already bright outside, sunny, hot, with a breeze coming in through the French doors. I'd wanted Mommy to put her arms around me and scream. Instead, life was spinning—just like that—into spirit.

This was significant, I knew. This was bigger than anything that had happened to me before. For years, the prospect of Daddy dying had terrified me, and I'd done everything I could to knock it away. Now, alone in the bathroom, I felt nothing at all. What was I supposed to feel? What was I supposed to do? Was I supposed to cry? Was Mommy sad? It was hard to tell. Instead, I thought of irrelevant things: if I cast thirty-eight stitches on my medium-wide knitting needles, how big would the sweater I wanted to knit turn out to be? Were my nails too short for the new pink nail polish I'd bought recently? If Daddy was gone, would my brother Peter even know the difference? I started getting dizzy.

A few moments later, Joey came in, dull-eyed, and began brushing her teeth. By now I was sitting on the bathroom floor fingering the twisty edges of the rug, when Arleka, an Israeli singer who was boarding at our house that summer, told us that Daddy had come into her room in the middle of the night complaining of chest pains. Daddy had knocked on my mother's third-floor bedroom door, but no one answered. Meaning that Mommy was probably asleep beside Ronny, in his bedroom. I barely knew her, but Arleka was the one who told Joey and me how my father had died.

Later that same morning, Joey and her boyfriend, Bob, met with the funeral parlor staffers, who had wrapped up and carted away the dead so often they themselves seemed to have taken on the carriage of corpses. I watched them take away Daddy's body before running back upstairs to my bedroom. Still unable to shake my own emotional flatness, I put on some makeup. If I'd had some wool, I would have started fiddling with the needles. Just for something to do with my hands.

That night, Joey, Lucy, Mother, and I stood around listlessly in the living room beside the little bar with the wheels on it, none of us knowing what expressions to put on our faces. Joey suggested a round of Bloody Marys. "Two olives and one onion," Joey said, and drank hers in a single gulp. None of us looked at one another, but under my lids I was constantly sneaking glances at Mommy's face for evidence of genuine sadness. Lucy, who had just come back from Tanglewood, the music festival in the Berkshires, was still crying when Arleka appeared in the dining room. As if acting out the denouement of a Verdi opera, Arleka confronted my mother, screaming, "You killed him, you killed him, you killed your husband! You're a whore!"

Mommy slapped Arleka across the face, hard, though it took less than a moment for my mother to pull herself together and recover her usual composure. As Arleka stalked out of the room, Mommy even let out a laugh. It was a shallow, quivering, unmusical sound, one designed to brush over what had just happened. Gazing at her three confused daughters, Mommy explained that Arleka, as if it wasn't already obvious to everyone, was insane, and not only that, that she'd always been in love with Daddy, and bullshit and bullshit and bullshit.

Going to the kitchen, Joey, Lucy, and I poured Rice Krispies into bowls. I had no idea where Mommy had gone, but before long the *Carousel* soundtrack began serenading the rest of the house from Ronny's third-floor room. Ronny was up there. Ronny was still in the house. The three of us sat around the kitchen table eating our cereal, the clink of our spoons competing with the strains of Ronny's distant, respectfully soft yet still abrasive baritone singing along with "What's the Use of Wond'rin'?"

We were all crying, sobbing, but in between, I managed to gasp out a few words. "Is there any more milk?" I asked Lucy and Joey.

No answer. "It feels *chilly* in here," Lucy said. She, or Joey, asked whether she should close the window, and then didn't. An oversized moth was banging against the screen. Every sound, every sensation, felt exaggerated, overvivid, overloud, as if I were seeing and hearing things through a new set of senses. After a few more minutes of stilted, pointless politesse through our crying, one of us—I can't remember which one—let out a laugh, and then all three of us did. We laughed and howled until we were clutching our stomachs. We were crazed. We were sad. We were freaked out. We were in hysterics. We had no idea what, if anything, we should think about laughing fifteen hours after we'd been told Daddy was dead. Did we have any rights? Could we demand that Ronny leave our just deceased father's house? Of course not. Lucy, who was studying to become a psychiatric nurse, told us that after so much pent-up tension, laughing was normal, and that we shouldn't feel at all ashamed or embarrassed. But Lucy was the one who cried hardest. Finally, in an attempt to reassert some control, Joey thought to start a hymn, "The Lord Bless You and Keep You." Though our crying never stopped, it was now joined by words and music, and the three of us were determined to sing it through to its end, mostly to obliterate the sounds of Ronny coming from the third floor.

On my way to bed that night, I remember walking slightly sideways through the hallway, then slowly up the stairs. The walls were covered with photos Daddy had taken over the years. Mommy surrounded by our dogs. Mommy, again, posed under the Arc de Triomphe. The three Simon sisters beside the pool in Stamford. Me, at the top of a swing, ready for my descent. I was very little; the grass was very big.

And some say he built his empire for wealth and fame
But if you ask him why, he'll say he did it all for her,
All for her, all for her.
He said hello little woman, she said hello big man.
   —"Hello Big Man," 1983

Except for that one train ride, that summer of 1960, the summer he died, Daddy and I had always lacked the closeness my two older sisters took for granted. Still, Daddy made the largest and longest-lasting mark on my character. Our relationship may have been distant, but on a single train ride from New York to Stamford, I realized, as if for the first time, that I really loved him, and I have to believe that he loved me back. As time went on, and even though I only really knew him as a sick man, I felt as though I incorporated him into my identity. A lot of my own struggles, good and bad, were the same as his: self-centeredness, shame, inadequacy, ambition—depression. The songs I would someday write, the music I would someday sing, were always accompanied by an image, or an idea, of Daddy, one seemingly locked inside me forever. Not only that, but whatever stories I told in those songs circled back always to the same things: Love. Longing. Virtue. Crime. Secrecy. Vulnerability. Monsters. Beasts. The Underground. What happens when you go through your life carrying another person's mantle?

Joey followed me upstairs. Bob, her boyfriend, who had been a rock through this whole thing, had made all the funeral arrangements. Joey was sleeping in a guest room with Bob, but she kissed me good night, and Lucy did, too. That night was just awful. Nothing was right. The next morning I called Nick, who promised he would come visit the next day.

The world, it appeared, could be a very cold place. The only exceptions were my siblings, our twin Labradors, Porgy and Bess, and Laurie, my dog, of course. I couldn't help but remember a few summers before, and how, despite the presence of Billy, and Ronny, I was untroubled then. My parents' dinner parties, one after another, like gold, shimmering beads strung on a necklace. Show people, and composers, new scores ringing through the rooms of our house: *What's the use of wond'rin' if the endin' will be sad . . . you're his girl and he's your fella . . . and there's nothin' more to say.*

Daddy: He walked straight—looking neither right nor left. 1960.

BOOK TWO

Nick Delbanco, 1963.

CHAPTER NINE

the hardships of the mistral

It was 1961, and Daddy had been gone for a little over a year. His ashes were dropped from a small plane over the copper beech tree on our Stamford property. It was a rough period between my junior and senior years, and I barely got into college. Lucy was attending Bennington College in Vermont, so I thought I'd have a chance there, but Bennington put me on its waiting list. Joey had gone to Sarah Lawrence, so surely that was a slam dunk, but Sarah Lawrence accepted me only as an "off-campus" day student.

The reasons why weren't terribly surprising. I hadn't done as well as I might have in high school, mostly because of my stammer, but in retrospect I also had a few undiagnosed cognitive problems—a psychiatrist later told me my brain was like a wild tossed salad. My speech handicap froze me from participating in most classroom discussions—just finessing the guttural *r*'s in French class was hair-raising—and when it was my turn to read aloud in my other classes, I would come up with any number of excuses as to why I couldn't. A tickle in my throat, indigestion, a terrible pain in my knee that I had to see the nurse about right away. Too mortified to discuss my condition with anybody, I would burst into frustrated tears instead, followed by even more excuses, including blaming my difficulties on allergies. Of course my stutter continued to affect my grades.

I'd also done abominably on my SATs. I was so worried about failing that I cheated, copying the marks of the girl seated beside me. Unfortunately, her test was different from mine, which meant that just about all of my answers came out wrong. Midtest, I also suffered a panic attack that caused me to flee to the bathroom, trailed by the proctor, whose high heels clacked against the floor of the gym and into the girls' room, where I locked myself into the stall and sat frozen on the toilet seat, my head in my hands, my throat stopped up, my heart beating in my chest like a captured bird. I didn't go back to finish. It was later arranged for me to retake the test at home, but my scores were still too low to entice any self-respecting college admissions department.

Fortunately for me, that year my beloved fourth-grade teacher from my school in Riverdale had joined the Sarah Lawrence admissions committee. Mr. Papaleo, or Pappy, as we called him, had eased me into his classroom once upon a time, thanks to his yo-yo tricks, his empathy, and his sweetness. Now, via the kind of excellent coincidence that has defined other areas of my life, Pappy put in a good word for me with the admissions committee, laying out the case that I was an "artistic" type—sensitive, yes, but a "special" girl who might in fact excel at a school like Sarah Lawrence. Half the girls in my freshman year English class at Sarah Lawrence, in fact, were "special" girls, with one kind of "sensitive" quality or another. Jessie, my best friend in my class, kept telling me how "interesting" I was, the same adjective Mommy used to describe my repertoire of "artistic" neuroses. In the face of all my various verbal anxieties, I should have considered attending Juilliard, as Mommy suggested. But I ended up at Sarah Lawrence, which was only seven miles away from our Riverdale house. Going there felt at once safe, hip, and normal.

In the early 1960s, Sarah Lawrence's student body seemed to be made up entirely of two all-pervasive types of young women. The first was the beautiful beatnik with pierced ears and straight, defiantly dirty hair to her waist, wearing a peasant blouse, tight, cut-off jeans, and sandals made by Fred Braun. Those girls could have been models on a Sarah Lawrence runway, and I hated them all instantly. The second group was lesbians, Sarah Lawrence being one of the most liberal, gay-friendly campuses in the country. It may sound hard to believe, but at the time I had no idea what being a lesbian meant, though someone advised me to be on the lookout for girls who resembled the famous painting of Louis XIV in his red tights. Overall, college in general, and Sarah Lawrence in particular, seemed to be all about which female body could summon the most admiring glances, with all females' eyes trained on one another. To hell with philosophy or art history—even though Sarah Lawrence had the finest professors of those subjects—we still wanted husbands, like college students in the fifties.

I was still going out with Nick Delbanco, and every swan I spied crossing the lawn, seated in class, or waiting in line at the dining hall made me think, If Nicky sees her, I'm doomed. But what else had I expected as the daughter of parents whose behaviors elicited more questions than answers on matters of sex, love, and loyalty? As a girl who'd been introduced to male-female intimacy with Billy in the darkness of my family's pool house, it would have been semimiraculous if I'd begun my college years with any confidence at all.

I didn't even have the questionable self-assurance that comes from having money. At Sarah Lawrence, no one considered me a rich girl, and except for one or two moments, I'd never grown up feeling privileged. Once, at school in Riverdale, a group of my classmates was talking about who had the biggest house in town, and mine, I remember, tied with another student's as the biggest. Another time, the kids found out that Daddy was the "Simon" of Simon & Schuster, the name on the spine of any number of library books. But true to the ethos of the Simon family, having money meant that you never spoke about money, and surrounded as I was in college by so many daughters of "name" families, I felt like the opposite of a big fish and lived happily on the twenty-five dollars a week Mommy put in my bank account. The big secret was that there wasn't much of Daddy's money left.

It was around this time that the dark force I'd soon identify as the Beast was forming inside me. It began when I started comparing myself to every girl I saw, feeling perennially "less than" them. My waist wasn't narrow enough. I wasn't as graceful as other girls were in dance class. I couldn't read aloud in the classroom. When I compared myself to other girls, my "not-good-enough" thinking came into play, gaining in force. This is a kind of Beast, I remember thinking.

The Beast was hardly a foreign presence, but it wasn't until Sarah Lawrence that I gave it a formal name. To me, the Beast was so many things. It began in my childhood, with my stutter, and intensified with trauma, thanks to Billy, a flourishing of a dark self-hatred inside an all-too-sad little girl who was not at fault, but vulnerable enough to allow underground spirits to infect and invade her thinking. The Beast was the feeling that I was never good enough, or loved enough—the persistent fear that I would forever end up a trivial second-best to my beautiful sisters Lucy and Joey. The Beast was self-consciousness, fear, and loneliness inside a house run by a mother and a father who only occasionally took their roles as parents seriously. Then and forever, the Beast was my envious feelings about everything I worried about not being. The Beast was, and is, whatever feels insurmountable in the moment. Its key words are *enough*, and *you should*, and *why can't you*, with me falling short, and feeling ashamed and exposed, every single time.

Nick and I had fallen in love in the little town of Wind Gap, Pennsylvania, where Joey, Ronny, and I were appearing in a summer-stock production of *Kiss Me, Kate*. It was the end of my junior year of high school and, with Uncle Peter's help, I got a summer job working as a makeup girl at the same theater company that had offered Joey and Ronny leading roles. I knew how to apply mascara, but I have no recollection of how I ended up onstage in the role of a butler, wearing blackface, singing "Another Op'nin', Another Show," or as the understudy for Bianca, the second female lead, which I was given with the assurance that I could sing my dialogue if I couldn't speak it.

One night, Nick drove to Pennsylvania to visit me, and the hint of romance that both of us had felt other times reached a new plateau. One day it escalated, when Nick and I went canoeing on a lake, the energy between us passing back and forth. The lake was lined with weekend houses, and Nick and I took turns rating their attractiveness, earning silent points with each other as we slowly paddled. "I hope they reconsider that roof," Nick said about a house in mid-construction that didn't even have a roof, a remark that made me like him even more. When we got out of the canoe, my dress caught on the seat, and he gripped my knee, steadying my step. "Tell me, have I ever seen such a knee?" Nick inquired, a flattering quip accompanied by a toothy half smile. A few minutes later, we were embracing, me standing below him on a gentle rise, making sure I positioned myself so that we were approximately the same height. I was completely enthralled. Hugging Nick was a lot sexier than I'd imagined it would be.

I later realized that I'd been initiated into sex countless times over the course of my life. I had been exposed to it, one way or another, ever since I was eight years old. Billy. Nora. Mommy and Ronny. A serious high school boyfriend named Timmy with whom I practiced the age-old concepts of first base, second base, and third base. But with Nick, I officially lost my virginity. Strangely enough, my deflowering took place on the very same cement bordering the swimming pool in Stamford where the majority of my summer encounters with Billy had taken place. Where to place Billy in my context of the sex/love duet, I still don't know.

Nick and I were walking around the Stamford property one abundantly starry night in mid-July after my junior year of high school. I was showing him all my favorite spots, including the red barn with the Ping-Pong table and the apple orchard, the windmill and the greenhouse, the tennis court and the pool house, Stoneybroke. The two of us made our way down the stone steps to the pool. It was a warm night, with a strong breeze. I had on a pair of Bermuda shorts and a T-shirt, and Nick was in khakis and a loose white linen shirt. I've always liked longish hair on men, and Nick had the perfect head and good looks to get away with it. As his name, Delbanco, would suggest, he was Italian on his father's side. "A pure product of the Italian soil," Chibie said when she met him.

The moon made the air lustrous, as though it had been polished. Nick took my hand. It was the first time for both of us. He was awkward, and I compensated by moving like a gazelle (or so I thought at the time). He urged me toward him until our bodies touched, and he kissed me full on the lips. This was my romance. Only mine. Nobody intervened. There were no ghosts. No memories. Just Nicky and me.

We sat down on the cement surrounding the pool. Nicky pulled up the legs of his khakis, and we both submerged our legs, calf-deep, into the warm pool water. "You're really beautiful," Nick said, which made me glance the other way, as if to say, "Don't look too close—you'll find a problem." He drew me to him again, and this time our embrace lasted longer and was more sensual. Nick made a sound in his throat that mingled with the sound of the wind, as he pulled me down on the cement, our ankles still in the water. We took our time, spending the next five minutes acting demure and hesitant, as opposed to being overtly, inexpertly, sexy. It paid off, too. We were naked by the time we were ready to have the kind of sex I'd never had before. It was surprisingly painful. It didn't yet bring the pleasure it would with practice, but being with Nick seemed to erase all the heartbreakingly hollow confusion I'd had with Billy.

Nick was a prodigious reader and writer, and by far my intellectual superior. He was responsible for igniting my interest in philosophy, poetry, and literature. I had done all the required reading for high school English classes and not much more than that, but Nick turned me on to Hemingway, Fitzgerald, Sartre, Lawrence Durrell's *Alexandria Quartet*, Malcolm Lowry's *Under the Volcano*, and James Joyce's *A Portrait of the Artist as a Young Man*. Nick was patient, too, helping me with my papers and sending me long letters to improve my grasp of concepts ranging from existentialism to the life of the tragic hero. The tragic hero, Nick explained in a long letter to me, was a man (or woman) of an "essentially good character and an admirable dignity" whose fatal flaw, or crack, in an otherwise admirable personality, precipitates his downfall. The tragic hero, he went on, is very often a great man who defies evil, or who comes face to face with "an indifferent universe."

All of which made me think of Daddy, and Nick himself pointed out the similarities. Why, Nick wrote in that same letter, should any man suffer out of all proportion to his sin? Why, indeed, unless the universe be evil and meaningless? "Tragedy depends on the notion of greatness, and a tragic fall can only be from the heights," he wrote, adding that Aristotle demanded that his heroes be princes, and that King Lear becomes a true monarch only when he is deposed. "Only and out of this misery comes his godliness . . . out of his fall comes a rise."

Who would ever write about my own father's tragic heroism? Would anyone care about his legacy? A publishing house that bore his name, but an empire-in-the-making wrested from him by thieves.

Just as I'd done in high school, I spent the first two semesters of Sarah Lawrence answering teachers' questions as rarely as I could get away with. During class, I would hide out in the bathroom, sometimes twice during the same class, to avoid being put on the spot. Did my professors suspect anything? Of course they did. Present or absent, I was the stuttering white elephant in the room.

By my second semester, I'd become a boarding student, enmeshed in the full Sarah Lawrence College experience.

Once I began living in a dorm, I brought my guitar from home—one Lucy had helped me pick out at Manny's Music, the famous instrument store on Forty-eighth Street—and stowed it under my bed. For the next few months I played my guitar every chance I could get. Lucy would come home on the weekends, as would I, and I remember closely watching her every move. I imitated the clothes she wore, and the songs she sang, until I could develop a style of my own. Lucy was imitating Joan Baez in a time when Joan Baez's first album was the dominating influence on an entire generation of girls. Bold, blond, blue-eyed Judy Collins was another great arrival on the music scene.

My sister and I hadn't started playing music together yet, but by the time she'd left for Bennington, she was getting comfortable on the guitar, and bought her first really good one during her freshman year. She learned a few chords, enough to play every song on Joan Baez's debut album. She had the same register as Joan Baez, a high, pure soprano with a strong vibrato. I had bought my first guitar sometime during my senior year of high school, and soon my friend Jessie Hoffman and I began writing and playing songs together. The first one's title was a combination of our names, the "Si-hoff Blues." Lucy would teach me chords on weekends and then over the summer, which reinforced my interest in both playing and singing. I bought a few albums and began imitating different singers. My voice didn't travel very far up the scale, but it had a deep, resonant quality. My reigning musical heroine at the time was Odetta. Hers was everything a woman's voice could be, its power deep, sonorous, almost demanding. Alone in my room at home, I sang along to her albums on my cheap little machine, whose needle scratched every LP I owned, tapping into my own lower register. Hollowing out my throat, shaping my mouth into a long-columned O, I trained myself to control my breathing in order to extend words with vowels like *home* and *alone*, stretching that *o* out comfortably in my lungs. I had a naturally strong, even vibrato, and various rooms with high ceilings and natural acoustics—like gyms, bathrooms, or any tiled room, for that matter— provided good settings for me to learn how to appreciate my own voice.

Sarah Lawrence required every freshman to learn a foreign language, and I picked Italian. My classmates and I were assigned to memorize a long poem, and mine, two pages in length, would have been a difficult task even if I spoke without hesitation. That night, I had an idea. When I got back to my room, I took out my guitar and immediately, as if the poem had been written as a song, I fell into the wide field and endless sky, the free and easy space, of music. My speech barriers—its doors, windows, bars—lifted away, and I wrote a melody to the song in less than an hour. More and more, week by week, it seemed, I was coming out of my "singer's closet" by remembering that the melody and rhythm were always there when I needed them.

When word got back to my Italian professor that I was composing music to the poems she'd assigned us, she urged me to sing one of them in class. Galloping back to the dorm, I grabbed my guitar, returned to the Foreign Language building, tuned up in the hallway, and began the song, trusting that the music would override my stutter, which it did. When I finished, the class's response was ridiculously effusive, which gave me a boy-oh-boy kind of thrill.

After that, one friend and then another asked if I'd be willing to visit the student lounge, or someone's dorm room, to play my guitar and sing. I was flattered, even excited. Rather than typing out a big paper on fourteenth-century painting in the Balkans, it was much more inspiring to write and sing a few songs for my friends. My roommate and other girls in my dorm would flop on beds, lean against bureau tops, stand in corners, and crowd

the already-messy floors as I led them through evenings when text and numbers, books and typewriters, were all left behind, and music was the only
thing that mattered. "Let me tell you something," I wrote to Nick around
that time. "I may be famous!! I gave a concert at school (in my bedroom) and
sang a combination of religious and folk songs like 'St. James Infirmary'
and 'Darlin' Corey' and 'Motherless Child.' The girls looked to be taken
into a very definite spiritual rapture. . . . Oh, Nick, we're going to grow together and make lots of money and kind of take the world over, you and me!"

Sarah Lawrence was a three-and-a-half-hour drive away from Harvard,
but nonetheless I was spending as much time as possible in Cambridge with
Nick, taking the train or getting a lift with a friend on Thursday afternoon
and returning Sunday night. During my visits, Nick was eager to show off
his "lady's" new singer persona and voice, along with my meager guitar
playing, which he'd always said he loved. Gradually I was finding my voice
through imitation, by hearing my own pipes overlaid on the voices of other
women, not just Odetta, but also Peggy Lee, Judy Collins, Annie Ross, Mary
Travers, Billie Holiday, and even Nat King Cole and Harry Belafonte. My
Odetta imitations included "Bald Headed Woman," "All the Pretty Little
Horses," "John Henry," "Circle Round the Sun," and a few more songs that
I belted out in the rooms of Harvard's Kirkland House and Claverly Hall.
But one day I sang "Bald Headed Woman" and my voice no longer sounded
like Odetta's, it sounded like mine. Not on purpose. It just happened.

Another benefit of spending more time with Nick was that I could avoid
school and therefore any additional classroom embarrassments. Nevertheless, my time at Sarah Lawrence, and especially my visits to Cambridge,
amounted to a series of unofficial out-of-town auditions. I continued to feel
the release and freedom that singing gave me, and the relief of not having
to talk (I hadn't yet made the transfer from "talking is scary" to "singing is
scary," which I would later). Many elements of my singing would need to
be corrected or even erased before I was ready to sing for "real" people, but
those months were an unofficial dress rehearsal for the rest of my life.

At the same time, Nick provided camouflage. I slid and hid beneath his
eloquence, his charisma, his good looks, his generosity, and the jealousy I
felt from senior Sarah Lawrence girls that I, and not one of them, was hanging off his arm. I was obviously, precociously, in love. Nick and I broke all

the rules by making love in his Harvard dorm room. I was under the spell of the romantic poets back then, and Nick was always quoting some poetry to me, elevating romance and sex into something unworldly.

Outside the bedroom, Nick was just as compelling in his wide-legged, slouchy corduroys and handmade shoes, his long black hair falling in a shiny blade over one eye. As a director at the Loeb Drama Center on Brattle Street—how Nick had learned to direct plays like Lorca's *Blood Wedding* and Sartre's *The Flies* was a mystery to me—he dressed the part in his long scarves and berets, his soft, measured voice, and his seductive, almond-shaped, dark brown eyes. I wondered sometimes if Nick was aware of the impression he made on other people. My guess is that he counted on it.

Lacking any deep knowledge of what the words actually meant, I knew enough to reject the "bourgeoisie" by looking and acting "bohemian," a distinction Nick made it his responsibility to teach me about, considering that I was obviously wrestling with being a bourgeois girl living through bohemian times, and trying my best to look and act the part. Following Lucy's lead, I got my own ears pierced, and wore my by-now extremely long hair in a light brown, lightweight mane down my back, even though it was always so thin and wispy it escaped any attempted braid. At home and at school, every young woman of my acquaintance was swapping clothes, songs, and jewelry. With Brigitte Bardot as our style icon, at least as far as heels were concerned, we spent our free time hunting down the lowest-cut shoes possible, imports from France and Italy, which we found on Lexington and Third Avenues, near Bloomingdale's. When my classmates and I weren't working the bohemian style, we switched over to the Audrey Hepburn look: black tights or extremely white sheer stockings with Capezios.

With my long earrings and pale pink lipstick, I was starting to become known around Sarah Lawrence not just as a singer but, for the first time ever, as a "hip" girl, an "in" girl—"cool," at least by the standards of the mid-1960s. Nicky's father sent him an article about the French singer Françoise Hardy, believing the two of us looked alike, and at one point my friend Lani informed me solemnly that she and I were the only two people on campus who had "shvank." It was a close cousin of *twirl*, the word people had once used to describe my father's style.

When I wasn't hanging out on campus or visiting Nick in Cambridge, I'd begun spending time below Eighth Street, taking the train from Bronxville and switching to the Fifth Avenue bus down to Greenwich Village. The Village in those days was a kaleidoscopic blur of sandal sellers, guitar makers, Indian drum stores, Spanish restaurants on Charles Street, and outdoor markets on MacDougal and Bleecker that sold tie-dye T-shirts, flared skirts, and cheap jewelry. My friends and I would return to campus wearing long, dangling Thai earrings, headbands, and pocketbooks with fringe around the borders. Music stores sold classical and folk albums stuffed in crates, all mixed and merged and spilling onto the sidewalks. Bookstores overflowing with photography books, sheaves of imported paper, books for class, books to impress, books that had called out to me for soulful reasons, like Arthur Schnitzler's *Dream Story*, a book my father published in America by an author Daddy had visited in Vienna, whose descriptions of sex and fantasy I found titillating, yeah, soulful! (The book was later adapted into the Stanley Kubrick film *Eyes Wide Shut*.) Not to mention books by D. H. Lawrence, Edna O'Brien, Truman Capote, Sylvia Plath, Virginia Woolf, Thomas Hardy, and assorted volumes of secondhand poetry and plays, everything from Rupert Brooke to Shakespeare, with pen-drawn illustrations of Ophelia floating lifeless in the water with a garland balanced between her breasts. The older, rattier, and more deliciously fragrant the book, the more in demand it seemed to be. Crowded around the book and music stores were even more storefronts selling beads, bell-bottoms, patchouli oil, hand-woven baskets, gongs, old postcards from Prague street fairs, baskets overflowing with astrological cards, and Nehru shirts whose vivid, blaring colors shone through the gunning exhaust and fading light of the city day.

The Simon Sisters. Lucy and I agreed that our stage name sounded schlocky and borderline embarrassing, plus neither of us wanted to be labeled—or dismissed—as just another novelty sister act. But in the summer of 1963, armed with only our guitars, we hatched a plan to hitchhike up to Province-town, on the tip of Cape Cod, and score a singing job. We had a fantasy of being little-girl Woody Guthries as we went from car to truck to car up and down the Cape, landing singing gigs left and right. In this fantasy we were brave and slightly decadent. Nothing more complicated than that—and we had no illusions about being "discovered." It was more of a lark than anything else, just one step more serious than singing at our mother's cocktail parties.

Mommy nixed our plan. We could either take the bus, she told us calmly, or not go at all. In the end, Lucy and I took a Trailways bus from Thirty-fourth Street in New York to Wellfleet, Massachusetts, where we got a lift from a friend the last fifteen miles to Provincetown.

Our first day in Provincetown, Lucy and I proceeded to stroll the entire length of Commercial Street, the town's main drag. Lugging our guitars in cheap cases as lightweight as papier-mâché, we stopped at each and every boardinghouse and small motel, looking for a room to rent, not wanting to call Mommy and say "Help!" By the time we found a single, inexpensive "bug crawl" room (an expression for lodgings with a spider here, an ant there) above a noisy restaurant, we had been traveling all day and were both exhausted. Our room was tiny and cramped, with a sink in the bed-room and a communal bathroom down the hall.

The joys of being young and on the musical prowl were hardly lost on either of us.

It happened last night we were feeling adventurous
We put on our heels and went out for a walk
More for a drink than to have a few eyes on us
Jenny and I slipped to town for some talk

Me and Jenny, twinklin' like crystal and pennies
Two hot girls on a hot summer night
Looking for love
　　—"Two Hot Girls (On a Summer Night)," 1987

Almost immediately, we heard that a local Provincetown venue, the Moors, needed a musical act, as the singer scheduled to perform had just been drafted to go to Vietnam and was leaving the next day. Without even bothering to audition us, the club owner said, "We'll try it out—just get here at nine tonight."

It was a good time for Lucy and me to get serious and ask ourselves: How many duets did we really know? How many chords? How many songs? But instead of practicing, we headed for the beach, where we decided to go for a swim. There, on the cold sand, something happened that—while unimportant in the overall scheme of things—I remember as a landmark moment. Wanting to impress Lucy as much as test myself, I conjured up the mental image of Bert Lahr as the Cowardly Lion. I was going in all the way, I told Lucy, shaking my fists as I cried out, "Courage!" with Bert Lahr's exaggerated, burring "C-C-COURAGE!" With half-girl, half-lioness bravado, I tromped ahead of Lucy into the freezing water. Lucy's applause and laughter greeted me when I turned around and dashed back, shivering, to my towel on the sand. Even if I was only in the water for a millisecond, I realized: you can always mime yourself into something better. You can become someone "other," taking a crucial step away from yourself, just as I'd done by singing over my stammer, or using an accent to answer the phone. Costumes, headphones, earphones, blindfolds—these were all steps away from the scary, pained, naked self.

Refreshed and exhilarated by being on the beach, my sister and I quickly adjusted to our new B and B, divvied up sides of the bed (one, two, three: shoot), and took turns in the shower. Afterward, we unpacked, hung up our clothes, and picked the least wrinkled ones to wear. We put on matching white, full-sleeved Mexican blouses fetchingly pleated and cinched in at the waist by colorful woven belts; our full, generous, knee-length linen skirts were supposed to be wrinkled anyway. Our slave sandals tied up around our tan ankles came all the way up to our calves. That night at least, we were all about our tans and youthful, head-turning bodies. Our hair was long and undone, natural, wavy, and slightly damp. Instead of focusing on the way we looked, Lucy and I should probably have concentrated on learning a few new songs to add to our repertoire, but for some reason, neither of us was terribly worried.

Dressed and coiffed to be adored, we hitched up to the Moors, guitar cases in hand, giving the finger to any and all cars that didn't pick us up, shouting after them, "See you at the Moors!" This became an expression Lucy and I still use, indicating "A pox on you who dare to pass us by!" Tonight would be the first time Lucy and I had sung together in front of a real audience. I had sung many times at Sarah Lawrence and in various rooms at Harvard, but this was professional. We were getting paid, or at least that's what they promised.

The stage of the Moors was an eight-foot-wide makeshift slab of plywood two feet higher than the rest of the floor. The audience clustered around tables that came so close to the stage they nearly grazed the plywood, both sexes sporting a sea of tattoos and denim—not exactly the same kinds of people who strolled along the paths and lawns of Bronxville and Cambridge. There was no backstage. Lucy and I used the tiny, funky restroom off the greasy, french-fry-smelling kitchen to apply our final coat of lipstick. From head to toe, the Moors had the distinct feeling of being smudged, and by the end of the week, despite appearing in our clean white blouses, my sister and I most certainly felt smudged ourselves.

As soon as we were introduced by the geeky, hillbilly, cross-dressing owner, Lucy said something and it got an immediate laugh. In fact, everything we said got a laugh, including "Hi folks, we are the Simon Sisters, Lucy and Carly." Our first song was "East Virginia," which we'd learned off Joan Baez's debut album. When we got to the lyric "There she laid her head upon my breast," the crowd at the Moors went wild, regaling us with wows and whews and yows and whoops and barking laughs.

Only later did we learn that the Moors was a gay-and-lesbian bar. What the mostly uncombed, ripped-jeans-and-motorcycle-jacketed audience made of these two sisters is lost to time. Lucy and I had taken our wardrobe at the Moors pretty seriously, and in return the audience probably thought we were twin milkmaids from Switzerland, or escapees from a nearby carnival. But anyone paying close attention would have seen how hard I, Carly, the younger sister, was trying to look and act like Lucy, the older sister. I was now taller than Lucy, but emotionally speaking, Lucy was still the high-up one, the light, the beauty, the center of it all. Then as now, my sister was my grounding influence, my heroine, my pilot.

Together, our voices made for an interesting, nearly ideal blend: the exact same pronunciation of words mixed with an entirely different vocal quality. Lucy has a pointed tone and delivery, whereas I have a lower, more smoldering voice. She provided the clear point to my husk, and in the end, we sounded like a single voice. We performed a few more songs: "Winkin', Blinkin' and Nod" (Lucy's soon-to-be-famous song), "Delilah's Dead and Gone," a Serbian folk song from the Theodore Bikel songbook, which required five chords—Lucy and I knew four and a half apiece—and two or three Harry Belafonte songs, of which "Day-O" was the unquestioned crowd-pleaser.

Charlie Close was a good friend of Lucy's, and may in fact have been pursuing her romantically at the time. He was business partners with Harold Leventhal, a well-known music manager, and together they managed Pete Seeger, the Weavers, Alan Arkin, Woody Guthrie, Judy Collins, and many other performers. Charlie came to see us at the Moors one night, and over the next few days taught us F# minor and a cool way to play an E major up the frets. In retrospect, he was grooming us for future management, as he was certainly in a position to escalate our careers. That week, Charlie, Lucy, and I went out to restaurants, cafés, and beaches. We talked about concepts, songs, clothes, and harmonies, and by the time Lucy and I took the bus back home to New York in mid-July, an idea had been hatched: the Simon Sisters would try to break into the Village folk scene. First, though, we had to audition for Charlie Close's business partner, Harold Leventhal.

Harold was a diminutive man, and when Lucy and I walked into his office and Harold stood up behind his desk, I kept thinking he was going to stand up straighter, but no, he leveled off a few inches over five feet. Alan Arkin, who started his career as a folksinger, was also in the room, playing a song called "Jenny Kissed Me." I developed an instant crush on him. More to the point, Harold, who'd been impressed by "Winkin', Blinkin' and Nod" and Lucy's songwriting skills, wanted to represent us, which was a major jump, though at the same time I felt I was only along for the ride, tagging along behind my older sister. Under her sweet, angelic appearance, Lucy, after all, had much more confidence than I ever did. After signing a contract with Harold's management company, we auditioned for Freddie

Weintraub, the owner of the Bitter End, the nightclub, coffeehouse, and folk music venue that's still standing on Bleecker Street. Freddie promptly booked us at the Bitter End nightclub for the fall, two three-week stints in all, and we were off and running. This all took place so quickly that I really forgot I was still a college student, still Nick's girlfriend and plenty in love, and still scared stiff at the notion of performing live on a real stage.

The rest of the summer I spent with Nicky in Cambridge, comforting him about everything he feared would happen to me once I entered the big bad world of show business. Nicky was aghast at the idea, convinced that my new future would consist of late nights and exposure to all kinds of seductions. Nick had brought me into the world of the intellect, and he feared I would ride into a *Sunset Boulevard* world while sacrificing a deeper, more thoughtful side. He had always insisted that I sing for the Harvard boys, but at the same time, he would probably have preferred to remain my own personal impresario. Why would I crave a bigger audience when, after all, I had him? I promised Nicky that the luster of showbiz wouldn't change me, or make me love him any less, nor would I attract the attention of all the playboys of the Western world.

Yet as Nick claimed to worry about my head being spun in all directions, it would be his head that turned first.

It happened in August of that summer. When Lucy and I got back from Provincetown, Nick and I rented a house in Menemsha, the little fishing village on Martha's Vineyard. It was a one-room house with multipaned windows all around, an outhouse, and an outdoor shower in the back. There was a stream beside the small driveway and a path meandering over a wooden bridge, past flowering bushes, honeysuckle, and columbine. Nick was working for a local fish market, delivering bales of fish to various seafood stores and restaurants on the island, and I was spending a few weeks hanging out and visiting friends. Sometimes I could hear him typing, and other times, he and I played gin rummy on the dock. Nick was also trying to teach me how to play chess. Lucy was in New York starting a semester at Cornell Nursing School.

One beautiful afternoon, I collected the mail from the post office and drove back to our little house on the pond. I planned to spend an hour or two on the beach while Nick was working, then come home and cook dinner for him and Max and Yvette Eastman, longtime friends of my parents. First, though, I riffled through that day's mail. There was nothing much: a bank statement, as well as an overstuffed envelope from a mutual friend of Nick's and mine from his Fieldston School days, now a student at Radcliffe. The envelope was addressed to Nick, but against my better judgment, and since it was from a mutual friend, I opened it anyway. I shouldn't have. Our friend said she was acting as a go-between. The other, more important letter in the envelope was from a girl named Nini. Among the things Nini wrote: "I can't bear to go around hiding our love in the shadows."

I sat on the bed and leaned back on my elbows. I was hyperventilating. I was taken over by fear. I was shaking. From what I could tell, Nicky and Nini's romance had been going on at least since the spring. Then again, might I possibly be misinterpreting things? Being wrong, in fact, was the only thing that could save me. The bubble of trust was suddenly burst, replaced by a feeling of pure invasion and hatred. I hadn't ever wondered whether Nick was unfaithful to me; I simply knew he had been faithful. As Jung once said, when you know something, you don't have to believe. Well, Jung—or I—was dead wrong.

When the truth hit me, everything flooded and broke. I went around our house, crying, smashing everything in sight. I broke dinner plates, wineglasses, even the big wooden salad bowl. I took some of Nick's shirts and shredded them with a pair of scissors. It was monstrous, but didn't this situation call for that? In my head unspooled a noir scene, all shadows and hair knifing the dark. Nini, the Radcliffe girl, wearing black tights, a long dark cape billowing behind her, golden hair knotting, creating wind in a rainstorm, red lips moist, calling out through the fog. Mastroianni in pursuit. I got in my mother's station wagon and sped to the Leventhals' house on the North Shore, which my mother was renting. She wasn't home, so I raced down about fifty wooden steps to the beach before making a left turn, running a quarter of a mile as fast as I could, slowing only when I began to lose my breath.

When Nick returned to our busted-up cottage, he knew exactly where to go: my mother's rental house. I'd left my car in her driveway, and knowing me as well as he did, Nick knew I'd be on the beach. As I tore down the sand, I was already making an emotional transition from "me" to "her," as if I were the character in a story. Not me, *Carly*, running, distraught, navigating razor-edged rocks, but some unnamed *her*, jilted, betrayed, and scorned, morphing into a heroine in search of a sandy spot where she could collapse, slumping and sobbing and moaning.

Nick caught up with me. I was too out of breath to fight him off. He denied everything: *No, no, no . . . there was nothing I could do about her . . . it didn't happen . . . you've got to believe me! I could never be that person. I love you. I love you! Carly, Carly . . . it's not what it seems . . . I swear . . .* And like so many blind, determined fools, I took his version to be the truth—or maybe, I should say, my character did. In the movie plot coursing through my head, I desperately needed to maintain Nicky's and my status quo. I had chosen to be blind so many times already, a choice I would find myself making again and again, for the rest of my life, in other forms, with other people. But on the beach on the Vineyard that day, I told myself that I had to believe Nick, that Nini was crazy, and that Nick didn't love or even like her all that much. I wondered how long Daddy had believed Mommy.

During my time at Sarah Lawrence, I continued commuting to Greenwich Village, meeting up with Lucy in front of Cornell Nursing School on East Sixty-ninth Street, the two of us taking a cab down to the Bitter End or to the other venue we played, the Gaslight. The Simon Sisters were the warm-up act for major up-and-coming performers like Bill Cosby, Dick Cavett, Woody Allen, Johnny Carson, and Joan Rivers, all rising stars on the downtown comedy circuit. As for us, we were two sisters who could harmonize like the Everly Brothers, with major-seventh chords thrown in just to be weird. We stood there, unmoving, onstage, in our matching dresses. Fred Weintraub, the owner of the Bitter End, introduced us—"The Angelic Voices of the Simon Sisters"—and then we'd break nervously into song.

Who doesn't react to being loved by a mass of appreciative people? I was no exception. All my college friends came down to see us, and my mother and other family members were in the audience sometimes, too. People told me I had a commanding stage presence and that I sang naturally. Mommy loved our songs, but always offered one small criticism or another along the lines of "Your voices weren't loud enough." Typically, the Simon Sisters played short sets, five songs in all, closing with "Winkin', Blinkin' and Nod." We opened for some seriously talented music acts, rising successes like the Tarriers, Judy Henske, Judy Collins, Randy Newman, and other solo folk musicians and groups. One night, when Woody Allen asked us both to critique his nightly stand-up routines, we did, handing him actual notes! By now, Lucy and I had started taking ourselves quite seriously.

At some point, we recorded "Winkin', Blinkin' and Nod," which became a hit in San Francisco—records have to break out *somewhere*, and some northern California deejay clearly loved our record—and it began climbing the national charts. If Lucy and I had been around to promote it, we were assured that with enough live performances, we could end up with a Top 20 record. But I couldn't leave Sarah Lawrence in the middle of my freshman year, and Lucy was already at nursing school. I was also daunted by the idea of being away from Nick for a year. For me, at least, romance mattered more than fame and fortune in the costume of a "sister act."

By the fall of 1964, Nick had graduated from Harvard and was preparing to go to Greece and England on a Woodrow Wilson scholarship. Lucy and I were on the road touring East Coast clubs and college campuses. I was attempting to keep up with my classes at Sarah Lawrence while getting more and more entrenched in music. It took us less than a week to record our first album, *The Simon Sisters: Winkin', Blinkin' and Nod*. I can credit the fact that our pitch was so good, and our total accompaniment was ourselves, one guitarist and one bass player. Our budget was less than five thousand dollars.

I remember waiting impatiently for the record to come out. I met Lucy at nursing school, and together we raced downtown. First we went to Harold Leventhal's office, where he gave us good news: the first album review had come in and it was actually good. Next, we ran over to the Doubleday record store—the three big record stores back then were Doubleday, Hudson Records, and Sam Goody's—and the first time we saw our record, Lucy and I jumped up and down and hugged each other. Then we each went into a different listening booth, put on headphones, took them off, then screamed and started jumping up and down again. I couldn't have been more excited by the idea of the Simon Sisters' first record (would Daddy be proud?). My excitement would always turn, to be replaced by a fear of appearing onstage and having to talk in between songs.

Over the next few days, Dave Kapp, the president of Kapp Records, our label, showered us with grilled-cheese sandwiches and Trailways bus tickets, and sent Lucy and me touring all over the East Coast and as far south as Knoxville, Tennessee. This was challenging, considering that both of us were in school, so our touring took place exclusively on the weekends. Wherever we went, we wore matching red dresses created by a Lexington Avenue tailor. Most of the time, Lucy and I served as the opening act for one boy group or another, typically attired in dark matching jackets and khaki pants—the Bitchin' Banjo Brothers or something like that—though occasionally the Simon Sisters were the main act. Better yet, our repertoire was growing. We were writing some songs of our own, and harmonizing new arrangements of classic folk tunes, as both Lucy and I had, and still have, a spooky ability to harmonize to melodies we didn't yet know. Lucy, I knew, would always travel to a fourth or a fifth above me, and I would adjust my voice until it landed in the right place. She and I spent hours with our guitars, with whatever new albums we'd just bought and some sheet music. Occasionally I would remember I was still a college student, but it was always a battle to return to Sarah Lawrence.

One night, Odetta came to see us sing. Lucy and I were performing in western Massachusetts, at the smaller of the two venues inside the Lenox Inn, with Odetta herself performing at the larger one. We had met after her show, and she told us, "Maybe I'll come see you tonight." It probably goes without saying that I worked myself into a tizzy. Lucy and I went onstage that night only to see Odetta sitting in the front, and I proceeded to lose control onstage, fainting—quite literally—onto her table. When I finally came to, I looked up to find Odetta fanning me backstage, me supine on the floor.

It took a lot of shows, and a lot of positive feedback, for me to feel at all comfortable. But with Lucy beside me, I knew that if fear overwhelmed me, I could always rely on her to step in until the panic skittered past. I worried less about stammering onstage. I was able to introduce songs, and even tell stories, with a fluidity that always surprised me. I had no explanation for my stop-start eloquence, and remember telling myself that if I ran into any problems, I could always take a long pause. My fear was unpredictable, too. One night, Lucy and I were singing in a college gymnasium when someone called in a bomb scare, and never in my life did I feel more peaceful or self-contained, more capable of reassuring other people. Which isn't to say that being onstage wouldn't be a tricky business for the rest of my life. I was always on the verge of implosion, of humiliating myself, of awakening the Beast.

The question was: What was next?

Back and forth to Sarah Lawrence, I was frankly enjoying my newfound status on campus, thanks to an appearance that Lucy and I made on the TV show *Hootenanny*. Kids now looked up to me. Professors gave me new leeway and accepted essays that were two days late. I got a lot of good feedback, and was a bit dazzled by it, too. Nick had already left for Europe, and I missed him terribly. During my Thanksgiving break, my family confronted me. Mommy insisted, rightly, that it was a waste of money for me to treat Sarah Lawrence as a "drop-in" part of my life. For her part, Lucy wanted to keep on playing the clubs, get the applause, make some money, and record a second album. In spite of my intermittent fear of performing, I was all too happy to follow her lead. As for the idea of me returning to Sarah Lawrence for the post-Christmas winter semester, the fact of the matter was that from kindergarten on up, I'd never wanted to go to school—ever. Now it was just more inconvenient.

So when Nick invited me to join him in Europe, it was the right idea at the right time. Plus, could anything be more romantic?

First, though, I had to get through the holidays, which I spent in Riverdale with my family. After Daddy died, Mommy had sold the Stamford property—a whisking, sudden packing-up of cartons and round trips to the Salvation Army. Gone was the white-columned Georgian Tara-like house. Gone was the childhood of midnight whispers and games beneath the apple trees. How that fantastic house in Stamford could be someone else's home was unbelievable to me. Who would find those secret notes tucked behind a shutter or in between pine floorboards? Who, I wondered, would stumble on the clue that would reveal the hiding place of the next note, which would lead to the key that opened the mysterious box, inside which a stranger would find a diary with its index of code names with, just perhaps, a tiny arrow pointing to a disheveled strip of wallpaper that read "I hate Hark" or "Please God, make Hark go to war"?

With the Stamford house gone, what was "home" for me anymore if not Nick? My fantasy, which would become a reality, was that my guitar and I would hop on an ocean liner and disembark in France or England, and Nick would be there to greet me. We would pick up a sports car and drive south to the Alpes-Maritimes, stopping along the way for some wine and a loaf of French bread, and I would play my guitar and sing songs for Nick and Nick alone. Adrift in those daydreams, I went ahead and took a formal leave from Sarah Lawrence, not knowing if I would ever return to college again. Instead, I would spend the next four months abroad, looking for signs. Nini was in the past. Once again Nick was my darling, my safe person. Moreover, going to Europe would give me the perspective on whether I should finish college in the first place. In Europe, I could take a leave from singing while glancing at road signs, exotic graffiti, messages in bottles, and tea leaves in Gypsies' cups.

When I arrived in Southampton to find Nick waiting for me under a doorway arch, the two of us literally buckled in each other's arms, each of us secretly primed to imitate the finer details of the American expatriate life. No Michelin Guides for us! I had it in mind to buy my first tape recorder to capture new songs, as well as writing the melodies to the lyrics Nick would write. Having just finished Fitzgerald's *Tender Is the Night*, and before that Edna O'Brien's *The Country Girls*, I already felt well acquainted with one of the best-known, most glamorous landscapes in the world as well as the Irish voice that would influence my folk songs. Nick and I were, I felt, a romantic-looking pair, ready to be invited to any dinner party that Gertrude

Stein and Alice B. Toklas could dream up. Europe would be the setting where Nick would write his novel and I would write my songs.

On a late February afternoon, Nick and I boarded the train from London to Milan, where I bought a crude Phillips tape recorder roughly the size of a shoebox. Eventually we were on our way, driving blindly into France in Nick's new Alfa Romeo, up the windy, narrow roads of the Alpes-Maritimes, in the extreme southeast corner of France. By the time we finally arrived in the tiny village of Châteauneuf de Grasse, it was so dark I could barely make out the stone from the stucco, and the terra-cotta from an olive tree.

As Nick unpacked the car, I glimpsed the far-off lights of Cannes and savored the prospect that when morning came, the Mediterranean would be visible. It was cold, but a new kind of cold, with a wet, throaty wind blowing in from unseen hills and waters. The trees made a French whistling, *sssss*, a single note modulating and cresting in volume. Nick's and my new home, at least for the rest of the winter and into the spring, was, in fact, a caretaker's house on a much larger property. The second floor had two bedrooms, with ours opening out to the ocean via wide ceiling-to-floor French windows. The bathroom had no shower, only a deep Japanese bathtub. The real drawback was there was no hot water. To draw a bath, first you had to heat pots on all four stove burners, and once the water was hot, lug the pots upstairs to the tub. "Prince Charles! Prince Charles! Courage!" I would call out, to remind Nick and myself that ice-cold showers and general discomfort were character-building strategies that Queen Elizabeth and Prince Philip used on their poor, freezing only son and heir. Still, nothing could induce either of us to linger in the tub any longer than to scrub each other's backs before disappearing naked and goose-bumpy into a waiting towel.

For a few days, the absence of hot water was romantic, but the romance fast soured once I developed a raging combination of three unwanted venereal complaints ranging from the uncomfortable to the ridiculous. Only a week after we arrived, just as the mimosa trees and anemones outside our window were beginning to burst and bloom, I found myself uncomfortably preoccupied with my own body.

Dr. Mouchotte, the doctor we found in nearby Nice, was a large man with big hands and a habit of bunching up his lips whenever he tried to pronounce anything in English. He had a distinct smell about him—an aroma both sour and unfamiliar. Ultimately, he prescribed what I supposed was a "douche bag," into which I was supposed to pour equal amounts of around twenty-five ingredients, most of which I suspected, but could never prove, came directly from an Italian restaurant, so vividly did they resemble the herbal seasoning atop a lasagna.

For the next two weeks, I heated up the water on the stove and poured it into the douche bag, along with a dropperful of tincture of Turkish mushroom cap and powders distilled from gnome-filled forests, all of which smelled unsettlingly like Dr. Mouchotte. The physical contortions that followed were unthinkable. Preparing the cure took up so much of the day. When I wasn't doubled up in pain and discomfort, I was writing letters to friends and family members, describing what Nick's and my new romantic life was like in our farmhouse high in the Alpes-Maritimes.

Thus, due to my maladies, Nick's and my physical relationship had a few rivers to cross. The magic of the trip, I knew, depended on my becoming healthy as soon as humanly possible, but I was already beginning to resent the whole process of the boiling-and-then-cooling of the water. At the same time, the plastic tubing hanging over the toilet was the inspiration for my earliest lyrics, which I wrote in an effort to get relief from my own pain and frustration. Writing lyrics became an emotional outlet, turning my own experiences and history into another person's. "I can't stand you" becomes "She can't stand him." "I no longer love you" becomes "She no longer loves him." By switching from *me* and *I* to *her* and *she*, I was able to free up the words and emotion inside me. Just like on the beach running away from Nick, turning into Monica Vitti or Sophia Loren.

Sometime during the first month, in the middle of the night, I first developed a symptom that would dog me for the rest of my visit. It was 2 a.m., and I awoke suddenly, quivering. It felt as if I were sitting on the hood of a car whose motor was running. I asked Nick to touch me, to confirm that I was feeling what I was feeling. Was my shaking—or "my vibrations," as Nick and I called them—the symptom of some underlying psychological or physical problem? Was I becoming more mentally unbalanced? Just as I'd once knocked against wood to prevent my father from dying, I did the same with my vibrations: *this night, you will not shake.* A day would pass and the same thing happened again, as it would every night, with a few exceptions, for the next few months. Nick was invariably tender, assuring me that my body wasn't actually shaking, that I was probably dreaming, that everything would be all right and I should try to fall back to sleep. I always did, but the next night it would happen again. If one morning I woke up without the shakes, my mood would be exaggeratedly optimistic, manic even, and as the day went on, it would begin swinging wildly back and forth as I faced down the prospect of another night of trembling.

My only distraction was cooking. I'd bought a French calendar whose black-and-white photos of local flora and fauna were accompanied by recipes. Taking my cue from the calendar, every day I prepared a new meal, nearly all of which were saturated with cream, mushrooms, onions, garlic, wine, spices, and herbs. Nick and I ate mussels and oysters, often followed by elaborate desserts I'd baked, filled with dried fruits, pine nuts, brandy, and wine. Every night, we washed down our dinner and dessert with a shared bottle of local wine, almost always a Châteauneuf-du-Pape.

Still, the shaking wouldn't stop. Nick and I went to the Picasso Museum in the little town of Vence. I bought a piece of pottery for my mother. That night, I awoke shaking and depressed.

We went to Eze-sur-Haute, and then Eze-sur-Mer. A brilliant walk on the beach. Drove back to Châteauneuf de Grasse. Night came around; I fell asleep and awoke, shaking.

At one point, six weeks into our stay, Nick and I drove to Spain, pausing along the way in ancient French towns that reminded me of the canvases of Cézanne and Van Gogh. We puttered past and through Aix, Les Baux, Arles, Montpellier, Cap d'Agde, Perpignan, and just over the Spanish border, Cadaqués, the town that Salvador Dalí painted, as well as a resting spot for Picasso, Miró, and Duchamp. Nick and I shared a sunny room in Cadaqués. It was the first night of hot running water in weeks, which we took full advantage of by filling the tub almost to overflowing. Our stay was enchanted, and I attributed the relaxation I felt to one thing: I didn't tremble. After a long hiatus, Nick and I made love, which also helped alleviate any symptoms of "the vibrations." The next day, we headed for Barcelona. When I first glimpsed what I thought was the city, brash and ugly and charmless, with factories and pollution filling the air, I felt my spirit break in half, and was relieved to discover that the city I beheld was *Badalona*, on the seacoast forty-five minutes to the northeast of Barcelona. What a difference a *d* makes. Nick drove at top speed to Barcelona, where a reservation awaited us at the Avenida Palace. A total relief, a magnificent city.

At dinner that night, I glimpsed a woman at another table who looked so much like Chibie I dissolved into tears. My grandmother had died of a heart attack the previous summer, a week after I fainted in front of Odetta. Since then I'd been having quiet anxiety attacks where I feared losing control the same way I'd lost control onstage in front of Odetta. That night at dinner the dam finally broke. I cried so long and so uncontrollably that the waiters and the formally attired diners surrounding us noticed, and the maître d' became so concerned that he arrived at our table bearing cold towels. Nick was worried, and prepared to call an ambulance. Instead, somehow we escaped from the dining room, me with my torso bent over, collapsed into Nick's shoulder. Both of us were bewildered. What exactly was going on? That night I stayed awake, shaking, sleep coming only after I took a hot bath and a phenobarbital.

Early the next morning, still in Barcelona, I called my mother from the hotel room and described my symptoms. Mommy had recently become intrigued by psychoanalysis, and from time to time saw a famous practitioner in New York, a disciple of Freud named Dr. Albert Lowenstein. Later that same morning, after consulting with him, Mommy called me back. Based on my symptoms, she and Dr. Lowenstein thought I might be suffering from a "nervous breakdown," the same thing Daddy had been hospitalized for twice. We made a plan: I would leave, go home, and get help.

A week before I left, I lay out by the twig-strewn pool on one side of our little house, reading Stendhal's *The Red and the Black*. Blowing in off the ocean up the foothills of the Alps were tiny water drops, reflecting the shimmering hues of the mountain flowers. It was, I found out, the local phenomenon known as the mistral—a strong, cold, ill wind, similar to the sirocco that bulldozes across Africa or the mystical Santa Ana winds in Southern California. Leaves piled up thickly on the bottom of the muddy pool as I read my book, riveted by its melodrama, longing, and romance.

Nick would remain in Châteauneuf de Grasse, writing his novel, as well as letters to me about the hillside and his excursions. I hadn't even left yet, but already I missed him terribly, missed our small house, missed our tiny, cold-water bathtub, missed the flowers and the cooking, missed our expatriate life together. I also regretted that our love wasn't more physical, or urgent. I didn't feel that my body was something he would want to spend time with. When he touched me, I felt *his* hand more than *my* body.

As I lay there reading, Nick joined me, and we had a depressing but honest conversation about the state of affairs between us. We both agreed that our relationship had grown middle-aged (ha!) and uneventful (how amusing to feel this way before you're even twenty-one!). We were both bored, and if another romantic opportunity arose, we agreed we would urge the other person to take it. Nick was as aware as I was of what was wrong with our relationship. I knew it and so did he, but I think he was surprised I felt the same way. My youthful conclusion was this: I should never have stopped looking things up in the encyclopedia, never stopped trying to keep Nick interested. Why hadn't I asked him about Jean-Paul Sartre and Simone de Beauvoir? Why wasn't I better read, more casually literate? Why hadn't I insisted upon reading the book he was writing? If only I had devoted more time to keeping Nick intellectually stimulated, I might have kept myself stimulated, too.

Has anyone ever properly explained love's weather patterns, low-pressure systems, cold fronts, storms? Surviving its tides and seasons, I've found out, is a feat exclusively for the strong of heart. With the agitation that had been building up all spring drained off, Nick and I were left to bask in the love we still had for each other. My last night in Châteauneuf de Grasse with Nick still lives vividly in my memory: The stove in our little kitchen. The woodpile just outside the front door. The mimosas beginning to sharpen their yellow tones. The sweet early green of the olive trees, the verbena, and the climbing roses subtly changing the complexion and color of our caretaker's cottage as the season began its softly spiraling turn. That night, I cooked our favorite recipe: Swedish meatballs with a lot of heavy cream, brandy, and noodles. We made love, and I packed, and there was more unspoken than spoken.

The next morning, Nick drove me to Nice. On the boat to Europe and throughout my stay, I'd fantasized about meeting French musicians who would show up at our house carrying guitars, lutes, flutes, and hand drums, all of us jamming late into the night, the entire scene ending up, inexplicably, with Lady Brett Ashley from Hemingway's *The Sun Also Rises* in the stands of a Spanish bullfight. Naturally, none of that had happened—not even close. But along with the homecoming presents I'd tucked inside my suitcase for my family, I would be returning to the States with my Phillips tape recorder and at least three songs I'd written, two with Nick as lyricist. While not as much or as many as I'd hoped, those three melodies represented some sort of beginning.

I began therapy immediately with an old-school Freudian analyst whom Dr. Lowenstein had recommended. Five days a week, I lay down on Dr. F's couch, never once looking at him, Dr. F unremittingly silent in return, which gave me ample time to dwell on the Rorschach-like paintings of trees and cucumbers covering the walls. Sometimes during my sessions, I suffered quasi–anxiety attacks. I'd sit up on the couch, hide my head between my knees, breathe hard, and try to find answers that could shed some light on the puzzle of what ailed me. I had countless dreams about both Billy and Ronny, but Dr. F and I never got to the bottom of their significance—or I just didn't believe his interpretations. Occasionally I could hear the sound of his pen scribbling, and entering and leaving his office I occasionally caught fast glimpses of a nice-looking man whose unfocused right eye lent him a slightly comical—or maybe it was magical—expression.

The most significant result of my sessions with Dr. F? I no longer had the shakes, not even once since returning to New York. I had come to believe that my trembling was the direct result of my relationship with Nick. Dr. F also spent a lot of time asking me about Ronny, though I remember being extremely embarrassed to talk about anything important, or intimate. In some essential core of myself, I'd always known about Mommy and Ronny, and their involvement was now out in the open. Four years after Daddy's death, Mommy and Ronny could be found everywhere: on the library couch in Riverdale, in the garden planting bulbs, kissing in the kitchen, walking my mother's Dalmatians, Mandy and Pandy. Everyone in my mother's social circle must have known. What did they think? I wondered. Did they gossip? Did they care?

I was never able to understand the unself-conscious ease Mommy obviously felt over her affair with Ronny, never able to accept that whatever guilt she might have felt ended the moment Daddy died. I still wasn't cutting Ronny any slack. I loathed him. His speaking voice always had a phony note to it, one that always made me imagine he was hearing his voice on a tape recorder and wondering how it stacked up against Ezio Pinza's.

At the conclusion of my analysis—coincidentally, at the same time the small inheritance my father left me had run out—Dr. F told me gently that it was time to graduate, that together, we had gotten to the root core of my psychological problems. From this point on, he said, I would be far more capable of handling any situation that came my way. Looking back, I assume he must have caught a whiff of that pungent, sour aroma of future bounced checks, the scent of a patient on the cusp of exhausting her funds.

By now, Nick, too, had returned to New York, and we went out to dinner at Chez Napoleon, on West Fiftieth Street, to celebrate my psychoanalytic "graduation." Among the offerings on the wine list that night was Châteauneuf-du-Pape, the same wine we had drunk every night in France. Over a shared bottle, Nick and I ate flounder, oysters, and onions in cream sauce as we reminisced about our days and nights in the Alpes-Maritimes, both of us aware we had been in that stage of our relationship where couples who love each other say good-bye, in very slow motion, before moving on to others.

After dinner, we walked all the way over to the East Side, where I was living with my sister Joey at Fifty-fifth Street and First Avenue. Nick left me there, as there was no longer a reliable question of his spending the night. I fell asleep watching a movie, and a few hours later was awakened by a rumbling throughout my body—the same shakes I'd had in France, the ones that had driven me into psychoanalysis. Here they were again. Why? Had I had a bad day? Did seeing Nick unearth some ancient memory of our relationship in France that had resurfaced at the restaurant? Then it finally hit me: it was the red wine, the Châteauneuf-du-Pape! The same wine Nick and I drank almost every night when we were in Europe. Like the final twist in an O. Henry story, it wasn't a nervous breakdown at all, but instead: allergies. If only I'd gone to an allergist instead of spending all that time, not to mention my inheritance, on Dr. F's couch, I might still be in France with Nick, buying little Mattisses and Picassos in seaport towns.

Allergies aside, I still had to decide whether or not to go back to college. My mother, Joey, and Lucy all saw me on a stage. Nick was alone in pressuring me to resume my education, and I loved him all the more for ultimately being on the losing side of this debate, and not least for accompanying me, hand in hand, through the hardships of the mistral. I honestly had no idea what I wanted. I would have gone in any direction anyone else seemed sure of. I could see nothing really positive about returning to Sarah Lawrence and was happy, and even relieved, to put my formal education on permanent hold. Lucy and I had hastily released a second album by then, and we were singing all over the country, but the problem was I didn't really want to continue doing *that*, either. If the truth be known, I didn't really develop any major new musical ambitions until I fell in love with Willie Donaldson.

"It Happens Everyday."

Lucy and me in London, 1965.

CHAPTER TEN

frog footman

In the mid-1960s, London was where everything interesting and offbeat was happening. It was the world of Henry Orient and *What's New Pussycat?*, of "Help!," "Ticket to Ride," "(I Can't Get No) Satisfaction," and "Downtown." Herman's Hermits, the Yardbirds, the Rolling Stones, Peter and Gordon, the Hollies, the Animals, and the Beatles—so much music to imitate, to interpret. Songs I could stand up and sing into the mirror, while dancing at the same time, or by singing harmony/descant or an improvised horn part at the top of my lungs. Alone in my room, I regularly sang along with the Everly Brothers, the Weavers, and other folksingers, but I was taken—captivated, enthralled, seduced—by the rhythms of rock 'n' roll. Clearly I needed a bigger mirror, a new one that could accommodate my entire body, and maybe London would be that place.

In 1965, with college on eternal hold, Mommy, Lucy, and I were supposed to take the *Queen Mary* to Europe and stay for a month, but at the last minute, Mommy elected to stay home—she blamed Pandy, the dog, I think. Lucy, who'd come down with a bad flu, followed suit, though my sister promised to come over to England later if I managed to arrange the Simon Sisters a gig or two. So it would be just me, sailing alone to England.

A week after the *Queen Mary* left New York, the boat docked in Southampton, and I took the train by myself to London. My first few days there, I stayed with a friend on Harley Street, eventually finding a room at the Russell Square Hotel. I felt extremely homesick, and a day later was relieved to find a phone number that had been given to me by a family friend who knew any number of London-based entertainment agents and performers. The name and number scrawled on the slip of paper, which would prove crucial to the rest of my stay, not to mention life, read only: WILLIAM DONALDSON, 18 HASKER STREET, followed by a phone number. The name meant nothing to me. The family friend told me that if I ever found myself in any trouble, to "just call Willie. He will take care of homesickness."

It seemed an overstatement, but when Willie answered the phone, the rapport and even attraction between us was instantaneous. What exactly was it that was so irresistible about even the sound of Willie Donaldson's voice? There are some people who just do it to you, and you get them, and they get you: Willie had a magic that seduced me from the start. Before I knew it, I'd accepted his invitation for breakfast at his Chelsea town house, and when the door opened, Willie handed me a glass of orange juice.

He was attired in a loose-fitting pair of cuffed pants and a charcoal-gray V-neck sweater over a classic white button-down shirt. The town house was elegant but also funky and dressed down, four floors of raffish English charm. Willie was easily six foot two, and as he walked ahead of me up the stairs from the vestibule, it struck me that even though he was barely thirty years old, his stride reminded me of my father's—long, unathletic, patrician, and vaguely effeminate. His accent was just as unusual. It seemed to take a particular route around his uvula, revolving up around the roof of his mouth and echoing back to his tonsils, this particular sound all driven from the sound box of his long head bones. His lips alone could have given more definition to his words, but I certainly wasn't the one who was going to make such a suggestion.

Willie was the president of a company called Players and Writers, and had produced the traveling English comedy revue *Beyond the Fringe*. *Beyond the Fringe* was the precursor to the Rutles, Monty Python, and *Satur-*

day Night Live. I had seen it five times in New York with my friend Jennie Lou, and we'd both gotten to know one of the four cast members, Dudley Moore, on whom Jennie had a crush. I fell for Jonathan Miller. When I learned he was a stutterer, I knew someday we'd meet. We haven't.

But on that July morning in Hasker Street, I had no idea who Willie Donaldson was, and knew even less what, if anything, he expected of me in return. Did he assume I'd called him in hopes of landing a secretarial position, or a part in a play, or a job as his cat walker? What had our mutual family friend told him about me? Had Willie ever heard of the Simon Sisters? I doubted it. I could still be a call girl. It could be a naughty nun reference. There was no gag on our imaginations.

The town house in which we were sitting, it turned out, belonged to Willie's girlfriend, the actress Sarah Miles, whom I had just seen in the film *The Servant.* To my mind, Sarah was the ultimate new-age English movie actress, on par with Julie Christie and Susannah York. Willie and I sat on a threadbare, dark brown Edwardian couch in their second-floor living room (the higher the social class, the more missing threads, is a pretty dependable rule of thumb), my back facing floor-to-ceiling French windows opening out onto Hasker Street below, Willie's face and foxy hazel eyes illuminated by the morning sun.

I already felt at ease, placed perfectly in the moment, lulled by Willie's fast, sharp British wit. Willie was the first *man* I'd met in my life who reminded me of my grandmother, Chibie. He had her mixture of the straight-faced and the absurd. Already Willie seemed a compatriot in my favorite kind of fun—the kind based on irony and mock formality, the sort where carefully choreographed pauses and inflections play a starring role, a humor that says *Life is a game to be played,* so must *we really insist on taking ourselves so damn seriously?*

For the next three hours, Willie and I sat there on the couch, pressed up against a row of needlepointed pillows covered with hair from two Abyssinian cats prowling underfoot. The cats manipulated their long gray hairs into the sofa like artisans. Willie noticed this and reprimanded them with class: "Hey, knock it off please, will you?" All the room's upholstery looked like intricately woven pieces, fashion, faux, fabulous! He reminded me of nothing so much as a formal little boy dressed up in his father's clothes. We talked about everything, including how my crush on Dr. Miller would culminate. The subject then turned to Lucy, and the Simon Sisters, and whether Lucy and I might be performing in England later that summer. "What a good idea." Eyebrows raised, and not even bothering to ask me if I minded, Willie spontaneously requested Lucy's number and reached for the phone. He was putting on a show for me, as I would find out he did for so many people. "Good morning," he said, practically singing his greeting and yodeling the syllables from high to low. When my older sister picked up, "Is this Simon Sister?" Then, "Have you had your orange juice yet?" Clearly the answer was no, because Willie suggested she fetch a glass, "and then we can talk about your hasty getaway from New York and get you over here at once, so you and the other Simon Sister can perform at the Palladium, and a week or two later, at the Albert Hall, and we can all make a great deal of money, not to mention in cash, too."

I was beyond delighted to be in the presence of Willie and could have spent the rest of the day sitting across from him. I felt uncannily comfortable being who it was that I was in his presence. Willie and I shared in easy bite-size pieces descriptions of our personal lives which trumped anything he might ever do for me as an agent. His brand of "funny" was a straight-faced absurd variety, followed by no applause signs. Willie was one who would take you over the line until you were bending back then tilting forward with the kind of laughing that often releases tears. But fearing I was overstaying my welcome, I finally picked up my bag, telling him what a great time I'd had. Assuring me he would easily find Lucy and me a job— "I've done it before," he said—Willie rose and, peering down the street to the left from the second-floor window, called out, "Taxi, taxi! Taxi for Miss Simon Sister!"

A few days later, over tea and biscuits, Willie and I figured out a plan to bring Lucy over to England—I would give Willie the money and he would be in charge of buying and sending Lucy a ticket, which he actually did—and plotted out a way for the two of us to audition properly for clubs and television shows. In less than a week, Willie had become the focus of my days, and already I felt closer to him than I did to many friends I'd known my whole life. He showed me London, walking the narrow streets with their cramped, unnamed pubs. We browsed boutiques, sat in outdoor cafés, leaned into the angles and sweeps of energy in the English summertime air. The streets and squares teemed with beatniks, as well as style mavens sporting new big hair: voluminous, full of colorful extensions, clenched in leather strands or Indian feathers or teased into beehives. We discussed whom we were going to meet, and what, exactly, we would say to them when that time came. Willie, we agreed, would introduce me to my future husband, Dr. Jonathan Miller, as well as to Peter Sellers, Spike Milligan, the Beatles, the Rolling Stones, and not least, Queen Elizabeth—for whom I, naturally, would sing.

Willie's optimism and confidence were infectious. When Lucy came over, and if Willie was somehow able to find work for us, as he'd promised . . . by this point I actually would want to perform. For me, *wanting to perform* was an entirely new feeling. More than anything, I was eager to be a part of the physical movement of the music I loved, to shed my nervousness and allay my anxiety by simply moving my hips. Another thing, too: after only a few meals, gallons of tea, long walks that always ended too soon, I was also falling head over heels in love with Willie.

Over our third or fourth lunch, Willie told me of a possible rift in his relationship with Sarah Miles. In turn, I told him about Nick and how, despite our closeness, he and I were ready to part ways. Still, if either Willie or I was in the dumps about our romantic circumstances, you would never have known it. In the days and weeks that followed, I learned all about Willie's dominant mother and his indifferent father, who, as the head of the Donaldson Shipping Line, had the privilege of getting a ship sunk by the Germans during the Blitz. Another cup of tea, another glass of wine, and it was again my turn to talk, this time describing my own indifferent father, and Chibie, and how much Willie reminded me of her. I elaborated on my schooling, and my family. We talked about the vacations we would take using the money Willie planned to earn producing (or convincing someone else to produce) any number of West End shows. Despite Willie's infectious confidence—he was like a little boy, dreaming big ideas—I was slightly skeptical that he had a drop of what it would take to carry off his ambitions. Still, he and I felt like coconspirators, rollicking toward some eventual erotic "showdown."

It took a week to get Lucy over to England, and when she did we immediately rented the top floor of a house at 6 Wilton Place, a few paces off Brompton Road in Knightsbridge. The house itself had a plaque right outside the front door, with the words TOAD HALL engraved in bronze, and I loved it on first sight, even the five-flight walk up to our bedrooms overlooking Kinnerton Street. I loved having Lucy around, but her presence also led me into the usual old paranoid thinking, that even though I'd already fallen hard for Willie, he was bound to become enamored of my older sister. "There's nothing to it but my endless-seeming competition with Lucy," I wrote in my diary, adding, "but I think I interest Willie more. I am his 'kind' of trouble."

For the next few weeks, Lucy and I polished our repertoire, which to my ears sounded surprisingly good. We both felt confident enough to audition for whomever Willie could find, the only problem being that the London labels didn't want to release our albums since neither Lucy nor I had any plans to stay around to promote them. But I didn't question Willie's judgment, or come down on myself too hard. In fact, I talked back to them when they gave us dismal answers, as only an American can, making jokes I knew they wouldn't understand, and I remember how much Willie loved my freshness and sauciness. Still, the fact of the matter was that Lucy and I needed to get lucky, fast, and soon enough we did.

In early August, within the first week of Lucy's arrival, the Simon Sisters auditioned at a place called Quaglino's, in the West End. In addition to two or three originals, Lucy and I sang a French version of Bob Dylan's "Blowin' in the Wind," Burt Bacharach's "Don't Go Breaking My Heart," Gordon Lightfoot's "That's What You Get for Loving Me," and the song that had become our minor hit back in the U.S., "Winkin', Blinkin' and Nod." "Well done, Simon Sister!" Willie said to us afterward, over and over again. But nothing came of our audition at Quaglino's, so the three of us went straight to a competing venue called the Rehearsal Room, a little club above the Royal Court Theatre, where we made a big impression on the owner, Nigel Corbett, who signed us on then and there.

Lucy had met Willie only twice when he told me he wanted to fix her up with the King of Wales. This pleased me to no end, since I took it as a sign that Willie was eager to keep me all to himself. Helpless in the face of Willie's sardonic, adorable, long-legged, coffee-scented charm, I spun around mindlessly, thrilled, casting off any suspicions that Willie might be even remotely untrustworthy. No, it was much more fun and romantic to believe that Lucy and I were meeting the King of Wales—who turned out to be not some doddering, muttering, actual king at all, but Richard Rhys, a close friend of Willie's from Cambridge days. He was actually a part of some royal lineage, and Willie was quick to move him up in line. From what I could tell, Willie and Richard must have been the two coolest, naughtiest, suavest upperclassmen ever to stride English soil, and I imagined that their wealth and offhanded, rumpled, imperious saunters had made them the objects of undergraduate worship across all twenty-nine Cambridge colleges.

After dinner at the Ritz, a quick stop at another restaurant, Chez Solange, and a visit to Danny La Rue's, London's transvestite club, the four of us took the long way home through Kensington Park. The night felt bewitched, as if any moment a common bench could have transmuted into a giraffe, a tree into a flamingo. The air was fragrant with oleander, and willows were silhouetted against a smoky, brightly lit London sky. It was clear by now that Lucy and the king were getting along exceedingly well, and when we got separated from them—*Please don't start searching for me, Lucy,* I silently begged her—Willie and I ended up on a bench facing a pond, riveted by the sight of a golden carriage led by two horses wearing equine formal attire. The coach had footmen! Or was I drunk? No, Willie saw what I saw too, dubbing them "Frog Footmen," words he relished repeating and which later turned into his own nickname for me: *Frog Footman.*

Once the carriage vanished, Willie and I seemed to be the only people left in the park. Indeed, it turned out we were, too; the park gates were closed, padlocked. Willie sat stiffly on the bench, and even when I put my arms around him from behind, he didn't melt in any discernible way, which both disappointed and excited me. He preferred to take his time.

"Do you find me strange?" he asked. "I mean reserved, odd . . . like something in me is missing and is slowly being regained?" He was clearly referring to his recent breakup with Sarah Miles. He told me she had come home from Ireland and found a woman's shoe under their bed.

Looking back, it was one of the most perfect moments of my life: for the first time, I felt I truly belonged somewhere, in this space of no space. My arms were enveloping a man whom I wanted, and there was no chance of losing him, since he wasn't mine. Once he was mine, and he would be, it would come into focus, the alchemy of it all, the possibility of an ending.

Somehow I knew that the dynamic was perfect and I wasn't in any danger of rejection. He couldn't reject me yet. I was on a brilliant edge. It was a moment of pure precipice. I didn't jump, though I was in position. As long as he didn't give himself to me, the seductive moment of possibility hovered. *Let it stay there. Let it last as long as it can last.* I wouldn't have liked it as well if he had pursued me at that point, if he had turned to me and given in with a little wan kiss, or a big passionate one. Instead, I relished the safety of *not yet having attained.* As a result of that heightened feeling of being, I can still remember details as though I were right there now: the vaguely crumbling oakwood bench with a wrought-iron frame holding it together, Willie's posture, leaning forward, the elbows of his jacket bunching, his hands folded in front of him as though sitting in a chapel. I looked to the right through the enormous willows and there was Kensington Palace, lit softly by a streetlamp filtering through mist.

It was almost five in the morning, we were still enclosed in the park, and I was getting chilly in my thin cotton dress. Willie was being careful not to touch me or be in any way "physical." He smoothly draped his jacket around my shoulders as the two of us made our way back to the park entrance, with me carrying the sling-heeled sandals I'd kicked off earlier in the night. According to Willie, the park would reopen at 6 a.m., but just then a bobby approached us, politely demanding to know who we were. As he was inspecting our IDs, Willie piped up that we were "friends of the Queen," and, in fact, distant relatives of Prince Philip's previous wife. He spoke so quickly and authoritatively that the bobby clearly believed his story, though it may have been the first and last time the word got out that Prince Philip had had a failed first marriage.

After trying and failing to get a cab in Trafalgar Square, Willie and I made our way by foot to Wilton Place by 6:30 a.m. The spell was intact: we hadn't yet kissed. The pale blue-green color of Willie's eyes matched the early morning sky as we approached the stone front steps of Toad Hall. Lucy, who must have been waiting up for me, called out the window that she'd be right down to unlock the door. "Behave, Simon Sister," Willie murmured to me, and then he was gone. Upstairs, Lucy and I stayed awake, debriefing each other about our respective nights out, Lucy telling me at one point how smitten she was already with the King of Wales. Switching on the radio, the two of us danced together to "I Got You Babe," "Mr. Tambourine Man," and finally, "Ticket to Ride." That morning, as we laughed and drank café au lait and ate peanut-butter-and-jelly sandwiches on sourdough bread, the Simon Sisters were blind to everything and everyone in London with the exception of Willie and the King.

My sister and I spent the week before our Rehearsal Room gig rehearsing, and even serenading the people whose house we lived in. Their response was extremely enthusiastic. When the day arrived, Lucy and I found ourselves backstage at the Rehearsal Room, where we were booked for the entire week. Our set was tight, nine songs, and during rehearsals, Willie told us approvingly how loose, funny, and relaxed we were both getting. In the days following our opening, I confessed to my diary that I had fleeting fantasies of marrying Willie and settling down in London, where I would launch a new career as a solo singer.

Willie was always telling me how much he'd "screwed" this person or that person, and I always thought he was speaking in a spirit of fun. He was, too, but he'd also left in his wake a long list of creditors, critics, and naysayers. I kept forgetting that Willie had little, if any, money of his own, nor did I know that what money he had he spent on drugs and hookers. Early on I'd let him know that my long psychoanalysis had drained my inheritance, but Willie likely believed my account would miraculously replenish and start yielding dividends the moment I turned twenty-five. I didn't care. As a twenty-year-old American in London, I continued to have no concept of money, had never cared much at all about it. Even if Willie was penniless, was there anything more romantic than a sardonic, impeccably mannered, stone-broke aristocrat? Willie always acted as though nothing and no one could ever hurt him—not Sarah Miles, not any one of his creditors or critics. Was Willie consumed with self-hatred the whole time I knew him? Did he have his hands full concealing himself, or leading a double life? I didn't know him well enough to answer.

I barely remember our shows, but Lucy and I always got a great round of applause, spurred on, no doubt, by the nightly claque assembled by the

King of Wales. (As is the case with most kings, his applause was instantaneously contagious.) We didn't get much press, but our shows went so well that our collective nerves, thus far kept in check, burst forth in a rush of manic exhilaration. We were an actual hit, and in London, no less, so much so that the rumor was being floated that the Beatles—then by far the biggest, most famous group in the world—were supposed to show up in the audience at the Rehearsal Room. Lucy and I were so lathered up by this news that we went out shopping for new clothes. At a Kensington market, I chose a brown-and-gold linen dress with a tiger motif and a low neckline. Lucy bought the exact same outfit. Still, there was the issue of which one of us would wear the dress in front of the Beatles. The solution was both of us, except before the big night, Lucy put hers in a washing machine, drastically shrinking it, as well as dyeing it blue, the dress coming out looking like a fitted, tie-dyed T-shirt, which turned out to be just as saucy as my tiger-striped version. Still, who cared? The *Beatles* were coming! Lucy and I both had the same feeling: we were in the right place at the right time, and Lord, we loved London! We loved the people surrounding us. We were living life as we'd never lived it before.

After finishing two sets with not a single Beatle in sight, Willie, the King, Lucy, and I had a few drinks and walked home. The Beatles rumor, it turned out, had been a publicity hoax dreamed up by the owner of the Rehearsal Room. As we made our way back to Wilton Place, Willie and I stopped in Hyde Park, making ourselves at home on a freestanding lounge chair by the banks of the Serpentine lake. "Frog Footman," Willie said to me solemnly, "you are the cleverest, wisest, most perfect girl there ever was." He grinned suddenly. "Well done!"

Was I the cleverest, wisest, most perfect girl ever born? If I was for a brief shining period, it was Willie who made me that way. He created whatever glitter tumbled in shiny clumps from all over him, and inspired whatever witticisms fell off my lips. He'd felt extremely possessive of me back at the club, Willie went on—jealous of the attention I was getting from other men between our two sets. That's when he leaned over and kissed me. When our lips touched, there was that moment of Okay, this has been there all along. I was right. Later that night, simultaneously, we moved toward each other, kissing again, this time for so long I could hardly believe we made it all the way to Willie's apartment. It was the very kiss, in fact, that kicked off the perfect love affair.

He started to introduce me as his wife; the "next Mrs. Donaldson," he would say. Our love life couldn't have been better. I felt quite possessed, in a wild and terrific way. Willie could be both tender and sentimental. Neither one of us, I remember, ever wanted to be seen naked, so we made love in the darkest of rooms.

I had already been in London for three weeks, and knowing that in three more weeks Lucy and I would be returning home to New York, the remaining time I spent with Willie felt urgent and enthralling, with an edge of desperation to it. We laughed at everything the other person said. We kissed the moment we found ourselves alone. Every day and night we went out: for music, for shopping, for lunches and dinners, for parties with Lucy and the King of Wales, and Peter Sellers, and Spike Milligan, as well as the casts from various West End shows, which now included David Steinberg, the American comedian and actor, and his girlfriend, the photographer Mary Ellen Mark. It reached a point where the two of us even began planning for the future, even the possibility of marriage. We had long talks about what my family would think of him and where the two of us would end up living. I couldn't picture Willie living in America, but at the same time, neither of us believed I would ever come back to England. We'd have to see.

A few days before our departure, Willie withdrew from me ever so slightly, which had the unfortunate effect of making me want to draw closer to him. Funny how that happens. Leaving London for a meeting, he promised to call me "every other minute." I took Willie's word more literally than I should have, camping out in my apartment waiting for the phone to ring. Willie called that night, and we had a long, loving conversation, but the next day he didn't call at all, and when I tried his hotel in desperation, the front desk had no record of any Willie Donaldson. The next day the phone remained silent, and at five that afternoon, Lucy ordered me to have a beer with her at our local pub. As the two of us were leaving our building, I glanced up to see Willie entering his flat two doors away. Naturally, he pretended he'd just this second returned home and was planning on bathing first before popping by to surprise me.

I had no reason to believe him, he was such a skilled and quick-witted fabulist. This particular lie wouldn't fly, not this time. But, overwhelmed with distrust and anger, I froze up. Immediately, I went to that place inside my head where I'd gone when Nick told me about Nini: denial. His lie wasn't true. I'd make up one I liked better. For the rest of the night, Willie couldn't have been more adorable, making love to me in a way he'd never done before. I couldn't help feeling he'd recently been in the company of a woman who had taught him a thing or two, but I bit my lip and feigned wonderment. There was no reason to seethe, or panic. It would all be over soon anyway.

In preparation for our departure, Willie had promised to pick up our passports at American Express—for some reason Lucy and I had entrusted him with ours, and he had lost them, and we'd had to order replacements. A day before we left, Willie still hadn't gotten them. For the first time I was openly frustrated with him, silently fuming and then apologizing for my silent fuming. Lucy and I were at Toad Hall, packing our bags and sharing emotional good-byes with friends, when Willie pulled up in front in a limousine. He was pale, I was teary, and that night we barely exchanged a single word. We slept back to back. More than once Willie had told me he'd had premonitions that we wouldn't get married, and while I suspected that his premonitions had less to do with divine and sensory mystery than they did with his own ambivalence, I dismissed my doubts. To commemorate my departure, I'd made him a crossword puzzle, all of whose clues and answers referred to my eventual return. I told him I was counting on his memorizing at least a few of my songs so that when I came back, he could fill in for Lucy. That last night, I left him a cassette of me singing.

All three of us took a taxi to the train that would, in turn, transport us to the inordinately fast American ship that would take us home. I cried softly the entire ride, hiding my head in Willie's jacket sleeve while Lucy gazed out the window, smiling sweetly and pretending not to notice. Willie handed us our passports and slipped something else into my coat pocket, though I didn't look at it then. At the station, the driver began removing our bags, but Willie remained frozen in the backseat. Suddenly he bounded out. "Wait for me, wait for me, I have something for you," he said. I mistakenly assumed this meant he might be taking the train with us to the ship, but no.

In a discreet and self-conscious way, he merely kissed me good-bye. As Lucy and I found our seats on the train, Willie was nowhere to be seen through the windows, which were now fogging over with engine steam. Whatever Willie had forgotten to give me would be secure until we met up again in a few months' time, maybe.

I suppose Willie was a "show business" person. A terrifying and accurate description of that showbiz type is written by Herman Wouk in *Youngblood Hawke*. "They can simulate anything—pleasure, anger, courtesy, love, hate, amusement, fear, grief, humility, awe, graciousness, and in a given situation, they'll give the right reaction. They do so in order to not frighten normal people . . . in order to get along with them."

A picture Willie (left) kept in his wallet of him and J. P. Donleavy.

As always I'm trying to follow in Lucy's footsteps, even in an arabesque.

---

CHAPTER ELEVEN

moneypenny

On the boat train to Southampton I wrote a letter to Willie. I didn't cry any more. I was just plodding through the shock of losing my days with him. When we reached Southampton, the porter swooped in to transport our bags to the ship, though Lucy and I felt more comfortable carrying our own guitars along the gangplank. At one point I whispered to her, "Isn't that Sean Connery?" Lucy took a quick glance. Yes. It was.

We were twenty feet or so behind him, and maintained our pace in an attempt to confirm a positive identification. Sean Connery's hair was light brownish-blond, almost curly, like a baby's hair, in contrast to the coiffed, Brylcreemed look he sported as James Bond, which Lucy and I and probably every other moviegoer in the world had assumed was his real hairstyle. For whatever reasons, he seemed to be traveling alone. Sean passed through the first-class line, at which point Lucy and I lost sight of him as a small army of uniformed ship concierges and porters stepped in to transport all his belongings.

Once we were on board and in the hands of our own steward, my sister and I boarded a tiny elevator that shepherded us down into the very depths of the boat, until we arrived at our room. It was tiny, windowless, and itchingly claustrophobic, outfitted with two extremely narrow bunk beds. A small table adorned with a small lamp doubled as both desk and dressing table.

With next to no room for our luggage, Lucy and I decided to extract from our suitcases only the absolute necessities—sandals, bathing suits, bathrobes, scarves—and stash the suitcases under the bottom bunk, placing our guitars in the narrow closet, beneath the few hanger items that fit. This residence compared unfavorably to our Provincetown room the prior summer. In between we'd had a palace in London. An unseen fan blew constantly into the room, its noise like a continuously flushing toilet, but I had no idea how to find it, much less fix it. The only practical domestic things I'd ever been taught as a girl were how to make a hospital corner on a bed and sew a hem stitch. (Lucy, on the other hand, knew how to use a sewing machine.) In lieu of learning practical matters, I seemed to have absorbed selective lessons about the power of long, tan legs, which knee looked better crossed over the other, and never to let another person wash your underwear.

After a day of tumult on the English Channel, Lucy and I settled into the womblike comfort of our tiny room. After pouring my heart out in the letter to Willie, he'd replied via a telegram that read, simply, "Come home, little fellow." If I'd thought I missed Willie on the boat train, and had written him telling him so, I missed him twice as much now. I adored him, was overwhelmed by him, believed I was ready to give myself to him forever, though at the moment, if I were being honest with myself, what I really wanted was to feel more secure about him.

Part of the boat's entertainment featured daily films, and the movie screening that afternoon was *The Hill*, directed by Sidney Lumet and starring none other than Sean Connery in the role of a British military prisoner. Lucy and I were in the audience, and when it was over, we walked the many stairs back downstairs to our cabin. I was about to write another letter to Willie when I had a sudden inspiration. I would write Sean Connery a fan letter, and invite him over for tea, or a drink! (Willie had always encouraged my "cheeky" side.) In short order, I wrote something along the lines of:

Dear Mr. Connery:

My name is Carly Simon and my sister's name is Lucy. We are not your ordinary "fans." We are traveling from London, where we were singing at the Rehearsal Room. We are both educated college girls, and our father was Richard Simon, who founded Simon & Schuster, the firm that published The Ginger Man by J. P. Donleavy. We understand that you are going to New York to do a Broadway production of the play based on that book. Would you come over to our very cozy little room and have a cup of tea or a preprandial cocktail?

I included our room number, closing off with *We would love to meet you. Sincerely, Carly and Lucy Simon.* I knew I could hook Sean Connery with *preprandial*, which meant simply "before dinner"—I was using that word because I thought it labeled me "brilliant"—though when I showed the letter to Lucy, she seemed taken aback, even shocked. "I don't really want anything to do with that letter," she said after a while. "Please write me out of it," adding that in her opinion, I was making a fool of myself. No amount of persuasion or badgering could convince her, so I rewrote the letter, this time leaving out Lucy's name, and handing Henry, our room steward, a five-pound tip to deliver it to Sean Connery in his Presidential Suite.

It took less than fifteen minutes for the phone to ring. All I could think of was how proud Willie would have been of me. ("Well done, Simon Sister!" I could hear him say.) Four rings later, I casually picked up the phone. The voice on the other end introduced himself as, well, Sean Connery. He was in the middle of getting a massage, but might he accept my kind invitation in twenty or so minutes? Of course, I said, thinking, Where am I going to hide Lucy? After proposing she take a walk on the deck, or inspect the game room, I was sort of relieved when Lucy told me she'd be a good sport and stay. Safety in numbers and all that.

Lucy and I both took a few minutes to groom ourselves under the ghoulish lighting. Even without her newly applied lip gloss and Veronica Lake hair, my sister was beautiful under any light; it was me I was worried about, but I didn't have time to obsess over it because just then a knock came at the door, and I opened it.

There he was: the same man we'd seen in *The Hill*, *Dr. No*, and *From Russia with Love*. The same Scottish burr. The only difference being that Sean Connery was far handsomer in person, and his manner nothing like it was in any of those films, which convinced me what a good actor he was. Lucy and I took up residence on her bed, the lower bunk, while Sean took a seat in the only available chair. I wonder if he thinks he's slumming it, I thought, remembering to file away details about this encounter for Willie.

Sean was obviously impressed by how I'd advertised myself as the daughter of the legendary publisher, Richard L. Simon. (We were still both very proud of Daddy's legend.) Over the next half hour, we dropped even more names: uncles, aunts, houseguests, dogs, professors. At one point I caught Sean gazing at our long legs.

We talked about Sean's recent trip on LSD, and about books. Later in my diary I wrote that Sean's eyes had no soul—as if he were all actor inside, with no one at home. Then I thought, No—he's looking for something in *us*. I also couldn't help thinking that he was like a jungle animal who'd found his way into the smallest cabin on the world's largest ocean liner, and was now foraging to see if he could drag any remarkable grub back to his magnificent cave seven flights up, a room Lucy and I would be permitted to see sooner than we both imagined.

The next day, Lucy and I had just returned to our room from a showing of *A Day at the Races* when the phone rang. It was Sean, this time inviting us to his suite for cocktails and dinner. A few hours later, Lucy and I were ensconced inside Sean's Presidential Suite. The suite's three rooms were ten times larger than Lucy's and my little room downstairs. There was lots of shrimp, bottles of champagne, laughs from the throat, laughs from the gut. Tom Jones, a Welshman to Sean Connery's Scotsman, serenaded the room from enormous stereo speakers with "What's New Pussycat?"

Eventually Sean took a seat on the couch between us so we could all study the dinner menu. The shrimp scampi and the vichyssoise, he said, were both a must. Sean poured us all more champagne, which it was possibly a mistake to accept, as I was almost drunk already. Lucy, I could tell, was flirting with him, which made me irritable. She hadn't been gutsy enough to cosign her name to the letter we wrote Sean, so why did she feel she had the right to flirt with him? The waiter took our order and left, and then Sean proposed that the three of us dance—all together—until dinner arrived.

Lucy and I both got up from the couch and stood there facing him, two feet apart, as though awaiting orders from a square dance caller or an Israeli hora teacher. I hadn't the slightest idea what we were supposed to do, and was puzzled by my own feelings. Could three people dance at once? How? Sean pulled us both close to him, murmuring something to the effect that we all might as well make the most of this night. "Ah, girls, you're so beautiful," he kept saying. "You're so funny . . . come here, you adorable college girls . . ."

Instead of Tom Jones on the turntable, a Dean Martin record would have better captured the atmosphere in the room. At the time, neither Lucy nor I were considering the possibility of a "Simon Sisters Sandwich"—an expression, or a hunch, Willie came up with later. Maybe Sean had simply assumed that anyone who used the word *preprandial* in a note would be equally well acquainted with *ménage à trois*, and want one, too!

As it turned out, Sean's expectation of fun for the evening ended up going nowhere, as it was beginning to dawn on him, sadly, that do-si-do square dancing was closer to Lucy's and my speed than any Simon Sister Sandwich. To his credit, he didn't force or even bring up the issue. He was extremely polite and not remotely aggressive. With the wine and champagne making us sillier and sillier, Lucy suggested that she and I sing some songs before dinner showed up. We sang two songs a cappella: "Wild Mountain Thyme" and "Sometimes I Feel like a Motherless Child." Sean seemed bemused by our performance, as it must have solidified his impression of us as square finishing-school girls, well-heeled, well-bred folkies. Or maybe he couldn't figure us out at all.

Having cast aside the sandwich idea, and with both Lucy and me clearly adrift in the Cabin of Bond, Sean now sought out conversational entry points. What was it like being a nursing student? he asked Lucy. The conversation then moved to whether or not Prince Philip was circumcised— one topic generally following the other—though I can't remember what, if any, conclusion we reached. He asked if we owned any pets, where we lived, if we had serious boyfriends, and what sports we liked, or played. He asked me if Lucy had introduced me to the guitar. Every answer we gave was polite, while also struggling to be witty and sophisticated. Why didn't we have our act down by now? By midnight Lucy and I had taken our leave, thanking our host repeatedly, and making a plan for the following night.

For the next two days, everywhere we went, the three of us went together. We hunkered down in Sean's suite, eating Presidential Suite–quality food, reciting poems—especially Irish ones: Dylan Thomas, W. B. Yeats—from an anthology belonging to the Presidential Suite bookshelf, visiting the ship's casino, attending movies and even lectures. Arm in arm in arm, we made a jovial threesome. When I think now on how Mick Jagger, Marianne Faithfull, and Anita Pallenberg were spending their time, I have to laugh, thinking about how our rowdy childhood hadn't turned us into anything but prudish schoolgirls. You almost *feel* the uniform. On the last day, we met up at the swimming pool before returning to our rooms to pack, which, in Lucy's and my case, amounted merely to relocating our guitars into the corridor so we'd have room to drag our suitcases out from under our skinny lower bunk.

That night, with a tentative plan to meet up with Sean after dinner, Lucy and I, slightly high on champagne, went back to our room at around nine, which is when Sean usually called us. Our cramped room was still littered with the detritus of a summer spent in London. As we waited for the phone to ring, we cleared things away—a stray bus receipt, a broken eyebrow pencil, a sample of Sean's handwriting on a cocktail napkin (Sean had given me the phone number of his New York agent). But the phone didn't ring. Lucy and I cleaned up even more, going so far as to straighten the sheets and blankets on our beds. Into the tiny garbage bin went three-quarters-empty cough medicine and nail polish and cologne bottles. By 10 p.m., with the phone still mute, we had five garbage receptacles piled high with stuff. By now, we were motivated to clean as a distraction, as well as to cut through the tension in our tiny henhouse cabin, with Lucy and I two sister-roosters sizing each other up for a fight. A half hour later, I took a shower, telling myself that if Sean didn't call by eleven, I'd set my hair using the beer cans Lucy and I used as rollers, my mission being to give it body and make it as straight as Julie Christie's.

Exiting the shower, I said to Lucy, "I guess that's it for tonight. He's probably not going to call, right?"

Lucy agreed, adding that if Sean was planning on calling, he would have done it by now. I proceeded to dry my hair in front of the mirror lit by two lightbulbs sticking out of the wall like two different-sized human ears. My nose, I thought, has never looked so fat. The Beast was making its shipboard appearance, having been in storage during most of my stay in London. The tension which had begun infiltrating our tiny room worsened when my hair dryer bumped into Lucy's things, knocking them onto the floor, which led to her swiping me with a poor and sarcastic imitation of Willie saying, "Well done, Simon Sister!" It was now past eleven, and the phone hadn't rung once. There the two of us were, then. We'd had our chance, and nothing had happened. Was this situation as debilitating to Lucy's ego as it was to mine? On the surface, the answer was no, as Lucy seemed completely unfazed, concerned only about the scattered cosmetics.

Having been the one who took the initiative in the first place, I decided to place the final call. I let it ring around thirty times, but no one answered, and I finally hung up. The Sean Connery "thing" was officially over. Reaching down into the shopping bag that held the beer cans, I reluctantly placed six of them in my hair, securing them with clips. I slipped on my nightgown, by now glad it was getting too late for a midnight postprandial drink with Sean. Now, as we neared land—probably Newfoundland, or an iceberg—Lucy was lolling fully clothed on her lower berth, reading, or pretending to read, a book.

At that moment, I felt more in love with Willie than ever before. I rationalized the feeling as follows: that the vixen inhabiting me had been attracted to Sean not because of Sean but because, as I later confessed to my diary, I wanted to show Willie how alluring I was to other men, to show him how assertive and naughty I could be. More than that, I wanted to win the lifelong competition between Lucy and me, my fantasy being that Sean would insist on seeing me alone, not that I had the faintest idea what I would have done if that happened. Willie, I knew, wouldn't be proud of this Simon Sister losing out to Lucy, who was tame and quiet, and always played her cards close to her chest.

Hair cans in place, I pretended to turn off the phone and forget about Sean. We probably wouldn't see him again before our boat docked in New York. Maybe we'd wave at him disembarking in the first-class line, surrounded, as

I was sure he would be, with women wearing flowered sundresses, wide-brim hats, and black sunglasses, one or more of whom would be tightly clutching the arm of our James Bond, our Ginger Man, our soldier from *The Hill*, our Sean Connery. Doubling down, we were Moneypenny.

At eleven forty-five, the phone that I, the eternal optimist, had only pretended to turn off rang. Lucy shot off her bed and a second later answered it, her voice mellow and seductive. It was Sean, of course, and I heard Lucy explain that I had just washed my hair and was in my nightgown, getting ready for bed, whereas she, Lucy, was about to take a stroll on the deck to take in some late-night air.

It was the dirtiest possible sisterly trick. Pure and utter treachery. "No more duets," I wrote later on in my diary. No more 'Blowin' in the Wind,' sung in French. Goodbye to 'Winkin', Blinkin' and Nod.' No more Simon Sisters," I wrote. "I'm through for now!!"

Lucy didn't get back to our cabin until 5:15 a.m., just as the ship was pulling into the Hudson. As we passed the Statue of Liberty, I knew that I had officially graduated from the world of Henry Orient into the world of probable sisterly treason and lies. I couldn't let it in; this was too dangerous an area. On one hand, my sister had every right to do whatever she wanted with Sean. She wasn't the Simon Sister who would be returning to London soon with a hi-fi system and a wedding dress in tow. Matter of fact, I should have handed Sean over to her from the beginning. I'd re-created, inevitably, a familiar triangle: Lucy, me, a man standing in for our father. But where was my grace? If only need didn't always grip me so tightly all the time. The next day, I remember daydreaming about someday singing a song for a James Bond movie, a recurrent fantasy that would culminate in 1977 when I recorded "Nobody Does It Better" for *The Spy Who Loved Me*. Roger Moore was an exceptional James Bond, but every time I sang "Nobody Does It Better," I pictured Sean Connery in my head, hoping he would hear it wherever he was and think back to 1965, and the two surprisingly prim Simon Sisters. But that night the Beast had me in its grip.

In retrospect, I was probably looking for a reason, a hook, a justification, to separate from my older sister. Willie had told me over and over again that I could have a very good performing career in the UK by myself, and the prospect of singing and dancing alone, mixed with the fantasy of becoming

Mrs. William Donaldson, was tantalizing. I spent less time worrying about how much I would miss Lucy than I did contemplating the possibility of a break, a movement, a shift in the direction of my life. It was almost as though Lucy leaving me that night on the boat to walk the decks with Sean gave me tacit permission to break free from my lifelong identity as the younger sister toted around the world by her older sister. It was, I realized later, when I felt it was all right to break away. As much as the concept frightened me, it was time. Maybe. Though Lucy was like no other. Ever.

Lucy and me back home in Riverdale. We both felt it was all right to break away.

One minute a star on the English stage—the next, a guitar teacher and senior girls' counselor at Indian Hill.

---

CHAPTER TWELVE

jake was the hub

For the first few weeks, there was a letter from Willie almost daily. Endless phone calls and quirky promises. Then, around the beginning of October, the correspondence stopped. I received nothing from him—not a letter, not a call. Finally, on October 24, just as I was calling around to all of his friends to find out if they'd seen him, I received one of the most elegant Dear John letters anyone could have ever concocted. It was erudite, honest, painful, and deeply compassionate. The gist was the news that, indeed, he had gotten back with Sarah.

I called my friend Jonathan Schwartz and told him. He'd been following my relationship with Willie, as he knew him from his days in London. I took a taxi right uptown to Jonno's apartment and he let me cry for a little bit, but we ended up playing piano and singing. Jonno was soon to become a D.J. and had an important role in starting the airplay of "That's the Way I've Always Heard It Should Be," my first single.

I was completely shell-shocked. Drained. Despondent. I'd been planning on returning to London in two or three months—assemble all my belongings, tie things up with Nick, and say good-bye to my friends and family.

I had already packed up my KLH stereo in a carton, in preparation for returning to London and Willie's apartment on Wilton Place, and was imagining our future residence, a modest duplex in Kensington Gardens, that would overlook an alley with a charming pub at one end. The idea of not returning to London, and to Willie, affected me physically, as if my whole being had been carved out. It was as though I'd had the fleeting opportunity to fall passionately in love with my boyfriend version of Uncle Peter, and now it wasn't going to happen. I didn't call anyone for weeks, and felt emptier, more confused, and less desirable than I'd ever felt in my life. By now having memorized its most tender targets, the Beast pulled in for an extended stay, knowing precisely where best to pry me open, leaving me vulnerable to all sorts of attacks, from within and without. *You are a shameful person. You stutter. You can't even open your mouth without embarrassing yourself.*

How much had I loved Willie, anyway? Had I loved him, or only parts of him, or maybe just the idea of him? He and I had spent such a ridiculously abbreviated time together. How was it even possible that I could be in love with someone I had known for only six weeks? In London, away from home, out from under various family thumbs, I had become my best self, and apart from the moon itself, London in the mid-1960s had to have been one of the most thrilling destinations in the cosmos. But had my own rose-colored glasses altered and possibly distorted who Willie really was? At the same time, Willie had altered my thinking, my desires, my core belief in myself. Without knowing it, he had changed my voice, pushing me toward saying the things I wanted and needed to say, a transformation that would stay with me forever. Not every moment was sweet, but the moment of the precipice—those golden, beautiful seconds before the liftoff—was just as good as any culmination. Subtly, through Willie, I was beginning to belong, finally, to myself.

Coming back to Manhattan meant that my sister Joey and I were once again roommates, with Lucy living right next door. A perfect sorority of sisters. Joey, as ever, was the boss of everything. I had never really "fit" inside her apartment at Fifty-fifth Street and First Avenue, and my presence there now made the fact more obvious than ever. I didn't fit *literally*, either. Joey had taken, and reupholstered in blue, almost every single piece of

Victorian furniture from Stamford, and as someone in the habit of slouching, how was I possibly expected to maneuver my long body into those prim blue chairs perched on those parquet floors? How could I live in a place that had a window cleaner who came regularly, in a neighborhood notable for supermarkets and dry cleaners and postwar skyscrapers? Let's face facts: Joey was a woman, I was still a messy girl.

By now Joey was traveling fast in the corridors of sophistication. She had always been a prima donna, but now it was official: she was a bona fide member of the New York City Opera company, flying off to Vienna and San Francisco, savoring the success she'd worked so hard to achieve. She was working alongside great conductors, including Leonard Bernstein, Zubin Mehta, Herbert von Karajan, Eugene Ormandy, and Charles Munch, great men who occasionally stopped by our apartment, and whose hair I could now and then find in my bathroom sink (which doubled as a guest bathroom). It was like watching a movie called *Joey!*, which added to the majestic theater of it all. As for Lucy and me, we were back together, working with a choreographer to reconceive our musical set.

In my despondency over Willie, I began decorating my bedroom with cheap Mexican furniture I'd picked up on Astor Place. My friend Annie Felshin had a store called the Mexican Art Annex. I spent hours there and always came home with a flowerpot or a scary Mexican spirit statue. The room, with its double bed left behind by Joey's former roommate, was definitely the "second" bedroom, and overlooked a courtyard where flocks of dirty pigeons gathered to defecate on the window ledge. As part of her sales pitch, Joey had said, "Look at all those glorious birds outside, Carly! They love you so much they want to come inside!" At least Joey could laugh at herself. The hall bathroom became my sanctuary, a place where I first heard a lot of great songs on my little mono radio, like Bobbie Gentry's "Ode to Billie Joe" and Procol Harum's "Whiter Shade of Pale." I would light a candle, sink into the tub, and sing along to the Stones' "Satisfaction," Herman's Hermits' "Mrs. Brown, You've Got a Lovely Daughter," and Peter and Gordon's "World Without Love." That music, and other songs from that era, began influencing and even honing my own writing and chord changes. I started playing around not just with changes of tempo midsong, but with ideas.

As for the fate of the Simon Sisters, Lucy and I might have stayed together, but our lives were rivers parting, diverging, and going in tender new directions. Soon she would be moving in with her boyfriend David Levine; they would be married by the spring. Having Lucy gone from our little three-sister housing project obviously changed the dynamic. I became more independent, though; in that vacuum I also formed another trusted and close alliance with the comic David Steinberg and the photographer Mary Ellen Mark, whom I'd met in London through Willie. David was a member of Second City, which was having a run in New York. They had moved into Lucy's just-vacated apartment, and they became part of a dazzling crowd of comedians, actors, and opera singers who mingled with my college friends Annie and Ellen in that exciting way that can happen when everyone is under twenty-five. Each night there was a featured guest and someone else would cook something new. The "hang," as we now called it, was superior.

David, Mary Ellen, Annie, Ellen, and I graced the town, often with a few more in tow. David was always fixing me up with his friends. He also tried to get Willie to come back to me with a not-too-urgent telephone call, but Willie didn't want to be in touch. He was already feeling guilty, having set the "cad phenomenon" in motion, i.e., not wanting to think about the person you've hurt and therefore completely dismissing him or her. I think I was a bit in admiration/love with David. He was so there for me and loved to make me laugh. When Second City opened in the Village, I became a groupie of the every-night variety. Many nights David and I stayed up late in one or the other of our living rooms and played the guitar, making up hilarious free-association songs: "I love you and the cows go moo." Decades later, he would go on to direct episodes of *Seinfeld* and many other TV shows. Mary Ellen would indulge me, listening to my woes on the subject of Willie long into the night. She was becoming one of the world's greatest photographers.

Before Lucy joined me in England, she and I had landed our first music manager and producer since Harold Leventhal and Charlie Close. John

Court was partners with Albert Grossman, and they had started Gross-court, a management company whose client roster included Bob Dylan; Peter, Paul and Mary; and others. John had been telling me the same thing Willie had: that if Lucy was going the marriage route, I should consider going out on my own as a performer, without my sidekick, the older, more spectacular Simon sister. John also believed I could benefit from other, rougher-edged, more Greenwich Village-y influences, that I was a posh uptown girl who, if she had any sense about her, would be acting more "downtown" like Nico.

A day before my twenty-first birthday, in 1966, I was in the living room of our apartment when the telephone rang. It was Bob Dylan on the other line. I was completely frozen. Dylan, after all, was a prophet, a modern-day link to Woody Guthrie, and though I didn't like all his songs, I was already in awe. John Court had choreographed the call, and a minute later, I'd accepted Dylan's invitation to pay a visit to Grosscourt's offices.

When I got there, John introduced me all around. "Go talk to Bob," he said. "He'll tell you some things."

If talking to Bob Dylan on the phone had paralyzed me, being in the same room made me, if possible, even more awestruck. There was, after all, no one else like him. But I did as John said. Bob and I ended up sequestered in a mostly airless office, and Bob began talking. Thank God, he was stoned, which meant I didn't have to worry too much about making a good impression or our conversation going down in history. Bob had just come back from touring in Australia and the U.S., and though he wouldn't record *Nashville Skyline* until 1969, he had just recorded his new album, *Blonde on Blonde*, in Nashville. Bob went on and on about the glory, the sheer magic, that was Nashville, and told me that if and when I recorded an album, Nashville was the place to be. He also told me about the music producer he was working with, and the sounds he was able to produce by pressing new buttons that effected echo, reverb, and EQ. Then he recommended a song that he said would be perfect for me: "Baby, Let Me Follow You Down," adapted by Eric von Schmidt from an older blues song, adding that he, Bob, would be willing to reshape or rewrite some of the lyrics to accommodate my voice and style.

As we talked, I couldn't help but think of Willie, who had claimed numerous times to have served as Bob's agent in London, but when I asked Dylan if he knew Willie Donaldson, he looked at me, faintly dazed, as if to say *Maybe you're thinking of someone else?* Briefly losing focus, Bob recovered, and for the next ten minutes went into another serenade about Nashville so incantatory it should have been reprinted on highway signs as you entered the city limits. Bob's energy was soaring, until finally, his eyes closed, his arms spread out evangelistically, he growled, emphatically, "Believe me! Believe me!" That's one of my hallmark memories.

Later, John told me that working with Bob was the chance of a lifetime, and that recording "Baby, Let Me Follow You Down" would change my life. From now on, he said, I would be known as "Carly and the Deacon," the Deacon in this case being Richie Havens, who I would do something with. What, I did not know. In the meantime, though, Robbie Robertson would come over to my apartment and rehearse the arrangement so the song would better fit my voice.

There was a lot of *holy shit!*–ness. Still, my very first thought was that I had to keep what was happening to me from Lucy. I didn't think it was even possible to succeed without her. I slowly started to tell a few close friends, and even my brother, Peter, who was crazy about Dylan, but the reality of it all only became clear when Robbie Robertson showed up at my apartment a week later, only days after Dylan had his now-famous motorcycle accident in Woodstock, New York.

As Robbie and I began discussing the song, it became clear that "Baby, Let Me Follow You Down" was nothing at all like the folk songs I was accustomed to singing with Lucy. Nor was it like the songs I'd been writing recently on my own, songs that felt, to my own crooked ear, like standards, jazzy, artsy. Listening to the popular vocal trio Lambert, Hendricks, and Ross, I'd become dependent on hearing jazz intervals. I imitated Annie Ross, and tried to scat-sing the way Jon Hendricks did. I was attracted to so many different styles of music, it was difficult to know which one to follow.

There was another problem. Even though Lucy and I had both taken our turns soloing during our performances, I wasn't used to being a solo performer. My whole life I'd always had Lucy to lean on. Being told that it was now me alone set my nerves on edge, and I had no choice but to place all my faith in Robbie Robertson. Robbie was fawnlike in his looks, as well as innately modest, and gave off a schoolboy vibe with unsettled hormones. When our first rehearsal ended, Robbie invited me out for a drink, and we eventually ended up in the Chelsea Hotel, the plan being to meet the Rolling Stones' Brian Jones for a drink, even though Brian never appeared. The idea of having a drink with Robbie and Brian made me feel I was inhabiting my own version of Rock 'n' Roll Heaven. It was like being allowed a sneak glimpse into the permanent collection of a great museum. There have been few times in my life where I've felt genuinely agog, and that was one of those nights. Brian may not have made an appearance, but that night his seat was filled by Mike Bloomfield, Richard Manuel, and other acquaintances who stopped by our table to make heavy, but easy, conversation about electric music. When the evening ended, Robbie and I eventually ended up in Robbie's room, where I spent the night at a tempting distance. Robbie and I were shy with each other. Too shy to get into a rock 'n' roll groove.

A few days before the recording, I took the subway to the Columbia building, where I met the Producer, to find the most flattering key for my voice. Right then and there I picked up something unsavory in his eyes. First, he asked me to sing a verse a cappella, and overpraised me too soon. *Fantastic, darlin', you got some voice!* After I'd sung four or five lines of lyrics, he offered me a drink. When I declined, the Producer removed a whiskey bottle from the well-stocked bar behind his desk and helped himself to a tumbler. His puffy pink eyes narrowed to a squint. "Honey, if you're nice to me"—he pronounced it *nasss*, in his thick, purring, polluted voice—"I'll make you a *nasss* record."

It couldn't have been the first time he'd used that line on a woman. Willie, I knew, would be in heaven over this, and would have come up with the perfect riposte. But I wasn't Willie. As the Producer came closer to me, I stared him down from my seat on the couch. Did he think I was some Okie from Muskogee? Did he think I was an "easy chick"? As he got closer, I noticed the mottled drink-splotches on his nose, at which point I stood, shook my head, and came up with what I thought was the perfect retort: "I'm sorry, I'm greener than that!"

What I meant to say was "I'm sorry, but I'm not that hungry," or "I'm sorry, but I'm not that green," but put on the spot, it came out wrong. I straightened my dress and assumed my finest "audacious" look, as if to say, If you're the kind of person who takes inordinate pleasure from insulting women, well, distance yourself, asshole. I would have stormed out of the room right then and there, but I couldn't. Unfortunately, I'd taken off my pink Capezio flats, and one was missing. I had to retrieve it from under the couch, kneeling before the Producer like a supplicant, while doing my best to maintain my dignity and my blazing eye contact. He looked at me as though he had some deep inner knowledge that he would screw me. It didn't matter how or when, but he'd get it done. I didn't look back at him as I sauntered out of the room.

The next day was even more devastating, one of the first of what would turn out to be many difficult experiences with men in the music business. It was the day I was scheduled to record my vocal. The band wandered in slowly until they were all assembled. Mike Bloomfield, Levon Helm, Al Kooper, Rick Danko, Richard Manuel, and Paul Griffin. Things couldn't get any loftier than that. Some of these guys had backed up Bob Dylan, after all, on his 1966 world tour, and a year later, as the Band, the core group would create *Music from Big Pink*, but to me, they were already brilliant stars, all of them. I knew Al Kooper the best, but I can't remember why—maybe because he and I had done something together at a Boston University fund-raiser when my brother was a student there. Al had been one of the many brainy, schooled musicians from Berklee College of Music in Boston, as opposed to me, who had left school without even knowing how to read music. Those men in that studio on West Fifty-seventh Street were men whose reputations were like a whiff of whiskey in a cool downtown bar. You'd see pictures of them in magazines like *Rolling Stone*, sometimes together, sometimes individually, or alongside Andy Warhol or Twiggy. They were the people at the coveted corner booths at the Lamplight and the Bitter End. You heard gossip about who Levon Helm was dating and why they were all collecting in Woodstock, New York. Names were dropped, other facts blithely exaggerated. I wondered if I was ready to fall in love again, and could it be Robbie Robertson? I shut the hell up.

As the band laid down its track, I ventured into the control room, standing beside Albert Grossman, who asked me to sing along with the track, even though the melody was pitched too low for my voice. That could be a breaker. It was the difference between a surround that caught the song, and my voice, in its very best light, and a surround that would make me clumsily try to fit into an unloving slot. Caught up in his own grandeur, Albert turned full on me and asked, "Carly—when is it going to be our time? When are you and I going to get it on?"

Albert's long gray hair was damp and sweaty, bound by a rubber band or dirty piece of twine. I forgot for a moment who I was. What is all this? Who am I? Why are they playing this in the wrong key? What was I doing here? My God, instead of trying to come on to me, why wasn't Albert checking to see how Bob Dylan was doing in the hospital following his motorcycle wreck? "You know, you're a nine out of a perfect ten," Albert added. "You miss the mark because you have too much money." I was confused; I had no idea what he meant. He must have assumed I was rich, which I wasn't, though I wasn't altogether sure, either. I'd grown up in a household where it was considered gauche to talk about money, where I never learned the difference between a hundred dollars and a thousand. My mother never gave me any money, and I was living perfectly well on fifty dollars cash a week. Even if there was more money squirreled away somewhere, did it matter, and who was he to say? It was obvious that Albert equated a bank account with a lack of soul and feeling.

Regardless, my sole mission was to make a great recording of "Baby, Let Me Follow You Down," the song Bob Dylan had rewritten for me. When I went inside the booth once the track was cut, and attempted my first vocal, I knew it was two keys too low for me. I tried to change the melody enough to get closer to my key, but the Producer and Albert kept steering me back to the melody. To this day I can't prove it, but it seemed that one or both of them had deliberately sabotaged the track, cutting it in the wrong key, as payback for me not responding to their sexual advances. The key they kept insisting I follow might have been Levon Helm's, or Robbie's, or Richie Havens's, but the Producer had set the melody two keys too low for me, which meant I couldn't belt it out with the pushy, sexy, rock 'n' roll punch, and they wanted. Over the next couple of months, I called Albert, and John, and even Robbie about twenty times in all, but it soon became clear it was all over before it had even started. The track was shelved. None of them ever called me again. Had what just happened even happened? Desolation followed. The track does exist now in my very own hands—a duet between me and Richie Havens, who had apparently come in separately to record his part. It certainly had the flavor of anticipation, but with *no* point of arrival that was satisfying.

Depressed, I started gaining weight, quickly getting up to 150 pounds, and then 158, which was heavy for me, as I was typically a size six, or eight. It didn't help that Joey and I had both become addicted to a frozen drink sold at a small Forty-fifth Street deli and advertised as having no more than 145 calories, a claim that was later proven to be completely untrue. I don't know how many times Joey and I stood in the long lines on West Forty-fifth Street, but I do know we drank three or four of those concoctions daily, each one a frothy quart of self-destructive comfort in exchange for the devastation I felt over my first big failure in the music business. The fall from feeling like a bit of a star in London to waiting in line with masses of tubby girls like me for another chance to gain a few more pounds was another Roast cue, and I was now on the alert for new, ignominious ways in which it could operate.

The men in my orbit didn't seem to notice how miserable and heavy I was getting. At the time, Joey was dating Henry Morgan, the well-known radio personality, and one night Henry brought his fancy friend, a famous writer, to our apartment. As if I were a calf at auction, Henry asked me to stand in profile. That night I was wearing knit pants and my swelling outline must have been dramatic, but unable to see myself as others did, and curious but not offended by Henry's request, I turned forty-five degrees to the left. Across the room, the writer made an alarmed-sounding noise. Henry announced, to no one in particular, "You see?"

The truth was this: Willie was gone, my solo music debut was a failure, and I was fat. One night, I reached into my pocket and my fingers closed around what Willie had slipped into my coat pocket in the train station. It was a tiny jade frog. I kept that frog with me at all times, and every time my fingers found it, I couldn't help but think how Willie had rechristened me Frog Footman and that maybe we would get back together.

Still in the dumps, and unable to pay the rent, I needed to find a day job. Jennie Lou, my old classmate from Riverdale and Sarah Lawrence, told me I should consider working as the secretary to her husband, a producer on a television show called *From the Bitter End*. It was a studio-produced variety show intended to duplicate the look and feel of the actual nightclub, the Bitter End. The idea absolutely horrified me, but I took the job. I had evolved, it seemed, from being a singer at the Bitter End, the club where Lucy and I had performed just four years earlier, to taking shorthand for the producer of the television show based on the same club. It was a real comedown. That ladder was active up and down. It was good practice, as I would go in both directions many times. The producers couldn't have been nicer, but my shorthand was nonexistent. I lasted there a month, though not before spending a few weeks serving as an on-set gofer. My first task: go to Marvin Gaye's dressing room and see what he needs. When I arrived, Marvin was bare-chested, and when I asked him what I could do for him, he replied that he wanted to see something, and would I mind sticking out my tongue? When I obliged, with the same innocence I'd shown when modeling in silhouette for Henry Morgan and his friend, Marvin lunged at my face, swept my tongue into his mouth, and began sucking on it. I extracted it without inflicting damage.

From there, I went into the dressing room of the comedian Redd Foxx. As I knocked and entered, Redd let his famous red fox fur coat fall to the floor, revealing his naked body underneath. Laughing at my startled expression, he gestured me over, but I'd already turned on my heels. Still, there was a problem. What am I supposed to feel? I asked myself once I was back in the hallway. Was what I had just seen attractive? Was it not attractive? Why was I always so split off? I gave Marvin Gaye a pass only after hearing him sing "I Heard It Through the Grapevine" onstage. That was my weak spot: Orpheus. Men blessed with immense musical talent. Those guys always got a pass.

Where was my compass? Why wasn't I more upset, more shocked? What was real, what was underhanded, what was aboveboard, what was underground, and what was the difference? What was my problem and what was someone else's?

Getting a job as a counselor at a summer camp in western Massachusetts may have sounded like a big step backward, but to me it represented a whole new group of people and a whole new environment. I would be teaching guitar to high school girls, making sure they were tucked in bed every night, though mostly it was a symbolic escape from New York.

The camp, Indian Hill, was located in Stockbridge, Massachusetts, in the Berkshires. At twenty-two years old, I wasn't all that much older than the girls I was charged to oversee, and looking back, it felt as though time was out of order. Wasn't a counselor the sort of gig you were supposed to have as a teenager?

Indian Hill was perfectly and eternally green, with huge elms, beechnuts, maple trees, beautifully maintained lawns, and a swimming pool. It was an easy walk into Stockbridge, too, where there was a row of little shops where you could buy fudge and feel the freedom of being off-campus. The day I arrived at Indian Hill happened to be my birthday, and pouring rain, too, and as that summer would turn out to be remarkable—not least because the camp was where I met Jake Brackman, lifelong friend and partner in many ways—I developed the unprovable theory that the best things in life begin in the rain.

All of the campers at Indian Hill were engaged in at least one of the arts: drama, music, dance, or the visual arts. Music flowed out of every building, tent, and dorm, or from a nearby amphitheater, with rehearsals usually taking place on the huge lawn. As a counselor, I shared a room with two other girls in the main house and had a small corner bed, my stuff packed in a three-hook closet a foot away, as it had been on the ship coming back from England. There was no mirror, no privacy. If I'd felt on top of the world in England, working as a summer camp counselor in western Massachusetts, and pretending to be officious and angry if the female campers were ten minutes late to bed, felt like an enormous humpty-dumpty fall. By the time I got there, my weight had fallen to 148 pounds, though food was almost always on my mind. I occasionally found the willpower to skip a meal, but eating and not eating had become an ongoing struggle.

From the moment I arrived at Indian Hill, I kept hearing the name "Jake." Jake, it seemed, was a Harvard student and a counselor who would be arriving at camp two weeks late, as he was recovering from a bout of hepatitis. People kept telling me how much I would like Jake, and they would say this even in front of Faye Levine, my roommate and Jake's girlfriend. Faye herself told me how similar Jake and I were, how the two of us shared a physical resemblance, and she couldn't wait until the day we met. Was she setting up a rivalry, or possibly deflecting a future one?

Jake, Jake, Jake.

When Jake finally showed up, I didn't meet him right away. He and Faye spent the whole day moving their various belongings into the camp's "couples" housing. That whole day Indian Hill, for whatever reason, felt strangely tense. No one seemed terribly interested in their Bach cantatas, their oil paintings, their pas de deux. That night, there was a big cookout on the lawn, with around a hundred kids and counselors in attendance. I arrived dressed in a polka-dotted peasant blouse, tucked tightly into a pair of cutoff jeans. Bare legs and bare feet. Bangles on my wrist, hair flying long and sassy.

Several of the counselors had plans to dance around the fire that night, and the mood on the lawn was faintly orgiastic. The first person summoned to the fire was, of all people, Jake. The second person was me, and the campers led me to a spot on the other side of the fire, directly across from Jake, but with our backs to each other, so we were ten feet or so apart with flames and sparks a barrier between us. At the count of three, Jake and I were to turn, face each other, and smile as broadly as possible. In their little brilliant minds, convinced that Jake and I looked alike, and that even our toothy grins shared the same teeth, the campers must have known, somehow, that the two of us would become friends. How?

To this day I've never been able to fully explain the elaborate, premeditated choreography surrounding Jake's and my first encounter, but in hindsight, it felt to me as though a group of strangers was arranging a cabalistic meeting that they knew would transform our shared destinies: word-man and music-girl . . . mother and son in a long-ago life . . . sardonic father and rogue, lanky daughter.

Three . . . two . . . one. Turning around, I stood there demurely, in my Daisy Mae outfit, smiling widely. When I glanced up, there he was—Jake. Our eyes met very briefly before we both glanced immediately downward. Both of us were feeling shy, I'm sure. Perhaps it was some absurd psychology experiment. Perhaps the campers thought, Here is a girl who can stand up to Jake. It didn't matter. The first gaze Jake and I shared made everyone around quiet enough to hear the crickets sing.

Jake was tall and lean, with long, thick, dark brown hair. He was handsome; not exactly a male version of me, but there were interesting similarities. Over the next few days and weeks, I would discover how smart Jake was, too, how keen, alive, and ever-moving his intelligence was. He would wait patiently until you had finished talking before delivering a savage insight. Or else he would hesitate for the longest possible time before thrusting a verbal épée into your solar plexus. Jake, it seemed, always had the final word. In a group, all eyes and ears would gravitate to him, awaiting his coda or final summation, his mischief, incipient and outrageous. The only hint of what was to come was a tiny, curling, shuddering muscle in Jake's lower lip that alerted you that a perfectly aimed bon mot was about to wreak havoc on the room. Later, after we'd known each other for years, I coined a term for this technique: *Jaking.* A short, simple gerund, loosely defined as someone lightly cutting you in a language too original to ever forget. And sometimes not so lightly.

Over the course of that summer, Jake and I became as close as everyone had vowed we would, with me laughing longer and harder than anyone else at the things he said. Clearly Faye, his girlfriend, "got" Jake, too, and during their years together at Harvard and Radcliffe, where she and Jake were intertwined as the publisher and editor of the *Crimson,* Faye was no doubt the target of some of Jake's fabulous cruelty. Still, over the next few weeks, Jake and I developed shared summer rituals: driving to Friendly's for ice cream sundaes, getting high (my first time), and getting Jaked.

For reasons apparent only to the gods, it seemed that Jake Brackman and I were destined, in some way, to merge. I say "in some way" because only for a single second might there have been a slight hint of romance between us. He and I never acted on it. But it was much more than a celestial field

that kept us truly intimate but also apart, knowing that if we'd ever gone
the romance route, it would have ruined everything.

His friends are more than fond of Robin
He doesn't need to compliment them
And always as he leaves them
Feeling proud just to know him

But when Robin gives his love to others
There's no one living in my heart
Oh yes, I keep others in my heart
But they're not like Robin.
　　—"His Friends Are More Than Fond of Robin," 1971

A year after my recording session, I'd still never heard back from Albert
Grossman and his posse. It was an in-between time for me. As the late 1960s
rolled toward 1970, my social life was split between East Coast writers and
intellectuals who were publishing in *Esquire* and *The New Yorker*—Jake's
crowd—and professional musicians who were putting in the time, but had
yet to see the glory. One of the places musicians hung out and gathered was
at a Greenwich Village guitar store called, simply, Dan Armstrong Guitars.
I met countless young, hungry musicians there, including Jimmy Ryan, who
ultimately became my guitarist, not to mention cowriter, music director, and
very best of friends. And of course I met Danny Armstrong himself, who
had just invented a Plexiglas electric guitar that was garnering a lot of publicity. Danny became my boyfriend, and one night he took me backstage
at Madison Square Garden where he was meeting Keith Richards to
show him—and possibly give him—his hot-off-the-rack Plexiglas guitar.

I accompanied Danny backstage. Ike and Tina Turner were the opening
act, and they were still onstage. I would have loved to have been in the audience, but Keith came first.

Danny and I were directed into a large locker room, and when Keith finally came out from one of the stalls, the Stones' road manager, Chip Monck,
introduced him to Danny. I was just the female shadow along for the ride, an

unnamed girl wearing a hat with fox fur lining and a tattered raccoon coat over a pantsuit. After conferring with Danny, Keith moved on, and Danny began discussing changing the strings on Keith's guitar with Ian Stewart, the Stones' pianist, a thick-waisted, sad-eyed, beer-drinking, softhearted Scotsman. Keith returned, now attired in his black satin stage jacket. Thanks to a shot of whiskey and a pair of pliers, Danny finished restringing the guitar while explaining how the pickups worked, and Danny and Keith started jamming.

Then Mick walked in. One expects superstars to be altogether too large to fit through ordinary doorways, but much to my disappointment, Mick entered the room with utter ease. My first impression was that he was like a diminutive version of Mick Jagger. He was my height, with narrow shoulders and an extremely lean chest, and I found him sexy not just from the get-go, but way before the get-go. He was like a life-sized doll, with a generous but small painted face: neat, correct, at once plush and angular. After greeting his bandmates, Mick ambled through the locker area into one of the stalls, while Keith and Danny continued jamming. Besotted by Danny's new instrument, the boys were as cool as can be, whereas I was all smiles: Jagger was in the room!

Charisma is an overused word. It's different from beauty, and it's not the same as cuteness. People who have it possess faces that change from moment to moment, from stunning to plain to gaunt to exquisite to ugly to pale to flushed, challenging you to put a name, an adjective, to what you're seeing, or imagining, but since you can't, you give up, not realizing you are continuing to gaze helplessly at them, still puzzled, never *not* puzzled, in fact, unable to take your eyes off a face whose angles and adjectives seem to whirl and spin before you. Right away I could tell that for Mick Jagger, all women, including me, were his, by divine right. Women existed to frame him, impress him, shimmer for him, illuminate him, jog themselves helpfully into his peripheral vision: a fast-click snapshot Mick might take out of the corner of one eye for future purposes and dalliances. By now Mick was huddling with Bill Wyman and Charlie Watts. I can't remember if Mick even glanced at me that night, but my memory is he didn't—that would come later. Nor could I bear to look at him directly. Then it was time for the Stones to do whatever it was real rock 'n' roll bands did before a show. There were groupies in the room, and Danny and I made our way out.

Thanks to our coveted all-access passes, Danny and I were led to seats onstage, behind the speakers, across a tangle of cords, amps, Coke, root beer, Perrier, and red wine bottles, plastic cups, tools, and stools, with at least thirty stagehands busy plugging things in. Our fellow all-access-pass holders were mostly dressed in funky velvet and lace, cool motorcycle jackets, and bell-bottom jeans. The stage was already warm, so I stashed my raccoon coat and hat behind the navy-blue curtain dividing the stage from the backstage. Between sips of Perrier, Danny and I bided time until Ian called Danny over to assemble the guitar stand for Keith's new Plexiglas guitar.

Things began pulsing, shimmering, throbbing. The stage lights flexed, lighters flicked on from the audience, and the strobe lights began a wavy rock 'n' roll dance. Hearing whispers and shouts, I experienced a surge of excitement and energy I'd almost never felt before in my life, one I found physically overwhelming, as I heard the crowed line "I was born in a cross-fire hurricane," from "Jumpin' Jack Flash." Then Mick was parading, dancing with his back to me, swept up by the sound of the crowd.

The first time I saw Mick was on television, either *The Ed Sullivan Show* or *Shindig*. It was 1965, and as he sang "Little Red Rooster," he gazed directly at the camera, toying with it, his face overwhelming the screen, his eyes fluttering and trembling in their sockets as he revolved slowly in a circle. I'd never seen another performer so bold, or in-your-face, or sexually explicit. (The only other person who did the eye-flutter trick was, of all people, Uncle Peter, but now that I think about it, his role models were the same southern blues singers as Mick's.) A poster of the Stones hung on the wall directly across from my bed, showing Mick in profile, standing in front of the band. Mick was the first thing I saw when I awoke in the morning, and the last thing I saw before I fell asleep.

Onstage, in between songs, Mick turned my way, but didn't look at me once. Sometimes he wiped his face with a towel. Sometimes he took a swallow of some clear liquid. Wearing a long-sleeved brown T-shirt with an inverted gold horseshoe blazing across the chest, he never stopped moving, never stopped interacting with Keith, like two young trees being tossed around in a tropical wind.

There was no question that seeing Mick was the birth of something powerful in me: I remember I wanted to be a dancer, one who was watched. One who was tan, tan on the inside too, so tan that it pervaded my personality. One who ran into the water unafraid. Tan, running into the waves, perfectly lit and observed by everyone who had ever denied me anything, anyone who had ever made a black mark on my self-esteem. When I danced, trying to be Mick who was trying to imitate James Brown, I felt a lightness in my being and a strong appreciation of my long-limbed movements. It was not the dancing I was used to. It reminded me of the teenagers at Windy Gates, running down the cliffs, as if they'd never seen a mirror, only hazy reflections of themselves in the ocean as they ran into it, naked and laughing.

In the summer of 1969, I finally moved out of Joey's Fifty-fifth Street apartment and into a great Stanford White–designed apartment on Thirty-fifth Street between Lexington and Third Avenues, the Manhattan neighborhood known as Murray Hill. Among assorted other benefits, my new apartment was convenient to Jake, who lived exactly one block north. Over the next few months, Jake and I developed an even closer rapport. I can't really say that our times together were wall-to-wall fun. Often it was just the two of us—and sometimes I felt the Beast pull up a chair—and it was hard to figure out whether Jake or the Beast was more demonic. Overall, though, Jake's good opinion meant almost everything to me. I worshipped him, in fact. I was no longer quite as afraid of him, or perhaps, influenced by his new girlfriend, Ricky, Jake had simply become kinder since our summer at Indian Hill. His career as a writer had taken off. He'd written movie reviews for *Newsweek* and Talk of the Town pieces for *The New Yorker*. In no time at all, he replaced Wilfrid Sheed as the film critic at *Esquire* magazine.

Around this time, I found out that an old Sarah Lawrence classmate of mine, who'd become a TV producer, was looking for a theme song to a television special called *Who Killed Lake Erie?* The show was about pollution and the public's indifference to the quality of Lake Erie's water. The song I wrote was promptly orchestrated into a melody that reappeared throughout the hour-long special. I was over the moon until a *TV Guide* review singled out my melody as "Weltzschmertzy." I looked up the word. It was pretty much my first taste ever of being denigrated in public, and I knew I would have to develop a stronger response to criticism. The bigger point is that this "Weltzschmertzy" theme song would end up changing my life. Romantically, it was the start of an interesting period, too. Jake's best friend at the time was Terrence Malick, who was just becoming a film director and whose presence ignited a mild rivalry for my attention, though I suspected neither Jake nor Terry was as interested in me as they were in each other's company. I didn't blame them. I was more interested in them than I was in me. A year later, Jake would go out to Hollywood, and he and Terry would eventually collaborate on one of the best films of all time, *Days of Heaven*. Jake would also become friends with Bob Rafelson and Bert Schneider, the producers of *Five Easy Pieces*, Jack Nicholson's first major starring role, and begin spending time on-site, at parties and around pools, talking up new ideas as screenwriter, script doctor, editor, and probably court jester (not that anyone needed a second jester in the building with Jack around). Eventually, Jake wrote a classic film: *The King of Marvin Gardens*, starring a glasses-wearing Nicholson as a disc jockey, and Ellen Burstyn.

Raised in Oklahoma and Texas, Terry was intimidatingly smart, a former philosophy student and Rhodes Scholar who had already translated a book by Heidegger and who was now focusing on writing and journalism. In the weeks after we first met, Terry and I went on enough dates to warrant calling whatever it was we were doing an "affair." Jake had told me that Terry was brilliant and great and deep, which turned out to be true. At the time, Terry was writing a story for *The New Yorker* about Che Guevara, and I listened attentively as he talked with the kind of fervid enthusiasm for Che that I secretly hoped he might have an iota of for me, too. Still, Terry and I weren't the easiest fit. If Jake and I shared a dirt driveway into each other's sensibilities and senses of humor, Terry was on another road entirely. Our dates were complicated even more by the already somewhat confusing relationship I had with Jake, who had fallen in love with an aristocratic English girl, Erica Johnston, who was working as an editorial assistant at Knopf publishers, and whom everyone called Ricky. With her breathtaking pussycat features, Ricky might have been a girl in a Modigliani painting, and together, she and Jake made a glamorous, sophisticated couple. Jake,

Ricky, and I fell into the same choreography I sometimes inspire, one where I was the third wheel on a sturdy tricycle.

In my stunning five-room apartment on Thirty-fifth Street I was coming into my own as a girl about town. The couple from whom I was leasing the place had kept all the apartment's peculiarities intact, maintaining it to nostalgic 1920s standards. The layout was unconventional, the rooms connected fancifully. The dining area, which combined a kitchen and dining room, was separated by a wicker divider and decorated to resemble an outdoor garden. Vines of all shapes and sizes snaked around the room, which was so small it could accommodate only the three-and-a-half-foot round dining table that the owners had left behind. I brought in four inexpensive thrift-shop chairs, as well as my Mexican bureau from Fifty-fifth Street, an ideal surface and receptacle for nail scissors, picture-frame parts, guitar strings, twine, Band-Aids, rolling papers, and the usual odds and ends. A winding hallway led to the other rooms, including a library and a bedroom the perfect size for a queen-size bed. Though small, the apartment nonetheless managed to seem large and, somehow, central.

By now Ricky had moved in with Jake, and as I watched their relationship unfold, I was also busy writing songs I could sing at Jake's parties. Jake had lots of get-togethers, his apartment overflowing with the most interesting people passing through town, all of whom seemed to be on the cusp of success, everyone seated at a round table where you could work, eat, or play poker. At Jake's, for example, Terry auditioned a very young and nervous Sissy Spacek for the part she eventually played in *Badlands*.

It was around that same table, invariably littered with wineglasses, empty beer bottles, ashtrays, and games, that Jake and I first spoke about collaborating on a song. I still had the melody I had written for *Who Killed Lake Erie?*, the first one I'd ever written on the piano, with chords that drifted into minor during the verses, backing up to a strong major feel in the chorus. I asked Jake if he'd be interested in taking a stab at a lyric. At first, Jake had no confidence he could write a song, and didn't really want to, either. He wrote for *The New Yorker*, not for Tin Pan Alley. Still, I went home and made a cassette, and in response, Jake, who had never written a lyric before in his life, wrote a perfect one his first time out, though being Jake, he waited a day before even bringing up the subject. Finally, he passed me a sheet of handwritten lyrics. We hadn't even discussed what the subject of the song should be. In the past, he and I had spoken about how every woman of my generation felt the pressure to get married, while not exactly loving what we'd seen of our own parents' marriages and lives. Then there was the beginning, the lines about "my father," which Jake picked up from hearing me talk about him. When I asked him how he'd moved so easily into the deep basements of my brain, Jake told me he'd had no trouble whatsoever. As for the phrase "me first, by myself," Ricky's recent move into Jake's apartment had made him acutely aware of his own loss of privacy and independence.

Jake kept an upright piano in his living room. One night, when Bob Rafelson and his wife Toby were sitting around the circular table with Ricky, Jake escorted me to the piano, where I sang the song he and I had been working on together. It was then called "We'll Marry." Facing the wall, I struggled to play it smoothly, but it turned out that the song wasn't dependent on "smooth." The response we received from our collaboration—my music and his words coming together in "That's the Way I've Always Heard It Should Be"—was electrifying. When the song ended, the room was utterly still, then my small audience applauded rapturously. Campfire redux. Everyone loved it, or at least said they did. I can't recall anyone else who was there that night aside from Jake, Ricky, and the Rafelsons, but the applause that Jake and I got lasted years. It was the beginning of a beat to a bigger life.

I was still so puzzled by my feelings about Jake that I simply followed his lead. Unlike me, he seemed to know what he was doing, at least in his head. Early on, during the first year of our friendship, I realized that some things will never be clarified, or straightened out, at least in this lifetime. They just go on and on, and Jake's and my friendship fits into that category. The two of us lasted as a songwriting team because he could almost magically interpret my experiences. With cunning insight, he kept close watch on my "path." What's more, he interpreted that path with a sophisticated irony that gave voice to my most profound, secret feelings. Jake told me later that in those days a lot of people considered him Svengali-ish, but he put it better: he was less interested in people (myself included) than he was interested in creating "situations."

Early the next morning, the night after the public debut of "That's the Way . . . ," my doorbell rang. Still in my nightgown, I went to the house phone and asked who was there.

"Bob Rafelson."

I buzzed him up, hurriedly placing my coat over my nightgown. When I opened the door, the first thing Bob said was, "I couldn't help it . . ." and he placed his arms around me, holding me tight there. He had only an hour, he said. The rest of his family was still asleep in their hotel room. It was now my turn to respond, and to be perfectly honest, I had no idea what to say or do. I wasn't even sure what Bob Rafelson wanted. Bob was funny and attractive. He also had an extra quarter-inch of what might have been foam around every sinew that skin can cover—an effect of comfort in an otherwise slender man. I liked Bob, but I also felt powerless, a slave to what I imagined Jake might be expecting me to do. Jake, I imagined, would expect me to report back on my activities, give him an interesting anecdote for the two of us to chew over. And because Bob was attractive and he'd surprised me in my apartment, he and I became off-and-on lovers, if such an expression can be used about something so short-lived, for the next few weeks. Bob eventually told his brilliant, beautiful wife, Toby, about me during a "karma cleaning" session and, by the expert way Bob must have told her, in no way did I feel uncomfortable with either Bob or Toby in the future. My brief relationship with Bob led to any number of encounters with other available or unavailable men of that clan who, after leaving Jake's, traveled the short block south where I welcomed them into my apartment for a night, a week, or longer. "I hate to think of myself as being promiscuous," I wrote in my diary around that time. "I know I am. I really don't know how not to fall for people. What does it make me think about myself?"

One of the men I fell for was Jack Nicholson, who showed up at Jake's apartment one evening with his arm around his gum-chewing girlfriend, regaling the table with stories from the making of *Five Easy Pieces*, which had just wrapped. I was goaded to play my musical repertoire for the guests, which had expanded to include a song I'd recently written called "Alone," an amalgam of "I Am a Rock" and "I Am a Rock" again.

I could tell that Jack was enjoying my performance. He asked me, very seriously, what more had to happen before I amassed enough songs to make an honest-to-goodness record. I had no idea, but immediately began explaining how I would produce it, first laying down the guitar part, followed by me singing on a different track, to be overlaid eventually with strings. "Yes," I concluded, "there will be a plethora of strings."

After a long pause, and everyone else staying quiet in anticipation, Jack repeated, "Plethora?" in that way only Jack could, and when he did, I felt the same rush of love that I'd had with Willie, and also with Jake: perfect timing, an elastic stretch of irony mixed with a hint of challenge and possibly even menace. Before I knew it, it was time to say good night to Jack's gum-chewing girlfriend, who, in her Mary Janes and her dress with its puffed-up short sleeves, looked like an extremely attractive eight-year-old girl. When she was gone, we all remarked how adorable she was and how, as she was leaving, she waved at Jack and said, "Thank you, I had a very nice time." Alone now with Jake and Ricky, Jack trained the full force of his attention on me, and when I rose to sing another song, he seemed to take it personally, as if I were singing to him alone. The song was "I'm All It Takes to Make You Happy."

"What if we go over to your apartment?" he said when we were sitting alone.

He was unbelievable, and it was outrageous, the idea of returning to my apartment alone with Jack. There was a flicker of evil amusement in Jake's eyes as he sent Jack and me off into the night. It was as if he were already imagining the delight Jack and I were about to find with each other, one that might conceivably provide me and Jake with a future lyric. Thankfully I was a little stoned, as well as drunk enough not to be too nervous, and Jack and I ended up in my living room, with its smoked-mirrored walls and fake-fur foldout couch. Jack lingered in the living room as I prepared a pot of coffee. When I returned holding two cups, I took a seat on the couch across from Jack, who was perched on the piano stool. We chatted for a few moments and then he said, offhandedly, "Do you ever drink coffee in your bedroom?"

I was inebriated enough that I literally couldn't remember how to arrange my body in the right way for intimacy, though it was one of the few times in my life that I was wearing the perfect undergarments. When the two of us awoke the next morning, Jack immediately needed to make a bunch of telephone calls. The phone was on my side of the bed, and Jack sat up, propped against the pillows, while I lay there trapped underneath the long curlicue cord. Jack's phone voice—and his entire persona—was supremely assured. At the same time, I couldn't help but think he was trying to impress me with the caliber of the people he was calling. He tossed out nicknames left and right. Candice Bergen was "Bugs," Art Garfunkel was "Artie the Garf," and it took me a few seconds to realize that "Mike the Nick" was Mike Nichols. I lay in bed next to him, unable to come up with any witty things to say, and feeling dumb about it, too, so I remained quiet.

That evening, Jack was back, after another day spent shooting *Carnal Knowledge* with Bugs, Artie the Garf, and Mike the Nick. He showed up late, explaining that the Lexington Avenue bus had run into traffic. It was winter, and cold out, and more than anything, I was amazed that Jack Nicholson ever took a bus anywhere. He and I proceeded to have an almost domestic evening, watching television, with a few bits of frolicking thrown in. That same night, Jack told me that he was starting to see a woman he felt serious about. He'd been seeing her all winter, and there were children involved, and the two of them were on the verge of moving in together. The discussion he and I proceeded to have was extremely rational. "I really like seeing you," I said, "and I'm glad you told me before I invited you to my wedding in which you were my groom." Jack told me I was a "funny one" and he was glad I understood.

Did I? It seemed to me I had a few options. I could see myself as a girl unable to keep Jack Nicholson's interest, or I could tell him off, or I could act the way I felt, which was like a stupid, rejected fool who felt like crying, and who would never, ever attract anyone ever again. I did none of these. Jack was a handsome, famous, funny, clever man whom I'd met three or four times. I wasn't in love with him. My ego may have taken a momentary whack, but the end of my brief fling with Jack was akin to a promising summer rental that gets canceled at the last minute.

In the wake of Jack, I was gently passed around, as if in a fraternity, not the first woman to experience this and not the last, either. Beginning with Bob Rafelson, his brother Don, Pierre Cottrell, and Michael Crichton, it felt like a club in which Jake was the hub, one where you had to please the man just below in order to graduate to the next. I didn't feel unappreciated, though I was always aware I was giving myself away too cheaply. In college I had read Margaret Mead's *Coming of Age in Samoa*, which described sex as natural, guilt free, and causing no deep feeling or rivalries. Could sex be casual, or was it reserved exclusively for two people who had dedicated themselves to a lifetime together, as my own mother had spuriously tried to instill in my brain? Mommy's words still resonated in my head as though I were twelve years old. If I had sex with someone I had no intention of marrying, I felt guilty, fake. Nevertheless, by 1970, I'd had sex with boys and men who, unlike Nick or Willie, were nowhere close to potential marriage material. Nobody, it seemed to me, had it right about sex, especially my mother. Sex was up to me to define, and I'd do it my own way. The only issue was finding coherence in all the dogmas I'd heard my whole life, while still feeling responsible toward myself. Did sex really have to be as formal as an evening at the opera? Couldn't some encounters be as casual as a midnight swim? Like so many women, I was trying to reconcile these competing thoughts, the difference being that all of a sudden I had a vehicle to explore them—the sheer wonder of an original lyric. The more I sang it, the truer it became. To help define what I needed to know about aspects of myself as a woman, I needed the help of the only man I loved so deeply without the encumbrance of romance. Together we wanted to know the deeper truths of our time, and what we might risk as we found our way.

The couples cling and claw
And drown in love's debris
You say we'll soar like two birds through the clouds
But soon you'll cage me on your shelf
I'll never learn to be just me first
By myself.

When Jake gave me those words to the music I'd written, his lyrics matched the melody perfectly. I sat before my Tonk piano in my south-facing Murray Hill apartment, singing the song over and over again, alone, poised, at least in my mind, to live a life where I was far more than just the "girl."

Jake Brackman and me writing our first song,
"That's the Way I've Always Heard It Should Be," 1970.

*My first band hits the road. Clockwise from left: me, Jimmy Ryan,
Andy Newmark, Paul Glanz.*

---

CHAPTER THIRTEEN

record numero uno

Everything felt new for me in 1970: my Murray Hill neighborhood, my physical and emotional proximity to Jake, and the fact that for the first time in my life I was living alone, just me and my fluffy fake-fur foldout couch, my clothes, my shoes, and my music, strewn around five wildly imaginative Stanford White rooms. (It was a look, a style, and a kind of architecture that I would try to copy everywhere I went from that time on.) I'd set up my new sound system—containing all my newest, highest-fidelity equipment—in the room I called "my office."

One night, during the winter of 1970, Jake invited me over to his house for an Indian takeout dinner. (Dinner at Jake's was pretty much an ongoing invitation.) Janet Margolin, an actress who'd starred in the film *David and Lisa*, was there, along with her husband, Jerry Brandt. Jerry was a music manager who managed the Harlem Boys Choir, among other acts. I wasn't entirely sure if Jake had choreographed this introduction for professional reasons, but sometime in between the raita and the naan, Jake asked me to play our new song.

When I finished singing "That's the Way . . . ," Jerry was incredibly enthusiastic. "Can you and I get together?" he asked. "Would you like to make a record?"

"Actually," I said, "I'd love to be a writer more than I'd like to be a performer." Being a performer just wasn't something I was ready for, I went on. "I never really loved being onstage with my sister, and now I just want to sit back and write songs and be the"—what was the word?—"composer-at-arms."

"Sure, sure," Jerry said, knowing, as he must have, that anything was possible under the tutelage of Jerry Brandt. Jerry suggested that he drop by my apartment for lunch the next day, before asking, slightly opaquely, if I happened to have a copy of the *I Ching*. I didn't have one, so Jerry said he would bring his.

Jerry arrived the next day with his *I Ching* under one arm. He was handsomer than I remembered, and had a thrilling, contagious energy. We made some intense small talk, Jerry's black eyes on me the whole time, and I offered him a Swiss cheese, chutney, and red onion sandwich on rye. Jerry seemed to delight in the strangeness of this combination. "Is this some style thing?" he asked. "Anything with anything?" He then suggested that we "throw the *I Ching*," and asked me if I'd ever done it before. I hadn't, but that didn't mean I wasn't intrigued. From his pocket he took out a few ancient-looking coins. "Ask a question," he said.

I demurred. "*You* ask one. This was your idea, Jerry. You must have some reason."

He did, too. "Will it be to our mutual benefit to work together professionally?"

Jerry tossed the coins, translating their meaning by turning to the page the coin pattern referenced. Then as now, I'm an *I Ching* novice, and I suppose the answer was likely to be interpreted in whatever way the coin tosser chose. In this case, if I'm remembering it right, the answer had to do with a bear declining to step on the foot of the mouse and choosing instead to take on bigger challenges, like, say, a *moose*. It could have been something else, but whatever it was, the bigger question of whether Jerry and I should work together was *Yes*.

Jerry asked if I knew the guitarist David Bromberg, and it turned out I did. Dave was a great guitarist, and Jerry proposed assembling a group of musicians to help make a demo that he could take around to various record companies and try to sell me to one of them as a solo artist, and maybe even ignite a bidding war. All of a sudden, we were in action. The next thing I knew, I was in an uptown studio along with Dave Bromberg and several other musicians, recording three of my songs—"That's the Way I've Always Heard It Should Be," "Alone," and "I'm All It Takes to Make You Happy"—and two other songs by writers I'd never heard of. Jerry looked on the whole time and left the studio with a cassette, as did I. Still, in the back of my mind was the unspoken question: Why was I recording two songs by other songwriters when I knew I only wanted to use my songs as demos for myself as a composer?

As far as I knew, I was merely agreeing to record some demos that would then circulate into the hands of other artists who might say, "Wow!—what a wonderful song—and perfect for *me*." They would record it and I'd be off and running to the bank, accompanied, perhaps, by some kind of minimal fame: my name on a piece of sheet music, that kind of thing. Whatever denial I was in, I still hang onto some semblance of it today. I can't seem to fully give myself over to being a performer. And even when I *am* being a performer, I keep hoping I can get off the stage sooner rather than later.

The first record company Jerry Brandt took the cassette to was Columbia. The president, Clive Davis, purportedly listened to two of the songs before ejecting the cassette and throwing it across his office. "What do I want with a Jewish girl from the Bronx?" he's said to have responded, though knowing Clive as I do now, I think the story must be apocryphal.

I think Jerry reported these words back to me, incorrectly, to make a point, that point being, *You'd better listen to his words, Carly, because you'll be lucky if anyone else ever wants you!*

The sadistic implication was that if anything worked it would be because *he*, Jerry, would use his persuasive powers. And then came this from Jerry: "I think Jac Holzman at Elektra will take you."

Apparently, Elektra Records held weekly lunch meetings where everyone at the label convened around a big round table to listen to that week's submissions. The voting was democratic. A photographer on staff told me afterward that when my tape was played, every single person in the room voted it down. No one, it seemed, could figure out who I was stylistically, or how to market me. Was I a jazz singer? A pop singer? A folkie? Jac Holzman, the president of Elektra, had the right to veto anything he felt strongly about, and this time around he exercised his veto power. "There's something about her I just *feel*," he said, news relayed to me by Jerry Brandt a day later. Elektra Records wanted me! I was *in*! I was *on*!

Immediately, Jac and I began discussing producers. Jac mentioned that he had just worked with Eddie Kramer on the Joe Cocker LP *Mad Dogs and Englishmen*. He set up a meeting with Eddie, who showed up in my apartment and listened to me playing piano and singing, "That's the Way . . . ," "Alone," and a few other songs before I picked up my guitar and played a few of my guitar-based compositions. Eddie was South African. Even if he didn't have a posh accent like Willie, I was still a hopeless Anglophile (and that evidently included South Africa and most likely Australia!), and could have happily dined out on dialects ranging from Cockney to Cantabrigian, plus anything in between. They brought back the very best memories of Willie. It was only a matter of time before Eddie and I found ourselves in the Electric Lady Studios on Eighth Street in Greenwich Village, *the* studio on the East Coast.

Among the many people I saw wandering the halls of Electric Lady was Jimi Hendrix, blow smudged around his nostrils, followed by throngs of half-naked, elaborately painted girls, their own nostrils quite white, the whole crew on their way to a back restroom that I later found out was elaborately painted in psychedelic colors.

The very first song Eddie and I recorded was "That's the Way . . ." It made sense, of course, and was the song with which I was most familiar, too. Eddie recorded it with only me playing piano and a metronome keeping time. I then met a very fine arranger, Ed Freeman, who not only arranged the string parts wherever they were needed, but helped me with what are known as "head arrangements"—that is to say, just enough information for the musicians to follow in order to communicate that "non-arrangement" feel, but enough organization or structure to keep everyone on the same road.

Then things started to get a little complicated.

One night, Eddie Kramer and I went out for dinner, ostensibly to discuss ideas for tracks and overall album themes. Then we went out on a few more dates. One culminated—or should I say deteriorated—into a drunken night out on the town. Eddie and I made out, and then went even further, the evening ending up with me under the covers in Eddie's bedroom. For reasons I can't recall, Eddie and I ended up having a terrible fight, but it was devastating enough for me to fire him, or for him to quit outright, and I can't remember for the life of me which.

Well done, Simon Sister! It's your first album. What are you going to do, produce it yourself? Believing I knew how to produce an album may have been a reckless vanity, but with Eddie gone, I couldn't exactly press the rewind button. I was fortunate that Jac Holzman was around to put me at ease, along with his quiet, thoughtful, conservatively dressed brother, Keith, who urged me to do everything I could to convince Eddie Kramer to return to work on the album. In the meantime, I did most of it myself, very unprofessionally, shepherding copies of rough mixes of songs up to the Gulf & Western Building on Columbus Circle, where Jac presided over his enormous lunch table.

With his good taste, his congeniality, and the intelligence and good manners with which he treated his staff, Jac was a model for other record executives. It was 1970, and Jac knew exactly where to be in 1970. He had just released the Doors' *Morrison Hotel*. He and Jim Morrison were close friends. The following year, when he heard Jim had died—Jac and I were having dinner at the time, discussing material—he was devastated, practically inconsolable.

The closest thing to an in-house manager in those days was a label's A&R man, A&R being short for Artists and Repertoire, a job title that often means that that person becomes your best friend and companion on trips and concert tours. Steve Harris was that person for me. Over lunch in countless Chinese restaurants or in the halls of Electric Lady, he and I discussed all current and future steps concerning the sound, shape, and image I wanted for my debut album. Taking our lead from Jac, it could be summed up as: "Add strings to 'That's the Way I've Always Heard It Should Be' and 'The Love's Still Growing,' and let's add some cello on 'Reunions,' and oh, wait, the lyrics in 'One More Time' shouldn't repeat themselves on the final verse!"

I was frankly uncomfortable to be alone in the studio with the engineer, Dave Palmer. Dave was very, very good at what he did, but as expert as he was, I balanced it by being pretty bad. Not only did I not know what to do, I pretended I *did* know what to do, and ended up mixing about half the album (today, a listener can definitely tell which songs I had a hand in mixing). In retrospect, Dave must have had conflicted feelings about this tall, unknown girl with an overbite taking over at the board, pushing the knobs up and down, and advising him to "lower the reverb and add compression, also bring up the snare, my vocal is too soft on the second chorus."

Another upsetting event was that Jerry Brandt told me he could no longer stay on as my manager. His wife Janet didn't want him getting too close to me, or Jerry and me spending so much time together. All I could think of was that Jerry had stopped believing in my talent or, aware that Eddie Kramer was no longer involved in the production, assumed my first record would be a disaster. I was so upset that today I'm shocked I even managed to finish the album, but thanks to Steve Harris, Jac, and his brother Keith, who stepped in to spend a lot of time in the studio, I somehow did.

Ultimately, Jac, Keith, and Steve also—don't ask me how—convinced Eddie and me to make up our differences, and persuaded Eddie to return to Electric Lady to finish the recording of the few songs that weren't yet finished, and especially, to mix "That's the Way I've Always Heard It Should Be." Of all the songs, that was the one Jac believed in the most and was most eager to hear in its *finished* version. Little wonder Jac was so important to so many artists he took under his wing. Elegantly fierce, he was a gentleman with a strong sense of self, whereas Steve Harris by contrast was fun and funny and lighthearted. The result was my debut album, called, simply, *Carly Simon*.

But what should I do about the cover art? A few weeks earlier, I'd posed uncomfortably on a studio floor for a full-body, leaning-on-my-shoulder, head-to-one-side photograph. The art director ultimately decided to crop the photo to create a frontal head shot, turning it forty-five degrees to the right, so it would appear I was gazing head-on at the camera. Still, one side of my face couldn't help looking as though gravity was yanking it floorward. My makeup added a big bruise to one cheek, which retouching never rectified. My brother Peter did a second photo session at his Massachusetts farm, during which I posed in a long pink dress, my legs crossed underneath me. Eventually, the other photo, which ended up on the back cover, would have an interesting effect. In it, I looked a lot like Mick Jagger. It could be that Mick and I actually looked somewhat alike, but that photo served to make people—including Mick himself—aware of the resemblance.

Once the album was done, I was damned if I was going to think further than the artwork and the credits. I needed a rest or, an even crazier idea, a vacation. I had no interest in promoting my record with a tour, or via television appearances. Why? Stage fright, pure and simple, or more to the point, my *fear* of stage fright. I had no interest in facing down my various phobias. I wanted only one thing: for my album to serve as a demo and a showcase for my songs, so that other singers might someday want to record them.

My fear of going onstage, mixed with various other free-floating phobias that were preventing my life from going forward, drove me into the arms of one of the smartest, most humane, and delightful psychiatrists I'd ever met. I'll call him Dr. L. He was also determined to help me overcome the obstacles in my way. Performance anxiety. High-strung-ness. Self-esteem issues. My therapy with Dr. L would last for years.

In the weeks after I finished my album, another album was on my turntable day and night, an album I memorized and sang along with, and no doubt millions of other women across the country were doing the same: *Sweet Baby James*, by James Taylor. One night, as Joey and I were walking home on Fifty-ninth Street from the movies, we passed by a newsstand, and there was the new issue of *Time* magazine, with a cartoon drawing of James Taylor's face on the cover and the headline THE NEW ROCK: BITTERSWEET AND LOW. Without thinking, I blurted, with confidence: "I'm going to marry him." How did I know this? People have asked me over the years. The only answer I can come up with is that he, James, was perfect for me in every way. If you believe in predestination or clairvoyance, that would be a terrific example of why you're right to.

The Taylor family was hardly unfamiliar to me, as they had been coming to Martha's Vineyard since the early fifties. I had met young James on the porch of Seward's, had been very curious about him since. The family patriarch, Dr. Isaac Taylor, was a strong, formidable-looking man, handsome and brilliant, the dean of the medical school at the University of North Carolina in Chapel Hill, where James was raised. In the summers, the Taylors lived in a modest cottage perfectly situated on the island's South Shore, down a dirt road that ended up on Stonewall Beach. Once, when I asked a friend of my mother's what the Taylors were like, she was elliptical, but implied the family had a complicated history. In fact, she said, they were quite "mad."

The Taylors, she said—having heard this from up-island friends—were "North meets South." They were a strange family, she added, with five children in all, very straitlaced New England, originally from Newburyport, Massachusetts, as well as North Carolina, adding that they socialized mostly with one another. The father, known as Ike, was a brilliant doctor but an alcoholic, and years earlier had bought a lot of land at the tip of the island. When the Taylor children were little, Ike spent many years as a naval doctor stationed in Antarctica, coming home infrequently. "There's a lot of talent in that family," my mother's friend had said, raising her foxlike blue eyes at me. "Every single one of those kids."

The first Taylor I officially met was Livingston, James's younger brother, in 1970, when I drove to their family home in Chilmark to rehearse with him for a duet we planned to perform at a film festival my brother Peter was launching in Vineyard Haven.

That day, Livingston and I sat down for tea with James's mother, Trudy. At the time, I was a little bit hoping to become Livingston's girlfriend, but Liv, as everyone called him, was in the process of falling in love with his girlfriend Maggie, who ended up becoming his wife and manager for half a lifetime. I liked Liv enormously, long believing, as I still do today, that his talent is huge, and very much his own. James's younger sister, Kate, was also living at home, and she and I were at the same stage of beginning to perform. Peter Asher, James's manager and producer, was recording her, and would eventually market her first album, *Sister Kate*. Kate and I were competitive but extremely warm with each other, and during that visit she bowled me over with her weaving and knitting. She took after Trudy with those talents, and to this day there are dozens and dozens of Kate's creations, both musical and textile, in my house. But at the time, I had no idea that someday—soon, too—every single one of these people would be a big part of my life.

My album was released in February 1971 to some very good reviews. In March of that year, as I stood in the tiny kitchen of my Murray Hill apartment, I received a call that would be pivotal. On the other end were Jac Holzman and Steve Harris from Elektra. "What would it take for you to open for Cat Stevens at the Troubadour on April 6?" they asked.

I froze. The date was less than three weeks way. I had no interest in or intention of performing live by myself—I had sung many times before, but never on a stage for critics, never without Lucy, never with an actual band or with something to promote. I lived in New York; the Troubadour was in Los Angeles; and my incipient fear of flying was only increased by what I'd be flying to *do*. I wanted to hang up, but I was thinking fast, too. James Taylor was on the road, backed by a band that included drummer Russ Kunkel. Russ Kunkel, I knew, was the best drummer to come down the pike in a long time. All one had to do was pick up the needle and replay the tom-tom fills on "Fire and Rain" and "Country Road." Smartly, I told Jac and Steve that if they could convince Russ Kunkel to be my drummer, I would agree to do it, knowing that getting Russ would be impossible. Jac and Steve couldn't have quite conceived how quick-witted I could be when faced with my own phobias, nor could they (or I) have reckoned on the ways in which destiny occasionally throws you for a loop.

The next day Jac and Steve called back to tell me they had tracked down a drummer whose sound uncannily resembled Russ Kunkel's.

"Oh yeah, and who would that be?" I asked, ready to say the deal was off.

"Russ Kunkel," Steve said.

James Taylor, they explained, had been in a motorcycle accident on the Vineyard a few days before, breaking both hands and several other bones.

His tour was off, or at least indefinitely delayed. I was suddenly struck dumb. My next thought was that Jac and Steve were kidding, as I'd been counting on Russ Kunkel's unavailability so as to avoid opening for Cat Stevens in L.A. But they had outwitted me. It was fate.

In a panic, I called up Jimmy Ryan and enlisted him to find a piano player and a drummer who could temporarily fill in for Russ Kunkel during rehearsals. In short order, Jimmy found one of the all-time talented drummers, named Andy Newmark, and Jimmy did double-duty himself on bass and guitar, hijacking keyboardist Paul Glanz from another band. We decided on a short set list: "In My Reply," Livingston Taylor's song, the one he and I sang on the Vineyard together; "One More Time," a country tune I'd written for my first album; "Dan, My Fling," a big ballad written by Jake and his friend Fred Gardner; Buzzy Linhart's song "The Love's Still Growing"—its Indian-esque tuning required a separate guitar onstage— and we'd close the set with "That's the Way I've Always Heard It Should Be." We rehearsed four or five times, and thanks to Jimmy Ryan, who also served as our musical director, I thought we sounded pretty good.

I didn't have a manager at the time, which meant I was relying pretty heavily on Steve Harris, Elektra's A&R man, to stay close to me and to book all our cross-country plane trips and hotel reservations. It was my first trip to California, and I was utterly terrified of flying. Still, Steve and I flew out west, first class, me floating on ten milligrams of Valium and Steve levitating above me on four times that much. It was the golden age of air travel, the era when 747s had swanky but likely bacteria-filled upper decks, bars, and even piano players. Steve spent the flight telling me Jim Morrison war stories. Three or four hours into the ride, Steve pointed out the Grand Canyon and the Rockies, guidebook destinations that I, a largely sheltered East Coast girl, had never seen before in my life.

Los Angeles was completely thrilling, and as we drove into West Hollywood from the airport, I was on a manic high, even as we—Steve, Jimmy, and Paul—passed through L.A.'s flat, unattractive parts. Palm trees, but inside the borders of America! Finally we pulled up in front of the Hyatt Regency Hotel, a famous music hangout on the Sunset Strip. I couldn't have been more excited to stay there. It was now forty-eight hours before the Troubadour opening, which would allow us to meet Russ Kunkel and have one rehearsal with him. Then we would have a lone sound check before we went onstage. The Troubadour gig with Cat Stevens was scheduled to last five nights in all, two shows a night, and after that, as far as I was concerned, I would be done with live performances forever.

As I was walking through the lobby of the Hyatt to check in, I bumped into Kris Kristofferson, who was with T Bone Burnett and Stephen Bruton, the guitarist and songwriter. Kris introduced himself, and he and I had a small conversation, the kind, I would later discover, that Kris excelled at, one where meaning and implication are packed into the shortest, punchiest exchange. Kris tossed out a few Texan bon mots while squinting his sunken, intense, icy blue eyes—eyes like a Samoyed, I remember thinking. He had the look of a man who had just undressed you, and there would be no more clothes needed for a while. Every signal Kris conveyed said, "I've got to have you," and I felt prematurely possessed.

Kris shuffled his scruffy cowboy boots and picked up his guitar, and the promise of something tinkled into my collection cup like coins as he said, "Here's thinking about you," and then he tilted his head toward the door and was lost to the Los Angeles neon. I didn't know how soon I'd see him again.

My room at the Hyatt resembled a den of iniquity. With its platform bed and noxious-looking, fake-velvet bedspread, it looked in retrospect like it came straight out of the Amsterdam red-light district. Then again, this was the Sunset Strip, hardly my ideal, though I was also tripping on the strangeness and newness of L.A. The next day, the fifth of April, I met Russ Kunkel for the first time at the Troubadour. Russ was a beautiful, beaming spirit, with eyes that made deep and immediately comforting contact. He would become one of the most important, and musically influential, people I would ever know. That whole day I was enfolded by a sensation of scary bliss. Fear first—I had never performed onstage without Lucy—then bliss, as I felt ever so slightly in love with everyone who was going out of his or her own way to prop me up before opening night. Is this what fate was? You couldn't get out of its way?

On opening night I discarded my usual late-sixties-chick look, with its lace, beads, and braids, in favor of a new, carefully chosen outfit: a dark brown, short-sleeved, midlength dress and high Chelsea Cobbler red leather boots, a gift from Jac Holzman when I signed my contract at Elektra. It would just be me alone, ever alert, ever paranoid, and most of all, worried about every possible fearsome onstage scenario. I worried I would pass out, and that my band would be unable to revive me. I worried I would throw up. I worried that after I projectile-vomited, I might not be able to convince the other members of the band to blame it on an audience member in the front row.

As for Cat Stevens, the two of us met briefly as I walked past his dressing room heading onstage. I didn't want to stop and divert him from tuning up and whatever last-minute checks he was doing. For the past two or three months, I'd been listening to his latest album, *Tea for the Tillerman*, singing and harmonizing along to various cuts. I was a huge fan of his music, songs, production, and guitar playing, and had no idea whether he'd ever heard mine. Cat looked like a dark gypsy, and he seemed kind and friendly. "Good luck, luv," he called out in passing.

Steve Harris gripped me by the elbow, propping me up as I made my way down to the stage with my guitars. The club was small, and a bud vase with one pink rose stood on every table. Jimmy, Paul, and Russ were already onstage, which was a small comfort, but my overall terror made my hands feel like flippers, moist and bulbous. Here's what I had to do: pick up my guitar, place it over my head by its strap, and play. Simple. Right now. My heart was beating so fast, I wondered if they would bring a phone to me onstage so I could call Dr. L and other doctors in other fields.

I stared in silence at the audience as if frozen, and it was then I heard a sweet, familiar voice calling out to me. Shielding my eyes in the glare of the lights, I caught sight of Kate Taylor's truly beautiful, shining face. Hers was a Vineyard voice, familiar, calming, and when I heard her greeting, my frozen right arm released and landed fortuitously on the first G chord of my first song, "One More Time." The audience broke into applause. I have no memory of what I said in between songs, but I felt a definite rapport with the audience, and by the time I got to the fifth and last song, "That's the Way I've Always Heard It Should Be," I walked confidently over to the piano. If possible, the piano made me even more nervous than the guitar, but as I began singing, the audience became especially quiet and focused. *My father sits at night with no lights on . . . I hear her call "sweet dreams," but I forget how to dream . . .*

During the song, the microphone began to drift to the left in slow motion. I grabbed it and brought it back to center, but as soon as I let go it began drifting again. Again, I brought it back to center, like a typist working on an old-fashioned machine. The only good thing about my ever-tipping moving mic was that it distracted my focus from my own nerves. By the end of the song, the audience, who had witnessed the quiet, ongoing struggle, were on my side and gave me a standing ovation.

Backstage, it seemed as though all of Elektra Records was packed inside my tiny, flower-filled dressing room, giving me the news that "That's the Way I've Always Heard It Should Be" had taken an enormous leap and was now number 24 on the *Cashbox* charts. At one point Cat Stevens showed up to congratulate me before vanishing into his own dressing room to grab his band and guitar. I had a second show to do that night, so once the hugs and congratulations had peaked, Steve Harris cleared my dressing room of everyone except one man—or was it a large boy?—sprawled on the floor in the far corner of the room.

It was James Taylor. For some reason I hadn't noticed him yet, but then I recognized him immediately. He was nodding off slightly, but since I didn't know that drug expression yet, all I could think of was that he, James, was probably exhausted. He was barefoot, long-legged, long-footed—and his knees were bent. He wore dark red, loose, wide-wale corduroys and a long-sleeved Henley with one button open, his right hand clutching a self-rolled cigarette. His hair, simultaneously shiny and disheveled, fell evenly on both sides of his head, and he wore a scruffy, understated mustache, the kind so fashionable back in the early 1970s. He seemed both kempt and unkempt. Even sprawled out on the floor, everything about him communicated that he was, in fact, the center of something—the core of an apple, the center of a note. James came to, and he and I had a two-minute-long discussion about the Vineyard. He remained sitting in the corner before the door opened (for me, too soon) and Joni Mitchell, James's girlfriend at the time, appeared, and without glancing at me said, "James, we have to go now." James rose slowly to his feet, nodded good-bye to me without making eye contact, and followed her out the door. I wouldn't see him again for seven months, though I thought about him regularly. In person he and I hadn't had an instantaneous connection—James was too stoned—but over the next few days, I cast my mind back to the crazy prediction I made the night I spotted his face on the cover of *Time* magazine: that the two of us would someday get married. But how many women had this same fantasy? I would fade, foolish, into the millions.

Me and Kris Kristofferson: "I've got to have you."

"Come let us drink again, before the second show . . ."
Cat Stevens and me in London, 1971.

CHAPTER FOURTEEN

soft summer gardens

I had done something very much like jumping into the deep end of the pool when I knew only the doggie paddle. Dr. L said: "Just jump in, and don't even think about it." That's really good advice if you're psychologically stuck and if you're absolutely sure there's water in the pool. It worked. I had gotten on the plane, rehearsed one day with the band at hand, and then opened myself up to the competition, politics, and envy of show business, filled with smilers concealing knives, and the sound of whispering behind closed doors. But I had met Arlyne Rothberg through David Steinberg. She took me on as her client and protected me. For fourteen years, I had the best.

I would be slow to understand the trap of showbiz, but by the time I had done a few more shows at the Troubadour, opening for Harry Chapin, Don McLean, and Kris Kristofferson, and then opening up at Carnegie Hall, Symphony Hall in Philadelphia, and in Boston Symphony Hall for Cat Stevens, I was caught under the udder of the cow. The smell of the crowd and the roar of the greasepaint. It was dangerous, but so very heady. As long as I was the opening act and the audience wasn't really expecting *some*thing from me, I could deliver a small set. I got comfortable speaking between songs. I didn't stutter very much. I can't explain it, though I think it had to do with having a good number of word substitutions. If I had had scripted introductions to songs, I wouldn't have had the easy mobility of being able to pause or to change a word. My stammer and I weren't paying quite the same kind of attention to one another. Maybe doing something that I admired myself for brought me out of it? With the exception of one review I remember that compared me to a whinnying horse, I was getting the kinds of reviews that said, "Watch out for Carly Simon, she's heading for the stars."

While in New York for our Carnegie Hall concert, I made a date with Cat Stevens. I invited him to my apartment for dinner. We had gotten to know each other while in L.A., but there had been other new friends there. Cat Stevens is a very cerebral and quiet-spoken man who dances out of that serene persona in his music when he goes for emphasis, for dynamics, for the big bang in a song. It has something to do with beauty by mistake. That chord that your fingers go to by accident and *that* takes the emotion around another corner from the one you expected, like the rock walls on the Vineyard. I learned it from listening to him while he was onstage, and from the hours and hours I listened to *Tea for the Tillerman*—till I was on my third vinyl copy. The night he was to come to dinner, I made chicken with cherries in a cream sauce and got a particularly nice wine. He was late. I got agitated. I closed my eyes in a deliberate attempt to relax and loosen up. I got lost in the boundaries of my expectation. Or was it fear? The darkness seemed infinite, which scared me. Would I ever be able to control my emotions? I let a sliver of light through my eyelids and by the time I did, the fear had changed. It became practical. I looked at my watch. He was still late. I took my guitar in my cold hands and determinedly wrote "Anticipation," sitting on my bed. It was all there. There was no time to wait for the song to emerge; he might arrive any second. The urgency brought it out. I sang it with a growl, the way he would: "I'm no prophet . . . I don't know nature's ways." I tore into those words with a gravelly passion, the way Steve (his name: Steven Demetre Georgiou) might break out of the placid phrase just before the arrival of the other side of the coin. Gravel, sparks, guitar on the offbeat! Dynamic lunge.

The song was all but finished by the time Steve arrived, but I didn't go anywhere near playing it for him. Curiously, I had much more energy before he arrived at my apartment. Being with him, I was willowy and slow. I dedicated my album to him, and it had that song as its leadoff, and "Anticipation" was always the title from that night on. He and I became lovers for a very fine, but short, while. It felt astral. It feels too private to speak of our two bodies together, and too tender and spiritual to actually refer to it as sex. I loved to watch him as he slept, as he looked at the sky, or a piece of art. He rarely asked questions. When he did, it was in a wonderfully scratchy bass voice that sounded like an old man of the woods telling a tale of those who had passed by his tree hundreds of years ago. He gave me whispers and drawings of Blake poems. He told me about his childhood, his mixed Greek and Swedish parents, and we made a connection that has lasted.

Paul Samwell-Smith was my producer that summer of 1971. He had come to see the show at Carnegie Hall because he was Cat Stevens's producer. Jac Holzman had wanted me to work with Paul and asked him to come and pay some special attention to the opening act. When I performed onstage, he liked me right away. He was determined to woo me. I couldn't have been more wooed. I wanted to *be* Cat Stevens if it was at all possible. We talked after the show, and it was right there with Jac and my new manager, Arlyne Rothberg, in the dressing room, that we made plans to start one month from then. Arlyne would come along, and I would take my band to England! My first recording experience in London. There would be a lot of Willie memories.

I began writing in earnest in preparation for recording in England. One day, standing in line to get my passport, I saw a headline in the newspaper a man was holding in front of me. It was about Hank Williams Jr.; the headline said: LEGEND IN HIS OWN TIME. I cast James Taylor for some reason as that particular "legend" and started a song about him, imagining that I knew him, and I indeed was advancing him into a "lonely boy when he goes home alone." I was going to rescue him.

I wrote another song called "Three Days," about Kris Kristofferson, whom I felt in goofy, fruitless awe of. I was playing as his opening act sometime that May at the Bitter End in New York, and then again at the Troubadour in L.A. We had a strong physical connection, but I couldn't be myself when I was with him. He made witty, flattering comments when he introduced me onstage: "Following Carly is like going from the sublime to the ridiculous." Mostly I was speechless. I looked and I watched and I tried to please him. I felt a little interchangeable with the many other girls he could have so easily charmed.

Those were the days when he was drinking so much that he was falling asleep onstage. Kris and I were not to be a couple, but it certainly fit the bill for a slam-dunk deranged month or so. Arlyne thought we made a great couple (we looked good together), and those were days, just as now, when those things were actually manufactured, or spurred on, by managers, agents, and press agents. There were no setup photographs or falsified dates, just an air of two pretty electric personalities who both found music quite close to laughter and sex, and our audience could be gripped in a possible plot—hot information worthy of passing on.

Mercifully, I found him fascinating, even though I didn't know how to find out who he really was. I did love singing "Help Me Make It Through the Night" with Kris, and I loved sitting on the bed in one of the many poorly lit hotel rooms he stayed in, learning and playing "I've Got to Have You" and helping to breathe new chords into the bridge, as if he could actually use them: "Wakin' in the morning to the tenderness of holding you asleep in my arms, dreamin' while your hair was blowin' softer than a whisper on my cheek . . ." How did he think of that utterly fragile combination of words? Kris, the man of soft lips and marble eyes sunken in snow? The simplest textures, the songs of a night bird? Every time I sing it, I think of him and what a wonder he is. I think he is magic, the bad boy who only shaves when he doesn't have to go to church.

I was already in London, living in a rented house across the street from Primrose Hill, that "soft summer garden," and recording with Paul, when I had to come back to do one concert in D.C. with Kris. It was one of the ones that acted as a deterrent to my doing other concerts. We were co-billed, and during "That's the Way I've Always Heard It Should Be," I had palpitations that launched me into one of the worst onstage experiences I'd had. Thank God it was the last song in my set. After Kris's last song, we had to grab our suitcases and guitars and get to the airport for the last shuttle to New York. We ran down the ramp inside the airport and managed to get in just before the door closed. We sat down (Kris in the window seat,

I on the aisle), and my pulse rate was about a hundred and wouldn't come down. The plane took off and I bent down and put my head in my lap. I was shaking as Kris read *The New York Times* and wrapped it around his head, like a tent. He didn't want anything to do with the possibly sick or frightened woman he had on his hands. He told me to call the stewardess. I spent the rest of our flight breathing into a brown paper bag. But both of us knew other things were coming. He was going in another direction where paper bags wouldn't be needed. And I was headed to where I didn't know, but I knew it wasn't with Kris. I didn't need someone who made me feel the onslaught of the Beast. I returned to London after that night. Funny how you remember things pared down to a single image: Kris with the newspaper wrapped around his head.

The rest of the recording went well, and the result is one of the more memorable records I have ever made: *Anticipation*. Paul was the ultimate producer for me in so many ways I needed. He was patient, and heard what he wanted and described it in ways that were just poetic enough but not overly flowery. He knew how to get a performance out of me, and was funny in a new way. I loved that way. I played on every track except "Summer's Coming Around Again." Oddly, the song that was hardest to cut was the title track ("Anticipation"). You'd have thought because I had sung it live so many times before going into the studio that it would have just rolled off the reel. Not to be. We were starstruck by the song already. Intimidated. We didn't know if we could make it as good a record as it already was a song. We could push it too far or leave crucial things out. Overproduction is a common enough worry. Paul would see how *little* production we could get away with. "Less is more" was his slogan. Andy Newmark, our drummer, was lying under the piano or beneath his drum kit for most of the day, and then was asked to play to my already clumsy (time-wise) guitar part, which is how the recording of most of the songs went. I almost always put down a guitar and vocal or piano and vocal first, and every other instrument was overdubbed by Paul and Jimmy and Andy, sometimes all together, sometimes one at a time. It made for an attractively empty, choppy, emotional album. My time was free flowing, erratic. I would linger long and not pick the time back up. One measure dipped or drooped into the next, hardly ever the same length as the next one or the one before. My band could only guess where the next downbeat might land. It wasn't going to be a dance record, but that was just fine with me. It is unlike anything I've recorded before or since.

Paul is an original, the likes of whom I have never known. I got to know him very well during the summer of '71, and we talked deeply, revealing our true selves. We talked about sadness, and I got furious in front of him and at him, and I walked out of the studio; we fought silently, viciously, then he very politely brought me back and fed me sausage sandwiches and very sweet tea. He was such a lovely, odd bird in the yard. He was elegant and had a marvelous vocabulary for subjects that were really quite obscene. He had worked with the Yardbirds as bass player for so many years and had plenty of experience with prima donnas. I was not a prima donna. Anyway, I sincerely didn't think so. I know that my demands can be ridiculous at times. They rarely come out of anything but fear. I can trace all my cancellations, all my refusals to perform, to when there is a plane trip involved. Of course it's all about being afraid. Paul spent lots of time patting me. He made me think it wasn't mad to feel the ceiling might fall in during the next take of "I've Got to Have You." He also gave every musician space and love. He appreciated every note and hesitation before a note.

Paul and I spent lots of time taking a day off here and there, driving all over the southern part of England in his Mini Cooper. There was a feast of delightful-enough B and Bs where we discussed the album, listening to it as we drove. We drank champagne, ate squab, made love in miniature bathtubs, and discussed matters that should have been private but weren't, because we'd had the champagne first. Then we'd drive back to London and its summer gardens, Primrose Hill and Morgan Studios. We conversationally assembled the new ideas conceived during our voyage into the hinterlands about backup vocals, string arrangements, and mixes. I didn't have any clear sense of having a singular emotional attachment; though I felt closest to Paul (Samwell-Smith), I have never been so influenced by any group of musicians as I was with Jimmy, Andy, and Paul Glanz, and people hanging out in the studio such as drummer Rick Marotta and Cat Stevens, who sang along with the rest of his band members on "Julie Through the Glass" and "Share the End." I was more Paul's girl than anyone else's, but the fluidity of relationships (at least mine) was such that you only changed a coat's lining, not the wool, cotton, or fur that made up the outer layer and thus the appearance. I was the girl of the band, and there weren't many in the mix who I didn't feel drawn to. I could see it all happening in the pages of rock 'n' roll literature and magazines. The seventies were dazzling and uninhibited, but in my dreams was that Golden Books image I would chase forever—the apple-pie-cooling-on-the-windowsill, married little wife with her devoted husband and perfect children swinging from the swing that was tied to the old oak in the backyard. Or was it a fruit tree? That tree would nourish love, keeping it safe from harm. It might be able to undo the haunting images of my parents' so-called marriage. I was counting on it.

What a perfect time to meet Warren Beatty.

Soft summer gardens.

*Me hailing a cab in New York City to get home
and cook crème brûlée for a big date.*

CHAPTER FIFTEEN

the potemkin hotel

When my charisma was at an all-time high, I had a visitor backstage at the Troubadour. In between shows during my first week opening for Cat Stevens, Warren came into my dressing room and feigned shyness. He was affecting a touch of the old "aw shucks" attitude. As he saw there was no one else around, he closed the door. He got very close to me, looked into my face, and looked down at my breasts, braless and curved bravely in an insinuating shape under my chamois shirt. He said: "Can I see you?"

I knew who he was, of course, before he introduced himself. In actual fact, there was no one who could match him. What a glorious specimen of man. He put them all to shame, if looks and charm were what you were after. He homed in like a tracking dog. It was mysterious because it worked and it shouldn't have. Now, when I say it worked, I mean it was irresistible. He had to have me as a notch in his belt, a belt where the greats could mix warmly with the rich, the famous, and the fair.

Warren was naturally skilled at keeping several women on the hook at the same time, but there was always one at the top. He had a list that he referred to as "the main loves of his life." We all likely have had lists like that. Warren's list was there on a piece of white paper in his pocket so he could take it out and show you. When he showed me, he added my name, to make me current (the main one at the top) so I could see that I was right up there above women like Catherine the Great, Marie Curie, Maria Tallchief, and Lillian Hellman. As I said, this shouldn't have worked, but this is a man who imitated nothing. He was completely himself, and though it is unlikely that he had had his heart too terribly broken, he could manifest both that sheepish look and the "bird with the broken wing" thing. He was such an actor that he could convince himself that he was vulnerable. Therefore by the time he communicated it to you, it wasn't false at all. The three or four women he held at any given time in his upper tier actually made his infidelity less onerous per capita than if there had been only one other.

Warren *always* phoned the next day. Sex was followed by a call. He referenced things only the two of you could ever know; the two of you together would be the only two in history to ever remember at exactly what time on the morning of June 17 the radio had come on with the Beatles song "Norwegian Wood" playing. He remembered the names of my mother, sisters, brother, grandmother, old boyfriends, streets where I lived five years ago. With this groundbreaking memory, he seldom if ever got confused.

I thought: What have I done to merit all this attention? Never have I had such a rush before. Not that I haven't been aware of my appeal to some men, but this was over the top. The only thing it could mean was that he was one of those men who believed that my interest in them would make them more attractive to other women. What did Warren want from the next woman before whom I was being dangled as a lure? Who could satisfy the craving enough to make him settle down? He was like Frank Sinatra in *The Tender Trap*.

But you must give Warren credit for loving women. He did and does love them. He's not alone, but he is privileged by being universally attractive. He became compulsive because he could. But in love he believed that you use everything you possess to make her play like a Stradivarius. You use your hands—every inch, pad, and tip—and your voice must be seductive and trained to envelop the object of your affection in the finest Indian silk.

He was just poetic enough, just passionate enough. How he was sincere is hard to understand, but he was sincere. I knew I could never have Warren even if I wanted him, so I didn't ever think to take him seriously. I was playing the game he was setting out.

Maybe Warren had questions about his lack of ability to maintain a relationship. If he questioned his ability to love, I can understand why he might, but I for one believe he can and does really love, and like the best of his kind, he can also "simulate" love. Maybe it was pure need, disguised as love, and likely he made sure he moved on before what was disguised as love would ever come to that.

I always imagined Warren as a train conductor. Potemkin was Catherine the Great's lover and the man who basically ran the Russian Empire during her reign. The story goes that Catherine had never seen the Ukraine before and was coming there to see how he had taken over as Governor of these devastated lands. Potemkin ordered his builders to construct miles of houses and splendid villages along the banks of the Dnieper River, so that when Catherine's barge arrived she and her visitors would see prosperity and order. But Potemkin realized that due to time constraints it would not be completed in time. He wisely instructed his builders to make exotic fronts of the houses and stores that could be seen from the river, much like a Hollywood set. "The New Russia" was a success. What a coup. So, I think of Warren as Potemkin, lining his psyche with such "sets." I can see him riding, the whistles starting to blow as he rounds the bend on the train. He, the conductor, would have a half smile on his face as he came within a mile of the station. He would get out his small case and polish his shoes. He would get off the train when it huffed to a halt and look up, now with a full smile, at his mark. I was where his gaze rested. I would wait in the second-story window, which of course was a shell, with two gauzy antique lace curtains blowing in the finest wind a stage director could imagine. I was in his hands.

The great slip-up, and there was one, yes, involved my analyst, Dr. L. The therapist who told me to jump into the deep end of the pool. The same one to whom I would have listened all session long on what he had to say about Utah. Whenever there was a slow moment, he would resort to travel suggestions, usually involving Utah. This is the way it went down:

Warren called me on a Sunday afternoon to tell me he was at the airport in L.A. and flying to New York. He would be in by twelve thirty or one, and would be over to my apartment as soon as he could get here. One caveat was that he was needed on the set for some early morning shots and would have to leave by 5:30 a.m. But he *had* to see me. He missed me. He couldn't wait to see me. I got undressed and put something on the stove, some buttery pudding-like thing with a brûlée crust on top in case he was hungry, but also, to live up to the whole fantasy that this amazing man, the most handsome and charming and sweet and funny and politically correct and extremely talented man, was coming to see me in the middle of the night. I think we had known each other for only about a month at that point, and maybe I had been his partner on the court five or six times. Evidently enough so that he had noticed by then that my thighs were, indeed, "poems." When he arrived at the apartment, he picked me up at the front door and carried me into bed (on which I had sprayed some very nice eau de cologne, which was supposed to pass as my inner self). We made love like in a movie. However, there were real sensations, for Warren was such a professional, the pressure points he knew about stirred a tremor in me, which meant that I left my head for a while, and all of a sudden we weren't in the movie anymore. Warren seemed to have just created a brand-new manual on how to make love—not too brazen, not just missionary, but not too many tricks either—and followed it so expertly while being at the same time attuned and sensitive to the response he was getting. He didn't speak. Didn't whisper, either. Didn't call you "darling" or "sweetheart" but used your name. How can one formula work for so many? That was his genius. Maybe I *was* in love. I certainly was starting to talk myself into it.

There was no heath or roaring surf, but Warren was a warrior prince and in his mind, there *were* those things; he conveyed them as he put his hand on the small of my back, balancing me just at the right angle.

He was up and in the shower by five and out the door with a piece of toast by five twenty. I then got a few hours of sleep and raced to dress and get in a cab and up to Ninety-sixth Street by eleven in time for my appointment with my beloved Dr. L.

"Whew!! What a night I had. Warren flew in at the last minute and didn't get to my apartment until one thirty, at which point I was already tired, but he had so much energy and my God, he's such a superman, I know what I've said about him in the past, how I believe he's better at playing him than anyone could ever be, and how it was even better having two of him: one 'him' and one him playing 'him.' But last night I felt as if there was only him, you know what I mean . . ."

It was then that I noticed Dr. L looked unwell. He had a pallor that scared me, and I thought he was going to be sick or do something violent or that he might die on the spot. I asked what was wrong and sat forward in my chair. He said:

"Under the circumstances, I can't withhold this. It's too much to believe . . . it's unbelievable, in fact . . . I suppose . . . I suppose I will tell you . . . that . . . You are not the first patient of the day who spent the night with Warren Beatty last night."

Well. Since I was his third patient, and it was only eleven, there technically could have been *two* others. If so, I wonder if Dr. L told patient number 2? Poor Dr. L must have in fact wondered whether we women hadn't put together some practical joke. He must have thought he was going crazy.

I wasted little time telling Warren. I knew he might have something to add, or refute. He did howl over the phone. I'm sure he was adding numbers and going over facts in his mind and maybe took out his calculator or his calendar. Could he have slipped up? Could this have really happened? All to his credit that he was up for the hilariousness of the situation. I suspect that the other woman (or women) wasn't any more hurt than I was, with her own protective gear, though I don't know that as a fact.

All the time, I could feel the speeding approach of some dénouement. And finally, all the players—myself and the two other girls (let's just say there were two, it's more fun that way)—were back at the Potemkin hotel, disappearing behind sets of diaphanous white curtains that flowed, getting more phosphorescent, dimmer and dimmer, into the nonexistent rooms. The train's engine became softer and more distant as the handsome, enigmatic train conductor stretched and took out a black notebook from his breast pocket. I could see that look come into his eyes as he slipped his hand into his back pocket and filled his palm with loose diamonds. He thought of the woman at the edge of the Caspian Sea and how he might anticipate her every whim—would twenty diamonds and a newly composed poem by Lord Byron suffice?

Me in the fantastic Potemkin Hotel.

BOOK THREE

Your smiling face.

CHAPTER SIXTEEN

carnegie hall

J oey saw a psychic in the early seventies and, when she asked about her sister Carly, she was told "cement is her enemy." This was already true, although I wouldn't have put it exactly that way. I don't like New York City very much, though I do respect it. Lots of cars have a detrimental effect on me, the surge of traffic intimidates me, and blaring horns horrify me. I hear everything louder than it is. I've been tested. I have always liked Mac-Dougal Alley, Washington Mews, Patchin Place, Beekman Place, Sutton Place, the out-of-the-way places, less-busy trails that I like to imagine lead into the woods.

As cars go faster and I am more aware of them, they obscure the things worth seeing in the city, like the architecture. When I was little, the cars went slowly, or we walked, and there was time to really *look*. My mother pointed out every lovely arch on every building. We had time for this kind of observation, even up to the late 1950s. And it wasn't possible in the same way afterward, once the speed limit was higher. Whizzing by the Dakota? The Empire State Building? The Chrysler Building? What if we had no cars and more magnificent new buildings?

I am a throwback to the nineteenth century—lamplight, horse-drawn carriages, long skirts, and coats with capes. Imagine how beautiful those nights would be. The Marble Palace and Macy's were the first department stores in the city, soon followed by B. Altman, Lord & Taylor, and many others. Bergdorf Goodman came along just after the turn of the century. I am drawn to that time period, and could sense it, just as it was totally disappearing when I was little. One's tastes are so affected by what movies we see and at what age we see them. I saw *Little Women* a few times and *Gone with the Wind* fourteen times when I was a young girl, so they obviously had an impact, and I remember watching Henry James's story *Washington Square* in its renamed movie version, *The Heiress*. I was born in the Village and lived there when I was little. And although I didn't like cars even then, I could see that some of them were quite lovely. I used to step on the running board of my father's wood-paneled Dodge station wagon from the 1940s, and I can still see him behind the steering wheel in his Don Draper hats and long tweed coats. I put one leg into the car followed by the other, and would have wanted to wear silk stockings and high heels, but Mommy said I couldn't balance until I was at least twelve. (Instead I wore overalls almost all the time, and sometimes if we went to the ballet I wore what Chibie used to call a "frock.")

I was home for the holidays, back in New York for Thanksgiving 1971, after a haze of last-minute plans. My diary for the first part of that year was lost in a checked suitcase on an American Airlines flight to Palm Springs, where I was going to an Elektra convention. Second in heaviness to the loss of my diary was the loss of my handmade Indian dress with sewn-in beads. That and a pair of chamois boots made up my alluring yet politically incorrect stage outfit (as the American Indians were being ripped off by Madison Avenue). Sure enough, so much was going on in a space of very little time that my calendars, which were luckily in my pocketbook on the plane, show a whirlwind of names, places, and momentous events that would come to shape the arc of my life.

On Thanksgiving that year, my single "Anticipation" was already high on the charts, and the album of the same name was just about to come out. I was just back from L.A. and coming off playing at the Troubadour, this time as the closing act. Drummer Ricky Marotta and I were spending time together. Our primary relationship was one of music, companionship, and the commonality of friends, and has endured many decades now. I sparked to him—his music and his humor were sexy to me.

At 7:30 p.m. on the night after Thanksgiving, I got a call from somebody in James Taylor's camp offering me two tickets to his concert at Carnegie Hall. ("Jesus-Mary-and-Joseph," as Allie, Chibie, and my mother all used to say when something came out of the blue.) I had no time to think, and moved fast. Ricky was up for it, and was incredibly funny in the limousine that was somehow extracted, as if by wizardry, from a garage in Queens to pick us up for the occasion. The lumbering twelve-seater was quiet as it took Ricky and me uptown, returning me to an older time in my New York psyche, back to childhood and those car rides into the shining nighttime city. Ricky and I had been smoking and writing some song or another and were dressed as we had been all day. I was wearing a white Nehru shirt made out of a cotton/nylon mix, a pair of jeans, and my red boots from Jac Holzman, all fitting for the folk-rock concert of my dreams. Rick's handsome face was dominated by his beard and long black horsetails that went halfway down his back. As we got out of the car, Carnegie Hall looked magnificent, like something thankfully emerging out of the past.

We entered and couldn't find our seats. We were late and our tickets hadn't been held for us at the ticket window, so we stood at the back of the theater until intermission. The first half of the show sounded just as great as on the records I was already addicted to. The band was the very same—and the most perfectly fitting band ever: Danny Kortchmar (or "Kooch"), Carole King, Lee Sklar, and Russ Kunkel, who had played with me in L.A. after James's motorcycle accident. The acoustics in Carnegie Hall then were the best in the country. James's voice was brilliant and clear and inviting. His band was so comfortable with all the songs, which they had performed so many times and played on *Sweet Baby James* and *Mud Slide Slim and the Blue Horizon*, the new album that had made James a major international star. As I watched him sing that title track, I could see the painting on the back cover of *Mud Slide Slim* written all over it. It was painted by

Laurie Miller, and showed the "cabin in the woods" that James had written about, the one built (as the song goes) by "Jimmy, Jimmy, John, Luke, and Laurie, No Jets Construction." (Little did I know that I'd meet all of them, and begin to see that shack come to life, only a week later.) He sang all the songs I loved and had learned by heart, material from his first two albums, as well as "You've Got a Friend," the single that had gone to number 1 on the charts that summer. It was thrilling that I was so close to him. I felt a zigzagging child's energy in my limbs, and I was smiling so broadly that my cheeks must have grown permanently wider that night.

At intermission, about forty minutes after we got there, Ricky and I walked around the lobby and were corralled by Nat Weiss, James's lawyer, who introduced himself. "Do you want to come meet James?" Nat asked me. "The intermission lasts another fifteen minutes."

Awkwardly, I asked Ricky if it was all right with him if I went backstage with Nat. Implying, alone. "You bitch," he replied instantly—and continued talking to some friends he'd run into. It was funny. Our friendship has lasted far longer than my relationship with anyone else who was there that night. Nat and I went upstairs to the band's dressing room, where food was spread out on a big table and there was a trash can of ice that had every kind of cola and spritzer and Sprite-like thing you could imagine. It served as the central fire pit of the room. Everyone seemed to be enjoying the sparks, as though there were marshmallows to roast.

James was talking to a petite beauty with a big personality and major voice, Abigale Haness, who I thought was probably his girlfriend. It turned out she was with Kooch, but I was still hit in the chest with unreasonable jealousy, just as I had been when I first saw a photograph of James and Joni Mitchell together in *Rolling Stone* at least a year before. I greeted Kooch, whom I had known since we were small children on the Vineyard riding tricycles and then bicycles down to Menemsha Village. I gave Russ a big hug. He introduced me to Carole King and Lee Sklar. I avoided looking at James with the energy of someone dying to look but not yet brave enough.

Kooch ran over the set list for the second half of the show and finalized it. Abigale slid her hand through Danny's arm, like an animal making claims on her turf. Once I laid eyes on James, a sense of possession overtook me, as if a dog fence of little white flags had sprung out of the ground around him. The women on the periphery knew just how far back they must stay from that fence to avoid getting an unpleasant little jolt through their system. Jock, the road manager, called out, "Five minutes," and James changed into a white button-down shirt. I noticed a turquoise belt around the waist of his pants. It was a dragon or snake of some kind. A fan had made it for him.

He turned toward me, and his eyes hadn't even met mine when I said, before I could think, "If ever you want a home-cooked meal while you're here in New York, I'd love to make lunch for you."

He looked somewhere in the direction of my chin, with a quick shutter-snap of his eyelids, and answered: "What about tonight?"

"Okay, sure, sure," I said. "Yeah, please let's. Sure, lunch."

The remaining half of the show was more of Ricky calling me "bitch" half kiddingly and sitting and watching from seats that had been vacated by a critic who'd gone home to put the flourishes on his review. Ricky turned to me at one point and teased, "How much would you pay me to convince one of the critics to say in tomorrow's review: 'God's truth! James Taylor must have fallen in love between the first and second halves of his show. He was a different man—vibrant in his step and delivery . . . before, he was just muddling through, a man with his beer in front of the television set waiting for another night to pass.'"

There was a party in someone's hotel room after the show. Peter Asher and his wife Betsy were hosting it, and the rest of the band, friends, partners, and lawyers were in attendance. James whisked me around the room, and I remember dancing with him fast, led by his hands and not his whole frame. He had a lot of energy or after-show buzz. I was thrust from right to left like a new thunderbird in the hands of a teenager. It was more of a polka or a square dance. Nothing at all intimate. What was the song? I don't remember, but after it ended, I was introduced to Betsy Asher, who had a lot of power and mother-hen aura about her. She was tall and strawberry blond. Elegant and proud, first class, but approachable.

Peter Asher was so many things to me over so many years, including being Peter of the mid-sixties pop act Peter and Gordon, but he was largely James's manager and producer, and my impressions were all good. He and Nat Weiss were both running the show at its highest level. James depended on Peter and Betsy like Mom and Dad. They were a sounding board for his new songs, and he'd lived with them in London when he made his first two albums. Of course I was anxious about the impression I was making. James and I were dancing pretty wildly—putting on a show.

This night . . . this night was going to mean so very much to me.

Intending to figure out later what the home-cooked lunch was going to mean at this hour, James and I walked to the East Side and then downtown on Christmas tree–lit Park Avenue, all the way to Jake's apartment on Thirty-sixth Street. James wanted to get some weed, and I figured Jake would be the most likely candidate. Jake's social life spun its net in his Bloomsbury-like living room, and there was always pretty much whatever you wanted in the way of intoxicants. I rang the bell and Jake was in, and probably quite surprised (Jake is hardly ever really shocked) to see me standing there with James Taylor. I don't remember the conversation except, as we were getting ready to leave, James put on Jake's shoes by mistake. Jake said something that wasn't meant to offend James, but did. He quoted the Dylan line from "Positively 4th Street"—"If you could stand inside my shoes, you'd know what a drag it is to see you." He could have misquoted the line, but whatever, the words hurt James's feelings, and as we left Jake's apartment and walked the block to my place, I saw the same sensitive side of James as I did in so many of his songs that I already knew and loved. The hurt little boy coming out was very appealing to me.

I was nervous riding up in the elevator in my building, which was old-world and slow. Once inside my apartment, we smoked the joint we'd started at Jake's house and then, with the grace of a couple of gazelles just learning to walk, made our way to the kitchen and the refrigerator for the promised home-cooked lunch, which was Sara Lee banana cake, first one whole loaf and then another. Perfect for our first meal together.

I'm sure we were thinking along the same lines: What next? I want to kiss him—will he think I'm forward? Should I kiss her? Oh my, I feel a little too stoned. And other baby gazelle thoughts.

I have a peevish urge to show off new things that I've just recorded. It's an unattractive trait, as I see it now—overanxious and forward. It was a crack in the façade that the Beast could find its way into. As I had just brought home the mastered version of the album *Anticipation* the day before Thanksgiving, I was eager to show something of myself to James, hoping it would cut the mustard. I played a few songs and James was getting either fidgety or tired. He said, "Can we go lie down on your bed? I do mean just 'lie down.'" He spoke like a southern gentleman asking if he might remove his rain boots in the mudroom.

We moved into the bedroom, where the bed was still unmade and clothes were all over the cramped space. I turned off the light and lit a small candle. Only some muted sounds of traffic out on Thirty-fifth Street altered an otherwise perfect silence. James undressed quickly, left on his jockey shorts, and got under the covers. I took off my clothes, almost as if we were camping out together, trying to underplay the obvious sexual tension, and left on just a black silk camisole and white cotton underpants. I got halfway in bed, beside him. The revelation was as shocking as I thought it might be. The connecting of our skin went more than inches. It went flesh to bone, seemed to move with our blood, through vein and artery pumping back through lungs. I was aware that my heart was beating fast. The soft and the hard, the first kiss on the lips, lingering and marveling at its perfect pressure. I moved away, down just a little, beneath the soft sheets and quilt. Then, I stabilized my hand on his arm, pulled gracefully away from his face and his perfect warm lips, and eased my way into his angles, as if I'd always known them. I looked for his eyes. It was almost completely dark in the room. I didn't know if he saw me. Then I lay half on top of him. Slung like a gun in a holster, ready to make a move. It was the nicest contact I could ever know, could ever have asked for, or ever remember. We were the same length in limbs. He was four inches taller and his torso was much longer than mine, but it felt as though a manufacturer of bodies had copied our limbs and made them a perfect double.

Soft. We were sheep whose fleece covered every hard place. We curled. We breathed on each other's necks, we moved our limbs gently and discovered the surface of each other's skin. Very little hair covered either of us. Not the wool of sheep, it was just skin, tender as rose petals. I was too trembly to know where the feeling was coming from, but James breathing on my hair and my ear made rise in me a desire which I couldn't move to the music of because I thought I must respect the decision that we would just go to sleep. I liked the notion that we could always say to our grandchildren, in-laws, shopkeepers: "We didn't make love right away." *Blossom smile some sunshine down my way* . . . my lips moved very slightly, silently. We'd see what happened when we woke. I placed my right leg over his thighs—I didn't know where else to go—and my right arm rested across his chest. I laid my head on his shoulder and found the cranny that sloped down toward his chest. This was a chest I had yearned to lay my head on. In the near past, when I'd harmonized alone in my room to "Circle Round the Sun," I had imagined being in the circle of his arms.

"We should just go to sleep" was the gentle, unspoken suggestion from the man I had already loved for a year or more. I had spent every day with headphones on, listening to his second album, *Sweet Baby James*, and harmonizing with every song, imagining looking into his eyes and singing with him. While singing along to James's songs, though, I felt a similarity of outlook on the world and a sense of becoming part of the song, part of the story, the voice, and even part of a future, as if I could visualize future generations. Years before, I had learned "Circle Round the Sun" and had performed it as my solo when Lucy and I were the Simon Sisters. This year, listening to James's first album, I had relearned the folk song as James sang it, harmonized and phrased as he did, only altering the arrangement a little. Our versions could have been superimposed on each other's. I was in the circle of his love.

These are things I thought about as James fell asleep and began breathing with a regularity and a soft sound that was sweet like the breath of a newborn baby. Awake still, I was left alone with my desire, but I felt the merging of a part of our union that went much closer. This was the same preadolescent, knobby-kneed boy who had been subconsciously making his way around my dreams for years. The same boy who had helped himself to my vanilla pop on the porch at Sewards when he was barely a teenager.

I don't think I experienced more than a slight dimming of my consciousness in the two hours between the time James fell into his soft space of slumber and the time he woke up. I was lying fairly awake with his songs going around in my head until there was a blending of sounds, both silent, of the feminine and masculine, and I coaxed my songs to melt into his. My lips moved silently. "His pastures to change . . . deep greens and blues are the colors I choose . . . down in my dreams . . ."

I was singing to him in my brain, the part of it that was so thoughtfully unthinking. Singing and singing. "Blossom, smile some sunshine down my way . . . lately I've been lonesome." The songs topsy-turvied on each other, and I remained restless and especially inspired. "There's a well on the hill, you just can't kill for Jesus, there's a well on the hill, let it be." And then I sang my own lyrics, already about him: "Then you turn on the radio and sing with the singer in the band, and think kind of sadly to yourself, this isn't exactly what you had planned . . .'cause you're a legend in your own time, a hero in the footlights, playin' tunes to fit your rhyme, but a legend's only a lonely boy when he goes home alone."

James was my muse, my Orpheus, my sleeping darling, my "good night, sweet prince," my something-in-the-way-he-moves. The bedroom was quiet and dark, with only a few slats of light through the louvered shutters. I ran the fingers of my right hand very softly on his left arm to his shoulder, over his slopes, lightly so as not to wake him.

He had said the night before, when we moved from the living room into the bedroom, "Let's just go to sleep." I agreed heartily. Let's put off what we're both pretty scared of, I thought. He added that we had both been playing the field and this shouldn't be like that. We knew it wasn't going to be a one-night stand. There were many things we both knew already. Many years later he would accuse me of loving him for "being James Taylor," which ironically he meant disparagingly. But it was right on, and a very accurate description of the way I felt.

It was just becoming light outside, and in the bedroom I could see the closet door with the mirror, which caught a part of our bodies in a gray charcoal mist.

Everything else was blurry, and the one candle that had breathed through

230 | CARLY SIMON

the night was still by far the brightest thing in the room. Our bodies were still in a graceful tangle. I hadn't moved once except to relieve numbness in one of my legs by very slowly gliding my ankle from beneath his calf. He hadn't stirred then, but when he did finally stir, he woke up amorous. He kissed me right away. So natural and simple was the gesture. I let his lips surround mine. With two sets of eyes closed, two sets of lips can find each other.

He was relaxed, and our bodies did that Bali Ha'i dance, hardly any sound but those of waves breaking and blankets moving and pillows muffling the high-end frequency of the sheets brushing together. The amount of energy that had collected during the two hours (mine, as I held still, and his, as he dreamed) gave way to openness unattended by self-consciousness. James lay on top of me and kissed me and I returned his love. There are different characteristics in the sounds that notes make when they are played together. That's what we were, just two notes.

I felt we were a perfect fourth. I came to feel that I was the F-sharp and he was the C-sharp. Lots of singing together over the years seemed to bear this out. Our voices were so perfectly complementary and harmonized so well. His voice, his tone so clear and fine, inserted itself like the sound of an oboe cutting through the breathy rise of an alto flute. This music theory, and theory of love, has not been confirmed or proven. Like some things, maybe it's only true if I continue to believe it.

At my sixth-floor apartment in Murray Hill, New York City, sometime during the first month of our romance. We have no secrets.

Building a tool shed and other spaces onto James's shack,
with Zack Weisner and No Jets construction, 1971.

CHAPTER SEVENTEEN

choppin' wood

The Vineyard is about a hundred square miles total, with six towns in all. Edgartown, Oak Bluffs, and Vineyard Haven are on the north-ernmost part of the island, and considered "down-island," while West Tisbury, Chilmark, and Aquinnah (known for a long time as Gay Head) are all considered "up-island." Down-island is where most of the commerce takes place—little shops, bigger shops, auto and hardware stores, bakeries, and groceries—and while there are a few scattered stores, up-island land undulates like a lullaby, and you see farms and huge green stretches of ocean-facing land, fenced in or surrounded by rock walls, some four or five generations old, farmers and their children, horses, pigs, cows, chickens. Crisscrossing the island are three main roads, South, Middle, and North. Off the main roads are funky offshoot places like Menemsha, a tiny fishing village on the northwest coast on Vineyard Sound, as well as assorted ponds, and the steep, dramatic Gay Head cliffs facing due west.

When I was little, my family would always rent or borrow houses up-island, either in Chilmark, Menemsha, or West Tisbury. Like us, the Taylor family, who started coming to the island in 1953, were up-islanders, living in a house in Chilmark. Unlike Mommy and Daddy, who always rented, the Taylors were serious islanders, at first summers-only until Trudy, James's mother, made the beautiful, rustic house on Stonewall Beach in Chilmark a full-time residence.

With our Martha's Vineyard connection, James and I talked about the island in a kind of shorthand, as if we shared a secret language we had both grown up speaking—which, in fact, we had. Almost as soon as we met, we started making plans to go there, excited to see places together that we both knew so well and had seen, without the other around, for decades. James's soul was on the Vineyard, on his land, and mine would eventually make its full-time home there, too. Like his father, who had bought a section of the tip of Gay Head, James had found and bought his own large piece of land in 1969, but on the other end of the island, in the Lambert's Cove region of Tisbury—175 acres of woods, mainly scrub oak, tangles of lady's slippers, wild berries, cedar, cypress, and pine. James had gotten a good deal, too, buying the land with the money Apple Records gave him for his first album. Aside from wild and rolling, it was private, close enough to his parents' place for easy get-togethers. He shared the property with an enormous pig named Mona and his puppy, David, who was part wolf, part German shepherd. James's plan was to build a homestead up on the hill, and he was naturally eager to show it to me.

After that first night, James moved into my Murray Hill apartment immediately, the seamless meshing of the gears of our lives already perfectly in place, as if they had been in place forever. There was no sense of pressure, no sense of hurry. Later that morning, the two of us collected all his bags and baggage from the Barbizon-Plaza, stuffing messages into a small suitcase that said JT on it. He packed another suitcase with lots of pairs of dog-chewed sneakers. James's hotel room was as chaotic as a teenage boy's. James left a twenty-dollar bill behind for the housekeepers, but everything else we lugged back to Murray Hill—and for the next span of time, he and I were never apart for more than a few days.

The day after we spent our first night together, we walked up to Manny's Music on Forty-eighth Street. Our entrance into the store turned into a milestone of sorts, marking us officially as a couple, the musical equivalent of a banner advertisement. Henry Goldrich, who owned Manny's, made a huge fuss, even asking if he could put our photos together on the store's Wall of Fame. Of course, we both answered, we'd be honored. Our pictures were already in residence, but far apart, so Henry moved mine over so it hung next to James's, prominently, too, at eye level.

Less than two weeks later, we drove to the Vineyard in James's green truck, to see his "cabin in the woods"—the "shack," as James kept on referring to it. Having spent my Vineyard summers up-island, I had always dreamed of having a house there someday, maybe in Chilmark, directly on the water. In contrast, James's formidable property seemed in some way out of place, as if it should be on the south coast. The land was closer to the down-island sections of the Vineyard I knew far less about, near the water, but with no access to the beach. It was as though James were emphasizing the importance, and value, of upholding a more modest workaday image—announcing to the world that he wasn't the son of an esteemed physician who'd gone to Harvard, but instead he himself was a man who worked with his hands and had the calluses to show for it. Neither of us imagined how the land would become a life-long work-in-progress.

I remember our arrival, our first night there. We turned off Lambert's Cove Road into James's driveway, driving the quarter-mile distance extremely slowly, as the moon rose up in the east, to our left, seeming to follow us as we made our way along the long dirt road. James told me later how nervous he was about what I would think, worried that I might be one of those uptight New-York-at-heart girls rigidly opinionated about the peasant hierarchy. Ahead of us I could see the outlines of what looked like a romantic music box of a house. It was James's cabin, silhouetted in the moonlight. The pitch of the roof was steep. The windows were high and narrow. Everything about the house was like James himself: tall, lean, modest, and beautiful.

Only two pale lights shone from the cabin—one downstairs, one upstairs. Before untangling ourselves from the truck, crawling over shopping bags, luggage, and McDonald's debris, James did a lot of fumbling around for the right disclaimers about the place, not only to alert me to things I might not immediately love, but also to apologize for how rough and unfinished it was.

He reemphasized that it was a "shack," and indeed, when I walked through the door, I could see that he was telling it like it was. There was no threshold for him to carry me across, not that I was expecting one, and I would later come to learn that that kind of fairy tale moment was not in James's mind-set anyway. I was the romantic, mistletoe-kissing one, not him. He was the no-frills, down-to-earth, Yankee-influenced, practical madman.

James's cabin was still at a pretty rustic stage in its construction—two tall rooms and not much more. Four steps down from a landing was a living room with a wood-burning Franklin stove, all lit up and keeping the house toasty. Above the stove was a wooden grate that carried the heat upstairs to a second story, and above that, a small loft. The wood trim throughout the house was oak and pine, and the bare floors were covered here and there by throw rugs. In one corner of the first-floor living room was an almost five-foot-high pyramid of letters—James's unopened fan mail, a white mountain that was beginning to spill down, cascade, and overwhelm the room. Nearby was a pullout couch where James and I would later turn in for the night, and the walls were lined with books and nails where coats, vests, towels, pants, shirts, bathrobes, pliers, hammers, saws, and other tools were hanging. The small bathroom featured an antique toilet with a pull chain, a deep tub, and a mirrored cabinet above a small tin sink. The bathroom had no door, and the bathtub had no curtain. James soon bought waterproof material and sewed one himself, using fishing line threaded through a needle with a huge eye.

On the other side of a counter, dividing it from the living room, was the kitchen. *Kitchen* really meant four burners, a sink, and a small fridge beneath a counter. Kate, James's sister, was there when we walked in, making Toll House cookies, and she welcomed us as if we were two tall, lost, rosy-cheeked children from a Swedish fairy tale. Since I had met Kate a few times, and loved her right away, I couldn't have been happier to see her.

The next morning, we took a long walk around the property (I borrowed Kate's walking shoes). James led me around low forests of crowded new-growth pine and scrub oak, autumn clematis, and blueberry bushes that the first frost had almost flattened to the earth, all belonging to James. The property felt so grown-up. What did landownership really mean? I suppose my parents—and other grown-ups—knew those rules and answers, but

I didn't, not then. There were deep crevasses in the land, rolling hills and steep ridges, as if the entire property had been carved during some kind of major glacial activity eons earlier. It was, and is, the hilliest part of the island. Like the rest of the north side of the island, the soil was generally sandy but heavy and fertile enough to nourish tall trees and fat vegetables over time, and though James's land wasn't on the water, it was close enough for the air to smell of salt and sea.

That day, and other times, too, James described his vision: fields as far as the eye could see. He would clear the woods in order to create them. Wheat and rye and oats. He would plant willow trees and a golden chain tree by the beautiful natural pond near the entrance of the driveway, a pond James would eventually christen Carly's Bottom, as a tribute to his new lady's derriere. He described the many varieties of trees he would plant, too—beeches, Atlas cedars, dogwoods, mimosas, Colorado spruces—and where exactly he was planning on building a shed for his tools, and a barn for the horses he'd soon own. He cared about trees the way I did. There was frequently some strong-armed man pruning, molding the shape of them.

I didn't doubt him for a second. Already he was having rock walls constructed by a local artisan, one of the many builders who were helping James bring his vision to life. There was a young group of hippies who lived off James's land and built things with their hands and hung out at James's cabin, contributing their ideas, aptitudes, and skills. At the time I couldn't have dreamed of the powerful hold that James's cabin would come to have over me. During my first few visits, not wanting to be intrusive, I remember I was hesitant about making any suggestions at all, especially as James's vision for the place was still developing, and he'd done everything from sawing and nailing wood to hand-sewing the shower curtain. Should I, maybe, propose he put a door on the bathroom? Or was that too conventional an idea, the sort of overly civilized suggestion that defied the very notion of living a plainspoken Vineyard life? Maybe it was only that I didn't want to let on that I was pre-nesting as hard as I was. *(Caution: comfort ahead!)* James and I didn't talk about any of this right away, and certainly not about where the two of us would live if we stayed together. But one night, full of love, James had a prescient moment. If our relationship lasted, and if we got married someday, he told me, we would have two children. First would come a little girl whom we would name Sarah, and then, a couple of years later, a boy, whose name, he told me, would be Ben.

During that first Vineyard trip, James and I spent a lot of time with Kate. A naturally talented beauty with big blue eyes and a kind, especially gentle spirit, Kate was living year-round on the island and sleeping on a second pullout couch on the cabin's second floor. Kate was a musician and a weaver—a singer with a guitar, a spinner with a loom, and she had a mutt named Rodeo—and James, her older brother, was highly protective of her during a vulnerable time in her life. At the time Kate was going out with a scary giant of a boy named Hank. Hank was a local, a former Green Beret and Vietnam vet, whose family had a reputation for extremes. His mother owned a shotgun that she would aim right at you if you got too close to her property, and Hank's sister, who was erotically fixated on James, once clung on to James's truck door even when he tried to drive away from her (James ended up driving over her foot by accident, without doing any damage). Kate's boyfriend—maybe *pursuer* was the better word—had come right out and said, or maybe threatened, that he had nine lives, three of which he hadn't yet lived.

Kate, though, was wisely getting ready to break things off with Hank. One night, "The Man from 'Nam," as James later named him, was upstairs on the second floor with Kate, and James, hearing a male voice whose tone he didn't quite trust, became nervous on his sister's behalf. Like the rest of his clan, Hank had an aggressive reputation, but that didn't stop James. He headed up to the second floor and, with a raised but courteous voice, asked Hank to leave. In no way could you ever describe James as a shouter. His personality style is like his music—quiet, downplayed, courtly—and his rare outbreaks of anger show themselves in the style of a southern gentleman, which he was and still is, I'm assuming. Tonight, though, he was facing a soldier and a war veteran who believed he still had a few lives remaining. What was called for was surely more than what James was accustomed to, or what made him comfortable, and his typical dulcet tones, irony, and dry subtlety would have been lost on Hank anyway. I waited downstairs, listening to a very tense back-and-forth confrontation. A minute or two later, Hank came down the stairs, swearing at top volume, slammed the door, and left the house. James came down, looking shaken, but when I told him how brave he was to have stood up to Hank, he shrugged, as if to imply: *Well, what else was I gonna do?* Then he announced that he was going outside to chop some wood.

James left the cabin, trekking through the woods to the woodpile. It was a frigid night, I remember, with a nearly full moon. I soon heard the sounds of hard, successive pounding. James must have been relieved, and proud of himself, for standing up to Kate's miserable Green Beret. Maybe he was punishing himself, too, picking up an ax and taking out whatever violence he fantasized doing to Hank against a pile of helpless logs. I couldn't help but think of the Philip Larkin lines in the book of poems Willie gave me: "This is the first thing / I have understood: / Time is the echo of an axe / Within a wood." Then, abruptly, the sounds of chopping stopped, and James yelled out into the moonlit night:

"CARLY, I LOVE YOU!"

When he returned to the house, he laid a few pieces of newly split wood inside the Franklin stove and lit it on up (James always "lit it on up," striking a match on the underside of the kitchen counter or against the sole of his shoe). Once he got the fire going, he closed the stove's glass doors and turned out all but one small lamp near our pullout bed. Before retiring, he went back upstairs to check how Kate was faring. The way I saw it, that night James had seized the moment, protected his sister, had a catharsis, and in a fit of love-crazed wood chopping, sung my name up to the moon. And I was letting that love shine in, shining it back at him in return. To me, being with James wasn't so much a decision as a kind of magical predestination.

Reappearing downstairs, James vanished into the doorless bathroom, where he washed the soot and ash off his hands. Still dressed and wearing his boots, he approached our bed in no hurry at all. His boots (I remember they were made by a company called White's) made him a good two inches taller than his already tall, toned, six-foot, two-and-a-half-inch frame. He wore a light-brown-and-blue-plaid workman's shirt. His turquoise belt buckle was loosened, and his jeans, baggy in the knees and unbuttoned at the waist, hung down unevenly over his boots. In the lamplight, I could see his eyes: blazing blue. Even though the room wasn't entirely dark, I'd never seen that color blue light up the dark in such a way, those two eyes gazing at me wide open, a breathing, cursing, loving, yearning blueness that touched me beyond all words.

As James came toward me, the space between us got smaller and smaller, and our perpendicular lines, with the surge of a waterfall, became parallel. Our life together would go on in just this way for quite some time.

From the beginning, James and I were linked together as strongly as we were not just because of love, and music, but because we were both troubled people trying our best to pass as normal. The lengths both of us had to go to *act* as though we felt at ease in the world was a strain. It was a comfort to have in each other a relief from our private, individual craziness. James, of course, had been famously written about before we met. As a student at Milton Academy, the prep school outside Boston, he'd left school his junior year and gone into McLean Hospital, which also provided schooling. Many of his songs from his first album, including "Night Owl" and "Knocking 'Round the Zoo," were written either about the people or the situations he had encountered there. Whatever his diagnosis was, it was likely complex, part of that marvelous, difficult brain that led him to depression and drug addiction. Both were, and are, so much a part of each other.

As for me, if I was in trouble, James always rescued me, though I knew he felt he didn't belong on this earth as much as I did. I don't know if he really understood my own alienation and feelings of being on the outside almost all the time. Except when I was with him. I preferred focusing on James, no matter the situation, and if I could be helpful I would always try. (Of course, this occasionally led to me trying too hard, and being a nudge, or annoying, or cloying, or in general overdoing it.) If James was suffering, his pain diverted my attention away from myself, the result being that I agonized about myself less. It's like being a parent: you may be suffering from the worst migraine on earth, but if your child is sick, your self-centered immersion fades into irrelevance and gives itself over instead to the purity and relief of selfless caretaking. In her novel *The Shadow Knows*, the writer Diane Johnson describes a character holding her children's hands as they cross the street. The woman wonders how her children can possibly trust her since her capacity to trust herself is so fragile. The same was true for James and me. For the next decade, he and I would grip each other's hands against the ever-onrushing traffic of the curious, the jealous, the smilers with knives.

For the first few months, James and I traveled back and forth from New York to the Vineyard, where we splashed on some new paint, pounded a few nails, and cleared some fields, while planting some new, real trees (anything but the prodigious oak or pine). On Lambert's Cove, there was always the beauty of the outdoors, wood to chop, sassafras to be plumbed for tea, a basement to clean. Owning a place, I was finding out, was a lot different from renting. For example, I never even knew if there *was* a basement in our Thirty-fifth Street apartment building.

In New York, we felt as though we didn't want to socialize other than coparenting James's giant puppy, David. We cooked, got stoned, and ate. James had a few dishes he would eventually become well known for: beans, for one, an altogether remarkable Jamesian recipe, containing lots of garlic and onions, steeping for days. James slept late most days, and at night, he and I went out with Arlyne or socialized with Jake, Carinthia, Ellen, David, and Mary Ellen. Neither of us was really comfortable with friends *or* idle time. Accustomed to being "on" when we were out in public, being alone in our apartment felt like an almost foreign notion—and almost always: a huge relief. We got antsy, restless, eternally juggling ideas about what to do and when to do it, quickly becoming irked with ourselves if we stayed home when so many people expected us to attend their shindigs, shows, or get-togethers.

Our relationship was only three months old when I went out to L.A. to record a demo, while James stayed behind in New York to help record a few cuts for Abigale Haness, the girl backstage at the Carnegie Hall concert who would later marry Danny Kortchmar. Early one morning, my phone rang. It was 3 a.m. Los Angeles time, 6 a.m. East Coast time. It was James, and the story he told me had nothing to do with Abigale's recording session but, instead, with the eccentric plumbing in our Stanford White apartment building. James had been taking a shower that morning when the hot water quit. Finding himself suddenly under a deluge of icy water, he shut off the cold faucet, forgetting to turn off the hot. He went about his business, spending the rest of the day recording Abigale up in Nyack, an hour north of New York. Sometime during the day, our building's hot water came back on—including, of course, the water in the shower stall. When he returned to our apartment, it looked like a Ukrainian steam room, minus the old naked men. The living room wallpaper was curling off in strips. The photos and posters had begun a slow curtsying peel inward, and my record collection was warping. All our photos were ruined, though some I eventually straightened out between the pages of heavy books. We ultimately had to move out for three months while the entire place got re-wallpapered.

Less important than the wallpaper was the moment I learned what had happened. "Is this Carly?" said the familiar gentle voice on the other end. "This is James Taylor." Not *James*, but *James Taylor*. As if, after four months of propinquity at its finest, he feared I might possibly confuse him with another James. In tension, James's good manners came out, his civility, his old-fashioned North Carolina gentlemanliness. I honestly couldn't have cared less about the hot water or the wallpaper or the condition of our record albums, all of which seemed absurd and could be replaced: the only thing I cared about was that the sweetest, kindest, least replaceable man on earth was on the other end of the phone.

"My Darling James," I wrote in my diary around that time, "you are so rare in my life. Such a special thing. I pray nothing will ever make you less so. I've never felt so close to anyone in so many ways. That's the thing—the combination of closeness. I've had sisters and friends I could share intimate thoughts with, and men I could love but not talk to—uncles and aunts I could easily live with, and men I could talk to, but not love—I've had a dog I could snuggle up to and bathtubs that could surround me with warmth, and a grandmother who impressed eccentricity in its dearest forms upon me—but you, my Darling, leave me in a new space. You're all in one and then some more."

It was true. From the first time I saw a picture of him, James was it—the ultimate Orpheus of all my fantasies. He was smart. He was funny. He was beautiful to look at, a long, lean, poetical stalk of a man. He was anyone's romantic ideal of a poet and musician, and listening to him, I felt sometimes as if no one had ever had to teach him anything, that he'd been born simply knowing things. There's little doubt that the amount of attention James was getting at the time also intimidated me. In the early seventies, James Taylor was the most talked-about singer and composer in music, and everyone wanted him, though I never would have believed that kind of thing would have impressed me. I felt another thing, too: if James fell in love with me, then I could never doubt myself, or my own attractiveness, ever again. (Yeah, sure. And no. But I'll get to that.) Then, too, James also reminded me of my own father—that combination of musicianship, worldliness, and dryness, as well as the physical height, mixed with an obscure darkness and sadness, qualities hinting at something beyond what was visible. My father had been present but absent, and James had something of this same characteristic: *I'm just visiting—this apartment, this city, this earth.* Daddy had almost never looked me in the eye for more than a moment, and James, too, had a habit of breaking his gaze, mostly to glance downward at his own feet.

Several years later, when Jake became a devotee and student of Sufism, I found out about an extremely intimate practice called *trespasso* that I persuaded James to do with me. Sitting across from each other, I gazed into one of James's eyes for ten minutes, after which we were supposed to reverse roles, with James's two eyes gazing intently into one of mine. After ten minutes, we were supposed to do the same with the other eye. James, I remember, hated this. He could only look at me with anger, as if I were violating his very mind and soul, possibly because I'd pressured him into doing this strange thing with me in the first place. I wasn't altogether comfortable with trespasso myself—it made me self-conscious, and I was acutely aware of James's own discomfort. I remember being taken aback by how furious James became during even the first two or three minutes our eyes came together. His expression was closed, but I could feel the waves of aggression coming off him, too.

When James and I became a couple, a famous couple—more in print and in the imagination of our fans, maybe, than in our bedroom and living room—I found out that the same fire that ignited our relationship could turn to icy silence, to "no-ness," to "can't-go-there-ness," to "we don't talk about that-ness." I accepted this duality along with the rest of the package that was James Taylor, probably because I was accustomed to the same quality in my own father. Besides, as Mark Twain once said, "Everyone is a moon, and has a dark side which he never shows to anybody." "Angry dawns" once again! James, then, may have been my charmed Orpheus, but he was also Heathcliff, flirting with shadows and demons both hot and cold.

There was also the matter that we were both performers, and both very much in the news. It—my career, and the attention I was getting—had happened fast. First came the shows with Cat Stevens, followed by shows with Kris Kristofferson, Don McLean, and Harry Chapin. After James and I got together, I'd joined him on a multicity tour, performing around ten shows in all. A few months into our relationship, in March of 1972, James and I went to Hawaii, and on the way back, we stopped in San Francisco to pick up a rental car so we could drive down the California coast to L.A. The Grammy Awards were taking place that night in New York, and both of us were nominated, me for Best New Artist of the Year and James for Best Pop Vocal Performance, Male. The two of us weren't planning on attending in person. I can't vouch for how James felt about the prospect of getting, or not getting, a Grammy—he was mum about the subject—but I was quietly focused on it, though I made it a point not to say anything to him.

By two in the morning, the fog was sweeping in from the Pacific and that, combined with our jet lag and restlessness, lay behind our decision to stop along the way and take a nap, though we didn't have reservations anywhere. Barely able to make out the highway before us, we somehow ended up at the Big Sur Lodge. Luckily, management had room, and the two of us made our way through the mist with our bags to a small cabin amid the redwoods. We found a telegram pinned to the door addressed to James Taylor and Carly Simon. One of us opened it. It was from Jac Holzman at Elektra, and it read: "Congratulations! Both of you won Grammies! Love, Jac." The most amazing part was that dear Jac knew only that James and I were driving down the coast from San Francisco to L.A., and had sent a telegram to every single inn and hotel along the route.

"Skylight, James?"
"Sure, I'll have one!"
Adding a wing to the shack.

"Everywhere I look I see your eyes."

---

CHAPTER EIGHTEEN

moonlight mile

June 1972. James and I were in L.A. to do some recording, staying at the Chateau Marmont. I was going into the studio the next day to make a demo of some songs. One night, when James was working, we had been invited to a party given by Ahmet Ertegun, the president of Atlantic Records, who had proudly signed the Stones and had delivered "Brown Sugar" to the world. I went to the party alone, driving myself into the hills of Hollywood, and found the Erteguns' mansion, where butlers opened car doors and front doors, handed out flutes of champagne, remembered everybody's names, and then closed the doors behind them.

Mick was front and center. I saw him, registered it, looked around the room, put my pocketbook down, and went to say hello to Ahmet and his wife, Mica, whom I knew by then. I was a couple with James. We'd been living together for more than half a year. We were sought out by the Ahmets of the world, and they acted as though they'd known us all our lives.

Naturally I flirted with Mick. I mean, who wouldn't? If a woman didn't flirt with Mick, it could only mean she had a cold sore or she'd been brushed off by him already. Every time Mick passed me while I was talking to someone, he looked at me with the same expression: *You and I know the same thing. I, personally, have no idea what it is, and neither do you, but it is the same thing.* He kept looking at me, even if I was dancing with someone else (as dancing had started up and couldn't be stopped, what with the combination of the volume, the booze, the time, the city, the personalities). We found ourselves together at the doors leading to the pool area. We left naturally, as if we had a purpose out there.

In the garden, we finally entered solidly into each other's orbit. We walked together just out of sight of the crowd at the manse and discussed the interview that *The New York Times* had suggested I do with him. Sy Hersh, who assigned the piece, imagined that I would be able to get a story out of Mick, for reasons hinted at but not fully established. I wondered what I'd ask him. "What size shoe do you wear? Do you ever write songs in the bathtub?"

During our walk around the pool, Mick mentioned Cocteau and Genet. I talked meaninglessly about neoclassicism, and then he dropped Rimbaud's name. Nothing made sense in our conversation, just nervous emanations: sexy disruptions of the air around us.

"Slavery is such an underdiscussed subject—how it's affected the South."

"Violence is a calm that disturbs you," Mick said, as though it was supposed to have relevance. There was a stiff potted tree in front of us. How different than the moves of Mick Jagger. I thought of him and Keith onstage like palm trees raging in the Caribbean wind.

"Violence is *not* in that potted plant." I didn't know what I was saying. I guess I might have been afraid of what I wanted. I knew I shouldn't be flirting with this kind of danger.

"Do you speak French?" I asked Mick, closer now to poolside, noticing a few inglorious cigarette butts lying at the bottom.

"Just a bit, enough to say *adieu*. In fact, I got married in Saint-Tropez."

"How nice," I said, lowering my voice and reciting a bit of poetry. *"Quand j'étais petite, je n'étais pas grande, je montais sur un banc, pour embrasser maman."* I felt I had to compete with him, for absolutely no reason. No, I guess honestly it was to impress him. Those phrases were some of the first things I had learned in French class, and they apparently parked themselves in my memory bank of useless, very short French poems. I didn't stutter. I don't know why. In fact, I didn't even fear that I would, or that my face would contort over a word. I knew if I had trouble, I could stop short. Even if I left out a word, it wouldn't be that awful. And, I could let my words come out real slow.

"Where is the bride?"

"Bianca's home buying some hats."

"Did you pick out what she was going to wear on your wedding day? Oh no, that's right, you're not supposed to see . . ."

"Really, Carly, aren't you going to do a real interview?"

We were checking each other out in the circle of seduction. I didn't think it was unusual for him, but for me . . . well, I could easily get lost and not know what to fall back on. No more French poems, no more questions about Bianca or clothes. That "Little Red Rooster" glint shone in his eyes as he looked at me sideways.

"Do you want to know what my favorite Stones song is?" I asked. It was innocent enough, but he stared at me as though I had become a young fan who was going to bore him.

"Be serious," he said.

I looked directly into his eyes and held the gaze. "I am deeply, deeply serious." Suddenly I was as sexy as I'd ever been. It came from him. I was reacting, more than initiating. But then I realized I no longer had to talk. I could just be quiet and look at him. Let him be uncomfortable for a minute. But he wasn't. "Mick," I asked after a moment, "you really don't like to show your soft side, do you?"

"You think I have a soft side? What's that? Like a pudding?"

I had no idea where I was coming from. I had tried to be seductive with Sean Connery, but this was different. When I was with Mick, I became a woman who was attractive to *me*. He made me feel fantastic. On a good night, James didn't give me one-half of the energy Mick was giving to me. I always had to meet James halfway, or more. Mick was all there, and present, while James was suffering from that thing that I, in my life, have come to know all too well as my own curse, not knowing how to show up for the day.

I loved James more and more. What was I doing with Mick?

Just then the ground under Benedict Canyon shook. Keith's opening guitar lick of "Brown Sugar" made an operatic entrance on the outdoor speakers.

Later, there was a gorgeous black girl whom Mick was paying attention to. I had to remind myself that it wasn't a competition. Once I'd made that smart observation, I had to keep reminding myself, because I *did* feel that I was competing with all the girls buzzing and flitting around him like intoxicated Tinkerbells. In return, he was quite a hummingbird himself, wings beating so fast, he seemed to be lifted up and down by them invisibly.

Looking at him across the room, I saw the definite physical similarities between us. Specifically: the long face, small jungle eyes, and full lips. Up close, our lips unfurled as certain flowers do on nature shows, filmed in time-lapse. Also, I saw that his were naturally wine colored, emphasizing them. His face was full of color that seemed to move with pixelation. It was kinetic, always moving. And each move was so interesting. There were similarities in our skinny, doelike, floppy limbs. We stood exactly the same height, and since he wore Anita Pallenberg's and Marianne Faithfull's clothes, I imagined he might later don mine. That night, before I left the party, he put on my wide-brimmed burgundy hat and gave me an enticing nod.

I wrote in my diary: "I look at Mick and see a beautiful baby creature of another species born with human instincts." Then I thought: I wonder what Willie would think if he could see me tonight?

I had wanted to work with Paul Buckmaster because I loved his work with the Stones on *Sticky Fingers*. "Moonlight Mile" was as perfect an arrangement as I'd ever heard. Jac, being open-minded and generous, had funded a demo so Paul and I could work together and try things out. We had gone to the studio the day after the Hollywood Hills party to record two songs: one of them "Angel from Montgomery," a song by John Prine that Bonnie Raitt later did a top-notch cover of. I was giving it a rock 'n' roll edge, starting in a low octave and switching halfway to an octave above. I was excited by the newness of the whole mad approach to the song, although I knew it could be too out-there for Jac and Elektra. But I was so pleased with it myself, I couldn't wait to play it for James.

We were sitting on the brown hotel carpet in our room at the Chateau Marmont, with the Sony tape player on the floor in front of us. James was behind me, with his arms around me, and as soon as "Angel from Montgomery" was over, he lowered his head to my shoulder. He had been down for a few days. I wasn't sure why. Did he hate the song? Why was he shaking?

I had had some telephone calls from Mick, which likely had made him upset, though he would have been too proud to say so. Mick was calling about the interview I was supposed to do with him for *The New York Times*, and had also invited me to the Stones concert in San Francisco on that very night. Mick said the plane would wait for me. And I was going—for the article that I needed to write. That's how I presented it. But something else was brewing, wasn't it? Was I even honest with myself? James was picking up a scent, though one that I was trying awfully hard not to emit.

I followed James into the bedroom of our suite and watched as he took a suitcase from the top of the closet. He opened it and reached into a side pocket, bringing out a piece of rubber a few feet in length and the width of a piece of rope. *OH SHIT*, what was he doing?

"This is what I do," he said. "Watch. I can't have you and the habit at the same time. I just can't. I've got to get rid of this. Maybe if you see me do it, it will take away the cat-and-mouse game. You have to watch me. I have to let it all go."

It took about three or four minutes to get it all assembled. But then he tied off above his elbow and, while his blood was collecting in his veins below, reached in his suitcase with the other hand and brought out a syringe and some powdery substance in a plastic bag. There was another bag that had something else in it. Whatever it was, he poured it into a spoon, went into the kitchen in our suite, and melted it on the burner. I couldn't watch well enough to describe it even a day later. My mouth began to dry up and my heart went into panicked rhythms. Chemistry was in the making, and somehow all the components made their way into the syringe, and as he pulled the rubber tight on his arm the veins became purple and frightening. He walked into the bedroom and sat on the bed. He took the syringe and injected himself. It took five seconds and then he fell back on the bed. When he pulled the needle out of his arm, he exhaled and made some sounds like those of an animal being freed. A few minutes later, during which time I was as still as a corpse—in shock and trying not to show it, just sitting there leaning on one elbow—James got up from the bed and flushed everything down the toilet. All the medicine was gone. He threw the rubber arm strangler into the hallway chute to the incinerator, right outside our door. After the full dismantling, we clung to each other like apes, and closeness got hold of us in a painful but towering way. We stayed that way until the downstairs bell rang to tell me that my limo was there to take me to the airport. I pleaded with James that I would cancel my plans and stay with him, but he assured me that the crisis was over and that he was all right. He was beyond it. Everything was so much better. "It's over," he said. "I don't need it anymore."

From my diary:

James, James, James . . . His showing me was the big thing, the coveted madness he didn't want to relinquish. I was angry and terribly depressed. Was he shattering an illusion of what I wanted him to be? Dr. L says an addict will always lie to protect his disease. Life is barren without the drug. Was I asking for too much? There were many elements. Mainly I didn't want him to die. I was so scared that he would, just like my father. I was even getting to that familiar habit of knocking on wood.

Jac didn't like my demo with Paul Buckmaster and vetoed it, though he loved Paul's arrangements. He had chosen Richard Perry to produce my next album and sent him to meet me in New York. He had wanted Richard on the record all along. Richard and I sat across the dining room table from each other, his Brooklyn self facing my Bronx self. He told me that *Anticipation* would have been "a great album" if the drums had been stronger. The drums kept going off beat. That really put me off. My immediate reaction to him did not hint at the forty years of how close we've been since.

It wasn't long before I put myself in Richard's hands, with the necessary stormy conflicts that would make for a stimulating and sexy relationship.

Richard had produced or would soon produce Barbra Streisand's *Stoney End*, the Pointer Sisters, Ringo Starr, Fats Domino, Leo Sayer, and Harry Nilsson's *Nilsson Schmilsson*, which included the number 1 singles "Without You" and "Coconut," orchestral arrangement by Paul Buckmaster! Arlyne and I took the nighttime sleeper flight to London, arriving in the early hours of the foggy dawn. We stayed at the Grosvenor Hotel until my apartment was ready in the Portobello Hotel. It was decided that we would record in London, at Trident Studios in Soho, where Richard was crazy about the clothes. He made friends with shopkeepers and store managers and had them roll in racks of clothes to the studio for him to try on. He would always ask, "What do you think, Carly?" Then he would get out his checkbook, pay for what he wanted, and off the chaps would go with the racks.

Richard Perry and I worked on my new song, "Ballad of a Vain Man," about a man who owned a yacht, a private jet, a hat that comes over one eye, and an expensive horse that ran at Saratoga, who had the ability to do French parlor dances, had some friends in the underworld, and who'd obviously had some extramarital dalliances.

Whereas "Anticipation" was written in fifteen minutes, the song originally called "Bless You, Ben" took many trips down many roads before it came fully into view. I'd started it as a song on piano—I owned my aunt's old Tonk upright when I was living in my apartment on Thirty-fifth Street—and I played an Am7, got a tempo going, and vamped between Am7 and F with a riff that followed the melody. The words fell into the grooves, though not necessarily the same words I would finish it with.

Bless you, Ben
You came in where nobody else left off
There I was, all by myself, hiding up in my loft
Talk and trouble took my time
And singing some sad songs
I had some dreams there were clouds in my coffee, clouds in my coffee

There were a number of throwaway lines, as we call them in the business. The only phrase that remains from that first effort came when I was flying to Palm Springs with Billy Mernit, my piano player and great friend since my summer camp job when I met Jake in '68. Sitting next to me on the airplane, Billy pointed out the reflection in my cup—something he'd noticed with his keen photographer-lyricist's eyes: "Check it out, you've got clouds in your coffee."

I took out my little black book and wrote it down. You never know. The talent is in catching the right casual quip.

A year or so before, at a party in New York, my friend Kim Rosen and I had watched how everyone caught sight of themselves in the front hall mirror when they first arrived and held on to their reflection an extra private second longer. One guy who was staring at himself even twirled his scarf around his neck as he was removing it. Kim observed, "Doesn't he look as though he's walking onto a yacht?" That line went into my little black book right away. It was a good line. I didn't know what for, though. And a year before that, I had entered another line into my book: *You're so vain, you probably think this song is about you.* Not an overheard quip, but a genuinely daft piece of original cleverness. But I had promptly forgotten about it. It wasn't until a trip to L.A. when I gave the song a new title, "Ballad of a Vain Man," that it clicked. The word *vain* did it. Suddenly I had a protagonist! A guy! He would think the song was about him. Flipping through my black book for ideas, I found my beginning, courtesy of Kim: *You walked into the party like you were walking onto a yacht.* I gave him a strategically placed hat and some other things that I'm not sure he would have owned (such as a horse and a private jet), but the story was finally there, even though he decidedly did not dance the gavotte. And no, the song is not just about one person. Let's just say Warren Beatty played second base in this particular infield, which he knows so well, but as for who manned first and third—ask the shortstop. In all seriousness, the subjects of the first and third verses don't know that this song is also about them, so it would be inappropriate and a rude awakening to disclose their identities until they, them (vain) selves, were notified.

And here's a verse that never made it into the final recording:

A friend of yours revealed to me
That you'd love me all the time

You kept it secret from your wives
You believed that was no crime
You called me once to ask me things
I couldn't quite divine
Maybe that's why I have tried to dismiss you, tried to dismiss you.

When James came to London he could only stay for a long weekend be-cause he was needed back in L.A. He slept a lot during his visit. I know he was depressed and now, looking back, it may have had to do with some guilt he was holding on to. Some crumbling of a promise to himself—about a drink, a snort, a girl, something. I didn't ask him if or what he was doing while I wasn't around. I could only guess. He was free of demons only for an interrupted and too infrequent period of time. Heaven was when we both hit a glide simultaneously: lovely moments when our love came and rescued everything on the outside. We were enough with ourselves and our enor-mous little lives. Heaven was when it was happening like that, and I wasn't taking its temperature and watching like a fearful warden.

After he left, I was missing him a lot, and thinking about him. About a week after, I got a letter from Lucy, saying "the most adorable thing hap-pened." James had gone up to Riverdale to ask Mommy for my hand in mar-riage. I was so overwhelmed that something of such magnitude could happen and I didn't hear about it until a week later. But I was swept away with joy, calling James immediately. "Yes. Please. Always. Now . . ."

Album-wise, Richard and I were coming down the stretch, almost done recording. We decided to make use of our time at AIR Studios, which had become available thanks to its owner, George Martin. We needed to replace some parts, especially background vocals, and a guitar solo on "You're So Vain." Right down the hall, Paul and Linda McCartney were cutting tracks and George Martin himself was sitting at an acoustic piano. Richard and I took the chance and just charged into the studio. Richard could get away with it. He knew everybody. Both Paul and Linda were dressed as if they'd come from the country, Linda in clunky boots with wool socks, an over-sized sweater, and an unfashionable midlength skirt. She looked so funky and beautiful she stopped my breath. Paul was so himself, I never knew if he was ever any other way. Bonnie Bramlett and Harry Nilsson were there visiting their friends.

At Richard's invitation, all of them came down the hall to celebrate the finishing of our album. This made me quite angry, as I knew I wouldn't be myself with all that company, I wasn't really sure how things would sound, and we still had overdubs to do. But they crowded into Studio B, where Richard played a few cuts that he was especially proud of. There were sincere compliments sprinkled with questionable ones, with a few obviously fake ones stuck in between sips of vodka. I was almost silent, I was so tense. George Martin was an elegant sod (I've never known what that word means exactly), but he was brilliantly handsome and tall and renowned. How could Richard be such a relaxed host? He was and is a comfortable man. He became the life of the party. There was a lot of laughter and wine and vodka. It had the feeling of a very large celebration in a very small place. Toasts were made to all the future albums that were being mixed into shape at this renowned studio.

We had done a hundred takes of the basic track and at least thirty lead vocals for what we called "Ballad of a Vain Man." I told Richard we had to stop at a hundred, that I refused to be part of a record that went beyond a hundred takes. It was too expensively embarrassing for anyone but Liberace. Drummers had been flown halfway round the world, more than once, to play on this song that Richard had believed in right from the start. He had asked me to do the harmony parts while a "circle of friends," as he called them (I called them highly intimidating musicians), listened. I begged Harry Nilsson to sing with me, and he didn't hesitate to accept. Harry was a close friend of John Lennon's and was one of the terrific artists who didn't promote his work by stage performance. He was handsome and tall, wearing sunglasses, and had tawny hair curling around his unmistakable face. We were comfortable enough with each other, and got in a few takes (which means fewer than twenty-five with Richard at the helm) before I got a call on the studio phone and stepped out to take it in the lounge.

"Hallow, is this Caughly?" I didn't have to ask who it was.

"How did you know I was here?" Had Mick ever not been able to find anybody?

"What aw you doin'?"

I told him I was putting some vocals on a track with Harry and invited him to come. "You know where AIR Studios are, yes? No?"

Mick was there almost instantly, having probably been in a car right downstairs, sussing out his possibilities for the night. Timing is everything. After some hugs and kisses that looked mimed, Richard invited Mick into the recording studio to join Harry and me on the vocals. Harry was already ensconced. Paul and Linda had disappeared momentarily with the elegant George Martin.

Mick and I said hello in front of Harry in the control booth. We kissed each other on the cheek (one cheek, and then the other). Again, it was a little formal.

"Right to it, man," Harry said, as he shook Mick's hand and bear-hugged him.

"It's pretty easy, Mick," I said, feeling jittery and trying to be calm. "Just sing the melody if you feel like it, or improvise and do any harmony you think of."

I remember only that after four or five perfectly acceptable go-rounds, Harry said: "You two do *not* need me, you sound as though you're joined at the hip." He left for the control booth to find his future in a drink.

Mick and I were alone for the first time since the party in Hollywood, just a few months before. Proust says somewhere that "happiness is the absence of fever." If true, those forty-five minutes in the glass vocal booth with Mick Jagger were an extreme example of unhappiness. As we sang together—Mick was a natural at singing backup—the energy was choreographed by the heavens, an unexpected fever that was certainly heightened by the music. The song that had been waiting to come to life for so long finally exploded. From the first lines in my notebook, the flight to Palm Springs, the party in New York, and now with Mick's just happening to drop by at the studio at the very moment I was recording "Ballad of a Vain Man," it was all, as if by wizardry, coming together.

It felt like everything in my life had led me to this moment. My earliest musical influences—Odetta, the Southern blues singers, the Delta blues of Mississippi, John Hurt and Muddy Waters, Lightnin' Hopkins, and especially Uncle Peter—fused with my jazz and folk roots. I had it all in those loops in my brain and in the twists and turns of my crooked musical ear, and it ran alongside the nearly impossible blending of Lucy and me and our guitars, Joey and Puccini, the Great American Songbook, and all the musicals of the forties and fifties that I studied and sang. Lordy, my parents were part of my performance in the glass booth—Mommy singing "Summertime," when George and Ira suggested she give it a go, and Daddy's dedicated long fingers on the keys, his head bent over his Steinway hour after hour.

It was shortly after midnight. Mick and I, we were close together—the same height, same coloring, same lips. I could feel him, eyes wide on me. I felt as if I were trying to stay within a pink gravity that was starting to loosen its silky grip on me. I was thrilled by the proximity, remembering all the times I had spent imitating him in front of my closet mirror. Only now we were both Narcissus, each desiring our reflection in the other; I was moving in step with him. Not trying to, but Richard gave us directions that seemed more football coach than record producer: "Mick, step back just a bit, your voice cuts more than Carly's. Try doubling your parts and stand a little further away, both of you."

The farther away we stood, the closer we got. Electricity. That's what it was. I wanted to touch his neck and he was looking at my lips. The electricity was raw and hardly disguising its power. Having sex would have actually cooled things off.

I started to withdraw, which I thought was the only correct thing to do. It corresponded with Richard's wanting to listen to a couple of playbacks and then—nobody wanting to miss a chance to see Mick—an opening of the studio door and the appearance of George Martin, Paul, and Linda.

Conversation struck up between the Beatle and the Stone and I went to the ladies' room to play with my hair, mess it up to be like Mick's—only mine didn't fall into the perfect shiny piece of glass that his did—put on some natural lip color, and try to dry off a little. I had taken a swig of Harry's brandy, but it hadn't relaxed me at all. It had just made me sweat.

When I went back to the studio, it was empty except for Mick sitting at the piano. I joined him and he asked me to play the chords of the song for him.

"How do you know all those chords?"

"I'm just a stuck-up chick," I said, and he started fooling around on a song he was working on, "Funny, funny, funny, funny, how love can make you cry." He looked right at me. Then back at the keys. I could feel my face flushing. I harmonized with him as it became a chorus, an improvisation that was later searched for and never found among the multitracks at AIR Studios. Mick is that genius of an artist who thrives on the dark and the daring. And you could say that the love affair between us that appeared to be brewing contained both of those things. And if Mick could have his way, it would be Romeo and Juliet tragic. We couldn't have each other. Mick had been married only a short time to Bianca, who was waiting for him in a first-class lounge or hotel suite somewhere not too far away. And more important to *me*, there was the seriousness of my love for James. He wasn't the horse Mick was, nor was James as naughty or as willing to destroy the status quo. Mick was compelled by a difficult situation as much as anything. He would not have been as interested in me, I believed, if there hadn't been an insurmountable obstacle between us. That is true for most men.

Funny, funny, funny, funny, how love can make you cry.

It did not end there, though. We spent some evenings together at the studio where he was recording, and some other times in rooms at the Portobello Hotel, which was dangerous and conspicuous. I was genuinely drawn to the part of him that I suspected he didn't let out for a walk all that often. The only reason that I got what I imagined to be the tender, appreciative side of Mick was that I wasn't asking for it.

I was holding back with Mick—not giving him exactly what he wanted—but I knew it was still more than James would be all right with. The most touching moment I can remember, almost ever, happened later, the night before James and I actually tied the knot. We were in bed, getting ready for the big day, when the phone rang and James answered. It was Bianca Jagger. She told James that he shouldn't marry me because her husband and I were having an affair. She muttered some things I couldn't believe she was saying and James couldn't quite make out due to the connection and the language barrier.

Then James said, "I'm sure that's not true. Carly has told me about it and it's not what you think. I trust my wife-to-be. I trust Carly."

Following were the complicated, awful, proud, guilty, and life-changing feelings that have remained with me since. I can still wallow in regret to this day about things I did, versions of the truth I perpetrated. James was more than a prince. He was everything that a man could level his woman with. And I loved him miles beyond.

Recording "You're So Vain" at AIR Studios in London with Richard Perry.
Paul and Linda McCartney were in the next studio and stopped by.

"I'm lookin' forward to lookin' back from further on down the track together in fact, forever my love."
— *"Forever My Love," by James Taylor and Carly Simon*

CHAPTER NINETEEN

we'll marry

The weekend before I went to London we had spent on the Vineyard. On the plane there, anticipating our imminent separation, James and I went so far as to write an informal prenuptial agreement on a piece of paper. He added his notes in ballpoint pen on both sides of a single lined page, and we both bent down to sign it. "This document will attest that James Vernon Taylor and Carly Elizabeth Simon will enter into a state of wedlock as defined therein . . ." it began. James's handwriting was childish, sweet, alternately neat and suddenly impassioned, wilder. All material possessions would be considered common property, and in the event of "the dissolution of this agreement," all possessions would revert to their original owner. Joint possessions will be distributed equally "to both parties." As for "divorse" (sp), James wrote that it would be "applied for in writing, listing grievances," adding, "Waiting period of three months before compliance." Under the pledge, "I hereby agree to the above stipulations," we signed our names, James's signature forky, all bent wire, like a Calder mobile; mine girlish, well behaved, prep-school-like, lined up underneath his. I still have this sweet, sad document.

Looking back, we must have intentionally made our decision to get married only four days before the wedding, leaving us no time to fret about the details. Twenty-four hours before the ceremony, James's lawyer, Nat Weiss, arranged for the license, the limousine, and the Wasserman test, and James and I made a hurried trip down to City Hall in New York for a stamp here, a stamp there. Danny and Abigale Kortchmar would be our witnesses. Yes, it was a huge decision, but in every way, it felt like the right one, especially when you have only a short time to tear your hair out anticipating and worrying about it. Once we'd signed our names on the City Hall ledger, the four of us celebrated with a drink and chicken wings at a Chinese restaurant.

With only four days until our wedding ceremony, we had to keep accordioning the various steps and rituals. That night after the signing, James and I took a long walk together through the Village, as unprepossessing as any two people could be. It was warm out, and almost dark on Eighth Street, and anyone observing us would have guessed we were just another couple out for a stroll, which, in fact, we were. A door or two off Bleecker Street, on MacDougal, we passed by a jewelry store advertising wedding rings at a discount—25 PERCENT OFF! said the sign in the window.

James and I entered and went straight to the full-price ring section. We knew to avoid rings that were on sale—not because they were tawdry, or suspicious, but because of some mutually agreed-upon superstition that they were bad luck. A dark, handsome woman materialized behind the counter. James glanced at her fleetingly, closely, familiarly, before his gaze found his own shoes. The saleswoman was tall, her posture aristocratic, her hair in a severe bun, her white button-down shirt tucked into a black skirt. Her sexy-frosty appearance was in sharp contrast to the tinny, exotic music playing overhead and the flamboyant chains, Indian fabrics, scarves, crystal rings, different-sized Buddhas, incense sticks, and handmade Christmas tree ornaments draped, blinking, gleaming, and zigzagging, around the shop. She looked for all intents and purposes like a Mexican painter— or a Mexican painter's muse, including the eyebrows.

But before either of us had said a word, James, I felt, had an unspoken moment with her. It was as though the two of them shared a history, or worse, a charmed, short-lasting flicker of a future. Over the course of our marriage I would come up against this same sort of woman, in various forms and guises. But at that moment, she was just a small twitch in my gut.

Buying a ring was not a trivial affair, and looking back, I don't know why James and I found ourselves at some cheap Middle Eastern downtown tourist kiosk. Thinking back on it, it was James at his most New England-y: farmyard wedding rings. James and I paid for each other's rings, each one costing $17.95, so there wasn't much wallet shuffling, with each of us handing the cashier a twenty-dollar bill. (Remember, these were the expensive rings.) The one we decided on for James was slightly wider than the one we picked out for me. James's was faintly curved and beveled, with a dull sheen, while mine was narrower, with a more polished look. They were both ostentatiously "non-statement." The rings went into the store's small, ordinary white cartons and, pocketing our boxes, we waved good-bye to the saleswoman.

Fred Leighton, a Mexican-import-clothing store that had recently begun selling precious jewelry, was our next stop. I was hoping to find something useful *and* original to wear at my wedding that I could maybe wear in the future, too. I found the right dress at once and held it up, silently offering James veto power. He asked me to try it on, but when I said, "It's pretty loose-fitting, and it's a medium. It'll fit," he said, "Done!"

A simple gray-and-white, long-sleeved Mexican dress, vertically striped and floor length, it reminded me of the outfits Lucy and I wore when we performed at the Moors in Provincetown. That dress—my wedding dress— is one of the many articles of clothing that, along with various other irreplaceable things, have mysteriously vanished from my house. Gone, too, is the beautiful diamond necklace that James bought for me after we were married. Over the years, countless pairs of my best, worn-in leather boots have gone missing, too. Some of James's belongings have also disappeared, including a beautiful book that Joni Mitchell gave him containing pen-and-ink drawings and handwritten lyrics to the songs on *Blue*, most of which were originally inspired by James. I remember distinctly Joni's drawing of a girl's face, with a gleaming diamond instead of a teardrop. A friend of mine said she'd keep it safe for me.

Even at the eleventh hour, James and I still hadn't figured out an exact time or location, much less gotten in touch with a justice of the peace. I was hoping a simple notary could handle the job, but this, it turned out, was beyond a notary's job description. I hurriedly placed a phone call to my mother in Riverdale, explaining that James and I wanted to get married the following day at five in the afternoon—James was playing a show that night at Radio City Music Hall—and that we desperately needed to track down a justice of the peace.

Even though Mother had already been asked by James, Mommy sounded exultant. She promised to call a Riverdale acquaintance, Judge Ash, the second we hung up, and if Judge Ash was unavailable, she assured me she would find someone else. "Darling, darling Carly . . ." she said. "Are you having a big gathering?"

No, I told her. It would be just her, James's mother Trudy, and, of course, Jake.

"*Cosa linda! Cosa linda!*" It was the same endearment my mother and father had used with each other. Mommy again assured me she'd call Judge Ash the moment we hung up.

Jake was the next call. Could he possibly show up at my apartment the following afternoon at 5 p.m. sharp? When I told him why, that James and I were getting married, there was a long pause. "Are you serious?" he said at last. "Carpe diem. What about tearful nights and angry dawns?" His lyrics for our first song infiltrated our conversation like smoke seeping under a door crack.

I knew it seemed sudden, and impulsive, I told him, but . . . that's the way it was.

"I guess so," Jake said.

I couldn't help it. "And that's the way I've always heard it should be."

There was no laugh—just thirty seconds of breathing, from one mouthpiece to another.

I may have cried. I can't remember, but that's how my memory shapes things today. It was a heavy moment nonetheless, a deep conversation, as our song, finally, had come to life, suffused as it was now with almost too much meaning. "I'll be there," Jake said before he hung up. "Of course I will. Dress code?"

James placed a call to his mother, Trudy, asking if she could be at our apartment tomorrow afternoon at the same time. I couldn't get a good grip on Trudy's reaction, but the conversation wasn't long. I felt a hole in my heart on behalf of our joint family members who wouldn't be present. Neither James nor I had wanted a big festival of a wedding. In truth, the optimal wedding would have involved just the two of us, and maybe our sheer haste, plus the question of "Whom do you *not* invite?" gave us the excuse to keep the ceremony very small. (I also think I would have been too nervous to carry out such an intimate vow in front of a big crowd.) The fact of the matter was that it would have been impossible to assemble the most important people in our lives in such a short time, and I knew Joey, Lucy, and Peter would understand. In lieu of a huge crowd, we'd created a time, and a date, and made our decision, with everyone invited to James's after-concert party at the Time-Life Building in Rockefeller Center. How on earth, I wondered, did James have the calm and steadfastness to even consider walking onstage at Radio City Music Hall only three hours after our wedding?

Once the plans were set, I hung James's white linen suit in the shower to steam out the wrinkles. James took a nap while I tidied up around the apartment and took David the dog out for a walk.

I couldn't help thinking about Daddy, and how much he would have liked and approved of James. James was a Harvard boy in spirit and style, one smart enough never to have attended the college. Ivy League or not, James, in fact, was too smart, too all-seeing, for his own comfort. When he slept at night, he moved around a lot, once telling me he'd dreamed he was emerging through a black hole, that he knew he wasn't from this planet, but had no choice but to bear up under the strain of living on this earth. I'm guessing half or more of James's thoughts or perceptions were ones he wished were someone else's. At the time I thought, and I still do, that he's an uncommon genius.

That evening, though, James was nothing more than a nervous groom-to-be, and I was pretending just as hard to remain calm and unruffled, with both of us tossing customary rituals out the window, including the wedding superstition of the bride and groom not seeing each other before the ceremony.

"How does this look?" James asked. "Should the ivory pin stick through the tie, or should I just keep the tie tucked under the jacket?" His only small stylistic eccentricity was a hand-painted tie with a camel on it, which we both agreed he should wear.

I fixed it for him, and then it was my turn. "Do you think I should wear my hair up, or would that look too sedate?"

"No, wear it the way it is. I love it long."

Our wedding style, if you could even call it that, could be summed up as a slightly ostentatious absence of style. Neither of us considered that the occasion merited any fanfare or toys, paper hats, or long-winded, solemn speeches, and anything more than the most low-key recitation of our vows would have no doubt darkened James's reticently jovial mood. We already had enough of a public life, one that would get even more splashy and un-hidden as the years went by. Already we had the normal number of people asking us for the normal number of autographs, James always signing his name with a fast "caged animal" scrawl, me delivering a perfect school-girl script, making James's, by comparison, all the more treasured. On the Vineyard, then and throughout the seventies, the attention people were paying to us would become even more pronounced. James was attracted to the Lambert's Cove property because of its beauty and privacy, but nei-ther of us had counted on the presence of a nearby camping site known as Cranberry Acres. Fans would come right up beyond the borders of our property, and even take pictures outside our cabin windows. James would get extremely angry, but in general his road manager, Jock, helped ward trespassers off. As the decade went on, things got worse, with cars driving down our road at all hours, snapping photos and taking videos, and some people even knocking on our door.

But at that moment, none of that mattered. To paraphrase Tolstoy, it's absurd to think of charm or lipstick, feathers or hairstyles, at a time when, if you lack a proper base of ethics, you might as well forget the union. You have the wrong partner. Or at least, the wrong one with whom to build a life. We had that base of ethics. With James's modesty and good manners, he would have been in his element living his whole life in the sand somewhere, unglimpsed from behind the blackberry bushes, perhaps stealing out for an hour or two a day for a fast, surprise appearance and a smattering of folksy applause. That same paradox lived inside me, too, wanting to disappear into the woods while simultaneously being recognized and loved for a few minutes of reassurance.

Side by side, with James on my left, we stood beside the Tonk upright piano in our apartment with me clutching James's hand and shaking evenly from head to toe, and Judge Ash standing before us, presiding. On the other side of us was one of our unofficial ushers, James's (and now *our*) dog, David. In search of distraction, my eyes found the colors of the camel on James's hand-painted tie. *Oh my Lord, James, problems have and will arise, but you are my whole life.*

James and I both wanted the briefest of speeches from the judge, without any allusions to religion. He finally spoke: "Will you, James, take this woman, Carly, to be your lawful, wedded wife in sickness and in health, till death do you part?"

"Yes," James said.

"And will you, Carly, take this man, James, to be your husband, in sickness and in health, till death do you part?"

I heard my own voice saying "Yes," while my brain, as was its lifelong habit, took flapping flight, tripping on far-flung trivia. How and why had *death you do part* become *death do you part?* Where did the *you* and the *do* really belong? Where were the adrenals in the human body? Were they in the back, or over to one side? But which side? Why was I still shaking so much, and where in my body was I feeling whatever it was I was feeling, and were my spleen and my hypothalamus (wherever they were located, though I imagined they were very close to the adrenals) both holding up under all this strain?

"I now pronounce you husband and wife . . ."

"You may kiss the bride . . ."

As Judge Ash removed a document from his folder, James and I kissed. Then we did it once more, my brain nearly bursting with *Oh-my-good-God*s. A few feet away from me, my mother was wiping away tears. Having evolved beyond her initial belief that James was a drug user (in the beginning, she referred to him as a "potter," not knowing exactly what "pot" had to do with drugs, or if and where a verb or a noun was needed), James surely reminded her now of Daddy in his younger days, back when she still loved him. As the years went on, in fact, I grew to suspect she had developed a crush on James, not exactly a reach for my mother where biblically inconvenient younger men were concerned. Then again, James could "charm the ugly off an ape," as his own brother Alex put it.

Next to my mother, Trudy Taylor was holding a pitchfork, a metaphorical one not yet visible to the human eye. I was eager to win her over, and had made her a needlepointed pillow six months after our first meeting, the first time I'd ever attempted a "craft"—in this case a bunch of flowers inspired by a Picasso print. Trudy loved it, and my gift bought us a good ten years of sweet talk and recipe swapping. That said, Mommy and Trudy were always slightly combative. Standing beside the two mothers, Jake looked slightly baffled and wore a typically impassive Jake look: the one where I knew he was expending vastly more time and energy deciphering other people's expressions than bothering to arrange his own. After Jake's first-night comment about James's shoes, and a rough, uneasy eight months of getting to know each other, James and Jake finally became close friends. I wasn't leaving Jake behind, either, as he and Ricky were still going strong. To me, Jake's little smile conveyed only, *We'll see. Many rivers to cross here.*

Afterward, our small group formed a celebratory circle, a group huddle of sorts. No one was officially designated to count things off in any kind of 1 . . . 2 . . . 3, but voices of the assembled joined together in a loud, exultant "*Whooooopie!*" Any song would have sufficed, so long as it was loose, informal, simple, and unchallenging, and Trudy started the one we all sang: "*Christmas is coming, the goose is getting fat / Please do put a penny in the old man's hat . . .*"

Once the gang was gone, I broke out into giddy, let-it-all-hang-out laughter that soon turned into tearful hysteria. My own nervous energy was contagious. James began laughing at me, and then at "it"—the whole crazy scene in which we'd just participated, and the fact that he and I could now, with perfectly straight faces, call each other "husband" and "wife." We shed most of our clothes and went straight to the fridge to take out the Sara Lee banana cake we'd bought especially for the occasion. Grabbing spoons, we both devoured the cake as if nothing we'd ever done, eaten, seen, heard, felt, or experienced before had been so over-the-top funny: banana cake, for God's sake! We were like kids scrambling to raid the fridge before a responsible adult wearing a sheriff's star busted us in the act. We ended up in the bedroom, lying in a warm, worn nest of wedding dress, suit, camel tie, blue bra, stockings, pearls, and garter belt, all happily, chaotically entwined on the carpet. On that floor we made love, looking ahead as married people . . . or a couple of kids making believe they were married.

The next day I wrote in my diary:

Nov 4th:

The thrill of feeling myself go, and becoming complete, the other half filling in as if by a warm infusion—a compound of excitement, relief, a summer storm building over a hot afternoon as it joins forces with fronts, a duet of clouds that crash without form, through mists and moving air. My skin grows bright and my veins, attracted to its surface warmth, allow a color resembling the hue of a feather in the hair of a flamenco dancer.

I'm losing myself—it's so good that I want to lose more and more as if I were traveling by opium boats but could notice every hair rise on my arms. No swarm, just the soft tumble into warm water from air that's only two degrees warmer than the water. Someday you might need something else—something more, or less—but right now, it's just me. Ours will evolve into another kind of embrace. One that is inclusive. More existential, less subjective. Your hands turning my face to face yours, your hips branching over mine. I hold you inside me for as long as you will stay, and I think it will never be this good but it will and it has been and then it isn't, but it gets good again and it's what I've always looked for. I can't believe I have it. I have it. I have it.

Love and marriage were one thing, the demands of performing another. The night of our wedding, James got ready for his show, changing into corduroys, work boots, a blue-patterned shirt covered over with a Fair Isle sweater vest, and his by-now-familiar "lucky" turquoise belt. I wore a blue full-length cotton skirt, James's favorite piece of clothing I owned, one I'd bought in Greenwich Village right after getting out of Sarah Lawrence. It was the best, most perfect weight, and the ideal length from the ground, the waist allowing room for the top to curve down toward my navel like a bib. I finished off my outfit with an Indian-made pink-cotton mirrored jersey I'd bought in London that came down to the top of the skirt, high socks, and a pair of clogs. Together we walked out onto Thirty-fifth Street and into a waiting stretch limo, one much larger than we needed, one to be slightly embarrassed about in James's and my shared reverse-snobbery way. As it drove uptown, James went over the set list. He would lead with "Baby, It's Cold Outside," but at what point should he introduce me? He was trying not to pounce on himself for nerves; that was my specialty, after all.

The biggest thing of all? Both James and I were wearing our wedding rings. I kept snatching glances down at mine, half excited, half disbelieving. My ring felt like an amulet, possessed of superpowers. *Nothing can hurt me now.* Over the next few days, I made things even more official by changing the name on my three credit cards. My Bloomingdale's card would now read, in bold print, MRS. JAMES TAYLOR, DON'T FUCK WITH ME. Never in my life had I felt as sure of anything as I did about my new marriage to James. I hoped, and could have sworn on it, too, that whatever fears, worries, and dark uncertainties I'd experienced over the last year and even before that would turn to vapor and vanish into the unseen ozone.

The after-concert party in the Time-Life Building was joyous. James and I were surrounded by every single blood relative we had, as well as every record-company executive who had created salable brands from our faces, bodies, and voices. Jac Holzman, Mo Ostin, Lenny Waronker, Peter Asher, and my manager Arlyne toasted us, as did brothers, sisters, ex-girlfriends, ex-boyfriends, mothers, and close friends (including a few smilers with knives). I thought briefly about the call the previous night from Bianca and dismissed any relevance it would ever have to have. My family was there, looking ever so faintly slighted at having been left out of the actual wedding ceremony—or maybe I was imagining things—and my brother Peter took photos, including one where under the room's ghoulish overhead lighting, James and I ate pasta, strands dripping from our forks over a shared plate.

James and I left early. As we boarded the elevator, assorted guests threw rice at us, a grain-storm that slid down our shirts and into our hair and eyes, though most of it ended up sleeting down the elevator shaft. Outside, it was freezing, and James and I were immediately accosted by a crowd of concertgoers asking for autographs. After piling into the waiting limo, James and I fell into each other's arms, exultant, half screaming, "Hi baby, hi baby, oh God, I love you." Ten minutes later, we opened our apartment door only to be met by David, looking guilty. While we were out, David had somehow burrowed his way into my lone clothes closet and chewed up all my shoes, rendering them forever irrelevant as footwear, and forever useful as dog toys. The ones we had carefully packed from the Barbizon weren't enough. David was a "shoe man."

As I got ready for bed, I looked in my eyes in the mirror. I wanted to put it all together, to not compartmentalize this one. I wanted to bring myself into a healthy union or perfect fourth with my darling. I saw no sign of the Beast. The boys in the trees would go away now. There was no reason to look at another man. I no longer felt the same. I no longer had the same name. I would maintain my professional name as Carly Simon, but if names are a form of music, my new name rounded out the original chord of "Carly Simon." I felt destined, almost, to be known thenceforth as Carly Simon Taylor, the look of it melodic, balanced, a harmony of the spheres. Then there was my new husband, a man easy to get drenched by, easy to leave my old self behind for as the two of us pushed forward, arms linked. I would continue riding on the James Taylor railroad, in sickness and in health, for a long, long time.

This document will attest that James Vernon
Taylor and Carly Elizabeth Simon will enter into
a state of wedlock as defined herein:

1. Belongings and possessions: Materialist possessions
will be considered common property, except where
assigned and agreed upon by both parties. In the
event of the dissolution of this agreement all said
possessions will revert to their original owner
where title is legally clear. Any possessions acquired
jointly will be distributed equally to both parties
on a 50-50 basis. This will include any monies
resulting from the sale of any jointly owned property.

2. Financing: responsibility of debts incurred
by spouse

terms of termination
management of joint account
(what to contribute what) relative to amt.
(%) or available amt.
paying of household bills
(which come under joint account)

3 Progeny + wards
financial responsibility to be borne proportionately
to earning of income (as in joint account)

decision re education, schooling,
camp, extra domestic activities
to be decided by child when of age,
subject to parental joint vote
(majority vote) — son to have custody until jr.
more up his mind

3 Divorce — (no grounds) to be applied for
in writing listing grievances. Waiting period of
3 months before compliance

Alimony — to be
decided upon relative to the
needs of the recipient and
the ability of the donor to
comply

Contract to be mutually
exclusive to all and any
other like contracts

I hereby agree to
the above stipulations

Co-written in the air on the way to the shack.

"Another bride, another groom."

That's my guitar!

emulsification

Many marriages rise, fall, steady out again. You blurt out something unmentionable, reconcile again, and on and on into the sunset. James's and my marriage was like any other, because when all is said and done, marriage involves two people, who need food to subsist on and a house to provide them shelter from snow, wind, rain, and too-hot August days, where they can bustle around, sleep, and rest their aching feet. The only difference here was that James and I were both performers, private people in the public eye. Blame that, or our individual natures, but the waves and surf patterns defining our marriage were, I daresay, bigger and more turbulent than in most marriages. Our love became bipolar, switching from love to hate, lust to loathing, and back again, sometimes within a day. The pleasure with James was pure euphoria, whereas the pain was, for me at least, almost unendurable. Throughout it all, I was ever aware of my watchfulness, a lighthouse sweep vigilantly seeking out clues that James loved me, that the two of us would be all right, that we would manage to get home safely. Because no matter how many years have now gone by, James, for me, will always be a big part of what I call home.

These days, I'm anxious for Ben and Sally, our two children, to believe their father was happy with me. Obviously, not all of me, and not everything, but that there was enough good in me, and in the two of us, that James would not want to exclude me from his memories. James remembers, I'm sure, that he was in the delivery room when Sally and Ben were born, that together we bought and decorated a house on East Sixty-second Street, where we spent a couple of years, while also jetting back and forth between the Vineyard and Los Angeles, before we moved to a sprawling rental on Central Park West. Today, James would likely forget a good many things that I remember being flooded with color, just as he might also recall sunlight on days that for me were gray and dimly lit. Whatever he thinks of me today, I daresay it's slightly less damning than the way I see myself through his absent eyes. I imagine, too, that even with the pacification of age and hindsight, he still has the right to thrash around in moody retribution, always a specialty of the house.

He might also remember this—that he came home one night to confess that he'd seen a girl from behind on the street and was utterly riveted by the sight of her. He'd gone so far as to tail her secretly for one or two blocks, adding that he felt guilty and creepy the whole time. She, the girl, was tall, attired in a hip-hugging leather miniskirt and chamois boots, and James felt deeply ashamed to have lustful feelings about other women just after getting married. Then, he told me, the girl finally turned around. It was me, right there on the street. We fell into each other's arms laughing.

Then there was a humid summer night when he and I were walking to Murray Hill after attending a Dylan concert at Madison Square Garden— James and I were both shocked by the high, nasal quality of Bob's voice, though it was pretty interesting, too, Dylan remaking himself for no discernible reason other than a love of change and experimentation, something that wasn't in either James's or my repertoire. Both of us, I remember, were dressed simply in airy, summer fabrics. When we reached Lexington and Thirtieth Street, and knowing that James was eager, as ever, to get to another Sara Lee banana cake in the refrigerator, I made a guesstimate out of thin air. "From here," I intoned, "it's exactly eighty-seven steps to our apartment." Without elongating our strides, he and I began walking the remaining distance, counting our steps as we did, marking, in the end, exactly eighty-seven steps. From that point on, I imagined that James was a little bit more impressed with me, and I would certainly use my impressive predictive techniques a few other times. How many seconds would it take before the elevator reached the top of the Time-Life Building the night we got married? How many minutes would it take the waiter to come by with the soup? How long would it take James's dog, David, to relieve himself when we took him for a late-night stroll? It was probably the same obsessive-compulsiveness that started when Daddy got sick, or even earlier than that, but I preferred to think of it as magical, uncanny, my own version of psychic time control. I didn't have that much confidence in it, though. It was only correct *a lot* of the time.

A month after our wedding, James and I flew to the Vineyard to spend Christmas. A crowd of workmen filed in and out of our property, just as over the next few years, James, along with a ragtag team of local carpenters and craftspeople, would forever be at work on the house and surrounding fields. There were always people around hammering, sawing, splitting wood, making fences, clearing brush, laying down rocks, building porches— "the circus that is my life," James used to call it. First came the kitchen wing, leading to the bedroom directly upstairs. Elsewhere, workers were busy planting, clearing fields, and building stone walls as well as a new, improved driveway. We planted a very small kousa dogwood tree in the center of the deck we were building. As the months and years went on, the sheer physical presence of so many burly or scrawny well-intentioned tradespeople—and the fact that James and I were seldom alone in our own house—began getting under my skin. But that first Christmas, the constant choral accompaniment of saws and hammers was almost mixed in with the arrival of holiday packages from Elektra and Warner Bros., reminding both James and me how much our record companies loved and appreciated us. Most of all, they seemed delighted by the progress of both our albums, *No Secrets* and *One Man Dog*, which were rising higher and higher on the charts and getting lots of good press along the way.

I was as happy as I'd ever been in my life. "How has life changed since we have been married?" I wrote. "Mainly from the outside. But I wake up, sometimes from sleep and sometimes from preoccupation, and look at James and realize with immense delight that he is my own dear husband. My every thought includes him. He is so many good things, and his virtues seem to overwhelm me at times. Marriage seems to suit us both but why I don't know . . . can't figure out . . . but I don't feel any more worthy inside than I did previously."

Where, oh where did that feeling of unworthiness come from? I knew only that it was something that was with me all the time. Why did I expect marriage to change how I felt? Were my expectations too dramatic? Now and again, I said to myself, You're married! You no longer have to cross that boundary! You're now a Jane Austen heroine! Nothing bad can ever happen to you again! These thoughts mixed in with another voice, the Beast's, intoning, But you're not quite good enough. These voices weren't with me all the time, but they were around enough. As James said to me once, "You're just difficult *enough*, Carly. If you were any *more* difficult, I couldn't live with you. If you were any *less* difficult, it wouldn't be nearly as fun."

With our house ridiculously messy and overturned-looking, James and I climbed into our equally messy car and drove over to Trudy Taylor's house for Christmas dinner, joining the rest of the Taylor clan. Despite the long, skin-deep history I had with some of James's family members, I was still the awkward newcomer, but they were an impressive bunch of welcoming, animated northerners of the southern variety, Trudy a lifelong Yankee, Ike a southern-born one. Of course I knew Kate and Livingston already—Liv handsome, hilarious, and by far the friendliest of all the Taylor kids—but that night I also had a chance to talk to James's two other brothers, Hugh and Alex. Alex, the oldest, had a blues singer's sonorous voice, and was discernibly different from the other Taylors, including the adorable youngest, Hughie, at seventeen probably the "cutest" of them all. I went home that night with the distinct impression that as a family, the Taylors could be insular, interested mostly in the goings-on of its various members, with a collective habit, one that James had come by honestly, of rarely looking you directly in the eye. They were like an island tribe who spoke a private, loving language only they knew.

Trudy, the complicated mother of this huge, musical clan, was always in the kitchen, cooking one of the hundred or so meals I would consume in her house during my daughter-in-law years. A true gourmet who had studied cooking in China and elsewhere, Trudy got the compliments for her cooking that she deserved, which were many, varied, and slightly hysterical (you always had to outdo yourself, genuinely, too, with superlatives). Still, despite or maybe because of the family's unusual closeness, what could have been a tense, competitive atmosphere—each member of the family was actively creating, singing onstage, or recording something—was mitigated by their genuine enthusiasm for one another's accomplishments. Everyone was in everyone else's court, and I left that night with the knowledge that the Taylors were a family who knew how to support one another.

Inevitably it happens that a new bride will start to compare her new family with her own family of origin. With Mommy and Trudy living in Vineyard houses not all that far away from each other, Mommy, I felt, was always competing with Trudy for the title of Best Mother in the Neighborhood. As for my sisters, there had always been a natural amount of sibling jealousy among us, which wasn't helped any by the fact that I was now married to a famous prince, and getting the princess treatment. The more that happened, the worse, and guiltier, I felt.

Again, that Christmas, James and I had little alone time. The cabin in the woods—all four rooms of it now—was densely populated with Jimmy, Jimmy, John, Luke, and Laurie, the No Jets Construction Company, as well as a steady stream of visitors, some well intentioned, others not exactly unwilling to accept a James Taylor handout. In order to carve out some times to ourselves, we took long walks through the nearly frozen woods on the land neighboring ours, stopping at an empty summerhouse to satisfy our still torrid just-married inclinations. It was great, though not as easy as you'd think—maintaining a state of ecstasy while laughing our heads off as we made a beeline for a nearby house. We never knew for sure if the house was empty, but most were. I was almost aghast at what a good time we had, stripping off our lower garments and bending over washing machines, perching on couch arms, angling ourselves astride perfect strangers' Shaker sideboards.

One afternoon, shortly after the New Year, someone from Elektra called with the news that *No Secrets* and its lead single, "You're So Vain," had both jumped the charts from number 39 to number 1. For me, a performer who in her mid-twenties still saw herself as the stammering younger sister, the one eternally lagging behind, it was a wholly new experience. By sheer coincidence, James's album *One Man Dog* and its lead single, "Don't Let Me Be Lonely Tonight," had been released at approximately the same time as mine. Even though James's new album was doing extremely well, it wasn't the monster of a hit that "You're So Vain" was turning out to be. You would think I might have permitted myself a few hours, if not days, of satisfaction, or pride, but I couldn't. I had a crush on the song "Don't Let Me Be Lonely Tonight," similar to the crush I had on James, and the only thing I remember thinking was that I wished it were him, and not me.

It was the first time James and I had ever directly competed, and it confused me, not just because I'd always assumed James would be more commercially successful than I, but because my desire to make him happy was woven so intricately into the submissive side I'd cultivated in my childhood by bringing Uncle Peter milk shakes adorned with four-leaf clovers on top whenever he finished a tennis match. What is it about men that allows them to be at ease as the successful ones, without feeling any guilt if their wives come up short? Like many women of my generation, I wasn't remotely at peace with the idea of winning any competition with my man.

James's talent put everyone else to shame, and I only hoped he could savor his own tonality and poetry and sheer musicianship. To this day, there is a song on *One Man Dog*, "Little David," which is so childhood Vineyard to me. I think of Davy Gude and David our dog and it blends and merges together into then and now. As for my success with *No Secrets*, James couldn't have been prouder, or more gallant, in praising my work, and he seemed to take genuine pride that he was married to me. Whenever we picked up hitchhikers, which we often did, James always made it a point to call me by my name in the car, dropping a "Carly" here and there to let the person know it was me sitting there in the passenger seat. But perhaps I'm mistaken. I want to think he was proud.

At the same time, I couldn't help but pick up a new disturbance in the air. To make matters worse, my mother kept relaying messages to me that my sisters, Joey and Lucy, were both individually ruined, like Anastasia and Drizella, having heard the news about the overnight success of their stammering stepsister Cinderella, once best friends with cellar mice and dust balls, now riding around in magical style long after her midnight curfew should have expired. Instead of gloating, I just felt guilty. In the Simon family dynamic, for me to come out ahead was senseless and wrong. Hopefully, it was just a passing worry.

The "thing" I sensed in the air between James and me came to a head one bright weekend morning during our first year together. I was taking a bath in the claw-foot tub in the bathroom, which still lacked a door. As I was scrubbing myself off, I noticed how dirty the bathwater was getting. "I feel like I should get up and wash myself again and rinse myself under the faucet," I called out to James. "All this soap is leaving scum on my skin. It feels grubby."

Undergoing an instantaneous personality change, James stared at me, his face pinched and condemning, blurting out, as if in response to the most egregious comment ever uttered by anyone ever, "Haven't you ever heard of *emulsification?*"

Emulsification. I wasn't well versed in chemistry, the way James, genuinely interested in chemistry, was. It was one of those words you've heard, but don't know the meaning of. I knew vaguely that it had something to do with the breakdown of fat globules into smaller particles. The exact meaning of the word wasn't the point; the larger point was that James, schooled in physics and chemistry, knew a term that I didn't, and had pounced on me, humiliated me by deliberately making me feel dumb. A few seconds later, he'd gone outside, leaving me confused, embarrassed, and feeling rather bullied. Later, with my great friend Libby Titus, I made a list of other words and phrases that might catch me unaware and off-guard in the future, including *détente, creosoted posts,* and *perestroika.* Who knew what would come next?

More stinging than anything else was James's sudden shift into coldness. I was reminded of how he had spoken on the phone to two of his ex-girlfriends, Maggie Corey and Joni Mitchell, and how his apparent callousness had stunned me. A year earlier, during the first weekend I spent at the cabin, Maggie had called him. James picked up the wall phone, mounted on one of the beams holding the living room ceiling in place. Very politely, never dropping his southern gentleman persona, he warned Maggie not to call him ever again, and when he hung up the phone he started swearing. At the time, I thought his terseness with her was a sidelong way of making me feel more secure in his life by providing proof that his relationship with Maggie was over and done with. Still, what had she done, what had gone so terribly wrong, that she deserved to be guillotined like that?

A similar conversation had occurred a week or two later, when Joni Mitchell called the house. At the time James was in the cabin loft, the small room above the second story, and he must have been fully aware that I could hear every word of his end of the conversation. In essence, the blade came down again as he told Joni, "You shouldn't call here anymore." Yes, I was relieved that his relationship with Joni, his most recent love before me, was over, but at the same time, how could anyone ever be "over" Joni Mitchell? Joni was brilliant and enchanting, and her love for James, I always imagined, was original and deep. When James hung up and came down the stairs from the loft, he looked steely and furious.

As a woman who loved him, the last thing in the world I wanted to say was "Don't ever speak to someone you have loved, or told that you loved, or made love to, in such a way," and I didn't. I never said anything, simply registered this facet of James's personality.

Still, it was a sign, an omen. I should have picked up the precision with which the guillotine fell, should have memorized the quality of his incisive, elegant baritone. I huddled in my own private cubbyhole of watchfulness, transfixed by my own innocent conceit in believing James belonged to me now, and that words so icy, and so final, could never, ever fly in my direction.

In early January of 1973, the two of us flew to Japan, where James was on tour. The Japanese press seemed equally fascinated by me, and, not least,

by our marriage. Every night, one of the tour promoters took it upon himself to introduce each of the members of James's band who had arrived without a wife or girlfriend in tow to a Japanese lady of the night. It was a way
of life there, just as it's a way of life for many musicians on the road, and the
guys in the band loved traveling to Japan for just that reason, the easy separation of the heart and the body. James and I spent three weeks in Japan,
using the Tokyo Hilton as our home base despite the concerts he was
performing in Osaka and elsewhere, and I couldn't help wondering
whether James felt a little bit excluded from the boys' club.

The Japanese tour held another surprise for me. Almost daily, I received
notification from the lobby that a dozen red roses were downstairs, addressed
to me. They were attached to a note signed, M.P. Michael Phillips was one of
Mick's many aliases, one he probably used in hotel rooms across the world.
What prompted this? I hadn't encouraged Mick, but neither had I discour-
aged him. He knew I was married, so why didn't I just call him and tell him
to stop? Any decent female in a Jane Austen novel would have done that. I
suppose that both Mick and I were hanging onto something, and I wasn't
sure enough of myself to disengage from him completely. When James
asked me who they were from, I hedged and told him they were a gift from
the tour promoter for both of us. The roses continued showing up.

At the same time, the jarring amount of attention that the Japanese press
was paying to James and me led us one night to a difficult but crucially honest conversation about the competition between us. I don't remember exactly what was said, but our talk centered around the gargantuan success
of "You're So Vain," the attention I was receiving in Japan, and the fact that
this might be one of the very few times in my career I was temporarily surf-
ing a bigger wave than he was. James had torn feelings about this—he
didn't want to feel jealous of, or competitive with, the person he loved most
in the world, he told me. His words were extremely painful for me, since I
continued to feel guilty about being "big" or "important" within the Simon
family. This was just the time that my mother decided she would write me
out of parts of her will, since I wouldn't need the money anymore. More worrisome, I never wanted to overshadow the man I loved. "What a good, if
painful, talk it was," I wrote afterward in my diary. "He did let me in. Very

smart he is. Glad for the opportunity of having it make us so direct and open with each other. He doesn't miss a trick."

The early 1970s was an era when hallucinogens and other drugs were freely passed from record company presidents and A&R men to artists and their sidemen, backup singers, and stage crews. Whatever you wanted was freely available: cocaine, mushrooms, LSD, pot, as well as a few new fabrications recently invented in cutting-edge laboratories. Which explains why one of the men connected to the tour had recently given James and me four tablets of mescaline in capsule form to take to Japan. (For the record, I was innately fearful of all psychedelics. People who knew me well, including Jake and James, told me I wouldn't do well with them, since my nervous system seems to reside outside my body rather than inside, or "in my plume," as my son Ben says), so I simply packed the mescaline tablets inside my cosmetics case and forgot about them. We didn't take them in Japan, and when we got back I forgot all about them, at least until a few weeks later, when James and I took a short trip.

James's birthday, March 12, was coming up fast, and I wanted to surprise him with a big, hush-hush vacation, where James would have no idea where we were going. By that point, in spite of traveling to Japan, I had become something of an agoraphobe. Having never been the type to travel far from the mother ship, and the safety of my books and my medicine cabinet, sometimes I could barely summon up the nerve to go to a new restaurant. For our destination, I finally chose Bermuda, which is only a two-and-a-half-hour flight from New York, and reserved us a kingly suite at the Pink Beach Club, where my mother had stayed with Ronny and Peter once after Daddy died.

One day, James overheard me talking on the phone to Andy Newmark, my friend and drummer, and an irresistibly quirky fellow, who owned a house in Bermuda, asking for advice on restaurants and beaches. It was enough of a clue for him to make a fairly good guess as to where we were headed. I deflected him with a howling burst of laughter, confessing that

I really, really hated to spoil the surprise, but Bermuda? Sorry, no, we were heading instead to a tennis camp in Cleveland. No sun. No sand. No crashing waves. No underwater lovemaking. But we'd come back home with vastly improved forehands, backhands, and serves. James and I had recently been discussing the possibility of taking tennis lessons in New York. Tennis was a good, healthy exercise and if we grew to love the sport, we might even consider building our own court someday.

When James was finally convinced we weren't going to Bermuda for his birthday, and that I was, in fact, taking him to a Cleveland tennis camp instead, he was visibly disappointed. Still, I managed to ramp up his excitement level by buying him not one but two new pairs of tennis shoes, and for both of us, top-of-the-line Wilson tennis racquets.

By then, James had been on methadone for a year, and he packed enough doses to last him a week. We packed innocently and strategically for cool midwestern weather, considering we'd be playing tennis indoors. Then I got sneaky: I called the American Airlines ticket counter and asked the employee who answered the phone if she would change the name of the destination on our plane tickets to Cleveland, Ohio, which she agreed to do. (Never underestimate the power of fame.) "Just go to the first-class counter," she said, "and I'll brief Rosemary there to keep your secret." At the airport, Rosemary, as promised, was a model of discretion. James and I boarded the plane, stashed our bags, tennis racquets, and big leather hats in the overhead compartment, stored our new, customized Whitebook guitars with the stewardess up front, and took our seats in the third row. Thank God, not a single pair of shorts, sandals, or white pants gave any clue to our actual destination. But once we were in the air, the secret was blown when the captain announced over the loudspeaker, "Good morning . . . our flying time to Bermuda today will be two hours and fifteen minutes . . ."

James gave a single "Gracious me," followed by a soft, pleased laugh. At which point the stewardess, who was in on the secret, handed us two glasses of champagne in honor of James's birthday, and we toasted to "Surprises, instead of tennis camp."

The flight was smooth and as we lined up to disembark, I put on my hippie-of-many-colors cape and James his corduroy jacket. When the stewardess handed us our guitars, we really must have looked like "rock stars." Why not? Long hair, guitar cases, floppy leather hats. Which is probably why the airport officials in Bermuda, a British colony, began asking us questions.

They put on a good show of being non-adversarial, but at the same time they asked to see each one of us separately in one of the little cubicles set aside for long-haired, guitar-toting, leather-hat-wearing rock stars. Fortunately, the cubicles were separated by the thinnest of walls, which allowed me to overhear the conversation between James and a young customs official.

In a fluid West Indian accent, he asked James to unzip his bag, and after inspecting the contents, noted that James must be visiting Bermuda to partake of the island's many tennis facilities. Then came this: "I see that you have a paper bag there. Would you mind letting me see what's inside? Oh, yes, and what exactly is inside those little bottles? Do all seven contain the same liquid? Methadone, yes. And what exactly is that for?"

James had a letter of permission from his New York doctor explaining the reason for the week's supply, which the official scanned, confirming with James that the medication was for a "mental situation." In the next cubicle over, I was eavesdropping on this entire conversation, while partially undressing in front of a second customs official, this one an attractive, middle-aged, no-nonsense woman whose nametag read CHLOE.

She opened my cosmetics case, which I hadn't unpacked since returning from Japan, and had, in fact, barely touched. It suddenly hit me: in that case were the four dark-green caplets of mescaline that had been given to us. I might have told James about them, or alluded to them, but neither of us had touched them. The four pills were balled up in a handkerchief that, in turn, was stuffed inside a plastic travel-soap container. As Chloe opened out the handkerchief, the quartet of caplets went spilling onto the floor.

Chloe picked them up: Would I be so kind as to tell her what, exactly, these pills were?

"Those," I replied, "are a special processed Vitamin B_{12}, which I was prescribed for my heliospondic knee." I made up *heliospondic*; boy did it hurt!

"I see. Well—we'll just take these, shall we? And let the medical corporal-in-arms take a look?" When I nodded, Chloe pocketed them in her smock. She excused herself, shutting the door behind her, and went directly into the cubicle next door, where poor James was sitting captive. Now I heard her tell James that she'd found four green caplets inside his wife's cosmetics bag: Did he know what they were for? "Have you ever seen them?" added the man who'd been interrogating James.

"Oh," replied my wonderful junkie husband. "I think those are vitamins she takes."

"For her knee?" Chloe pressed. Not a well-honed detective!

Yes, James replied, and if memory serves, he added, "Can't be sure, but that sounds right. For her heliospondic knee."

A few moments later, Chloe returned. She apologetically explained that she was sorry to inconvenience me, but she had to take the four pills with her for additional testing. She thanked me for cooperating. "The Bermudan government has to take every precaution to keep our little island in the sun safe," she added. "It's for your benefit, as much as it is for mine."

Oh shit. What had she picked up from James's childlike, birthday-boy eyes? My heart started beating fast. James's and my celebratory vacation was over. We would be locked up. No doubt Chloe's "little island safe in the sun" speech was one she'd delivered regularly to any number of miscreants attempting to start a new life here. James and I were goners, and on his birthday, no less. At this point, compared to whatever else lay in store for us, deportation would be the best news we could receive.

The upshot: James and I were free to go, but our pills would have to stay. We could go to our hotel, and customs would contact us once they'd finished their investigation.

Slightly under a cloud, we took a cab to the Pink Beach Club in Tucker's Town. It was midafternoon. Once we settled into our room, we changed into our tennis clothes (white pants and white shirts—de rigueur for the Cleveland Professional School of Tennis) and headed for the courts. James was being a good sport for my sake, but that night I felt jittery as the two of us ate dinner in our room.

The phone rang first thing the next morning. James got out of bed and answered it just in time. It was the customs official who'd interviewed James in the airport cubicle. Further studies showed beyond a shadow of a doubt that the four pills confiscated from my cosmetics case were . . . nothing.

"Nothing?" James repeated.

No, the pills turned out to be nothing more than "just an 'armless 'erb," the man said, adding, "Would you like to come down to the police station in Hamilton and pick them up?"

"That's all right." I could hear the relief in James's voice. "You can just throw them out. Thank you so much. Have a nice day."

James laughed his way back to our bedroom and repeated the entire conversation to me, his favorite words being *an 'armless 'erb.*

I was still lying in bed. "So what did he do with them?"

"I told him to throw them away." A long pause. "Wait a minute—why did I do that? Shit! I have to call him right back!"

A few moments later, James was on the phone, explaining that he'd made a mistake, and his wife still needed her pills. In response, the officer told him which buzzer to ring at the station, and he would come down and deliver the *'erb* in person.

Like most Bermudan days, it was sunny and in the mid-seventies, and after getting directions to Hamilton, James mounted a bike and an hour later was back at the Pink Beach Club armed with four pills of pure *mescalito*. He gulped one of them down with his morning orange juice, and though I didn't take one myself, I was happy to go along for the ride. James and I spent the rest of the day walking along the beach, lying in the sun, and staring intently at individual grains of white sand. I'd very much wanted to take half a pill, but again, with my temperament, I didn't know if I'd be able to distinguish a good or even a bad trip from genuine, wall-dissolving madness. Regardless, it turned out to be one of the nicest days I can remember. That night, James and I played cards before he tuned up his Whitebook guitar and started a little island music going.

I was reminded of some of the ukulele rhythms that Uncle Peter played for me when I was very young, which is why I started dancing. "Do you remember the day your uncle taught us his dance?" James asked.

He goaded me to show him the dance again. "Come on, sweetheart, you can do it." He amped up the volume on his guitar, his playing getting wilder, which in turn loosened me up. How gorgeous and complete an experience it had been for me to see my uncle Peter simultaneously singing and dancing, moving the lower half of his body like a motor gone crazy, his movements and motions belonging to a dance as yet uninvented, from a country on no world map whatsoever, his hands jabbing at his upper torso and face like some beatifically smiling Indian princess as his legs performed what I can only describe as the Monty Python version of an African boot dance. Just recalling Uncle Peter's dance, James and I laughed so hard that my face hurt. That night, we skipped dinner, but celebrated James's birthday in the bathtub, surrounded by candles, toasting Uncle Peter with flutes of champagne.

Well done, Simon Sister!

At the end of May 1973, upon my return home from the most recent James tour, I found out that I was pregnant. I'd accompanied James, along with his flagship band—Russ Kunkel, Lee Sklar, Danny Kortchmar, and Clarence McDonald—and when we returned to New York, I remember keeping the news to myself until I was positively sure nothing bad would happen. The first few months of my pregnancy, I did the usual sleeping around the clock, and James and I spent those sleepy months on the Vineyard, building the new "wing," its forty-five-foot-high tower the crown of the neighborhood. The wing had a new living room area, with a real (though very tiny) kitchen, attached to a central room, with a brick fireplace, and a dining room table with extra leaves for when we had people over. And there were never *not* people over. In the times between sleeping and carpenters sanding the floors, surrounded by dusty people, many holding guitars, most smoking pot, all of them wearing bathing suits, I remember cooking massive amounts of Trudy's clam chowder for the assembled hordes. My own marijuana days had ended a few months earlier when a hash brownie nearly had its way with me. (In those days, there were no specific warnings about pot smoking while pregnant, though caution, I seem to recall, was the prevailing mood.) The only thing I took occasionally, for sleep, or seasickness, or airsickness, was Dramamine.

June 18th, 1973:
We're off to New York in a couple of minutes. The day is cold and depressing. I'm not lightening it any. Last night James got drunk

again. The problem is grave. He doesn't know why he needs to get drunk, but says that he needs to at least four times a day. I don't seem to satisfy much in him. I don't understand him when he says he needs me. He's so down on himself that he relies not at all on himself but on chemicals for happiness. He only seeks me out for affection when he fears its loss. I'm so sad.

He is more physical toward me in the presence of other folk than when we are alone. He thinks when I say "I love you," that I am asking a question, that I need something in return. Patience, I guess.

James was just off a two-week detox when he and I traveled to Europe in July to visit two of our best friends, Ellen and Vieri Salvadori. I'd been friends with Ellen since the seventh grade, and Vieri was my first partner in ballroom dancing class. In Rome, we were met by a record-company executive, who drove us to Siena, where Ellen and Vieri had a madly beautiful house overlooking what looked like a painting: Tuscan olive groves amid a landscape of charming, choppy, impossibly green hills. It was an extremely romantic setting, except for the fact that James was almost untouchable, suffering as he was from skin-hypersensitivity whenever my leg so much as grazed his, and declining all efforts at closeness or intimacy. "James just doesn't seem to want me," I wrote in my diary. "Bastard, I hate him. Why do I love him so? Why don't I love a Giver? I suppose I need enough elusiveness to keep me feeling as unworthy as I believe myself to be. Perhaps James has given his heart away. To opium. No—it's me being over-needy."

A week or so later, the four of us drove north to Switzerland and Austria, where my sister, Joey, was performing at the Spoleto Festival. It was always shocking to see my sister in the environment where she thrived, to hear her sing in that big, trained voice, the mezzo richness of it all making me wish I had studied singing and could do more with my phrasing. Joey was stunning, and I hoped I showed her how proud of her I was. The next day, we took a night train to Paris, stopping at an inn along the way, ultimately deciding to rent a car and drive the last fifty miles to Paris through scenic woodlands.

James had been fairly cool to me the entire trip, but when we got to the inn, he emerged one night from the bathroom a shaven man. His mustache was gone. It was a complete shock: in the two and a half years we'd known each other, I'd never seen him without one. (James had appeared on an album cover without it, but I'd never seen him clean-shaven in person.) Without his mustache, he looked embarrassed, almost, to show me his face, as if he'd never let me see him naked before. He was instantly transformed into the shyest, most vulnerable southern baby. Removing that rigid Prussian-soldier barrier seemed to affect his personality, too, as all the goodness of his nature came forth, and after my period of feeling unloved and missing being close to him, we made love just like a pregnant wife would with her clean-shaven husband.

But I'd also come to a realization: James needed his space—physically, emotionally—and was liable to reject anyone who deprived him of that raw square footage. If a close friend like Ellen Salvadori wanted a hug hello, or a kiss good-bye, that was no problem, but a sharp observer could easily intuit that the whole time James was looking for the exit sign. This same hypersensitivity to closeness, mixed with James's coolness—if not actual revulsion—to anyone who trespassed on his physical space, happened in the wake of every single one of his detoxes. His detoxes were from methadone and opiates, not alcohol. It got complicated, especially when he drank, when liquor made him want me physically. For James, those nights were double-edged.

By that September, we were both out in Los Angeles, recording. James was working on his new album, *Walking Man*, and I was working on my new album, *Hotcakes*. Jake was in L.A., too, living in Malibu, and he and I kept fiddling with songs, some of which we would put aside for future albums. In Jake's house, he and I worked on a new song, "I Haven't Got Time for the Pain," whose lyrics Jake wrote right in the middle of recording the album. Originally, Jake intended for it to be an I-love-you-and-you-came-along-and-changed-everything kind of song, but when I asked him if it was about Jennifer Salt, the woman in his life, he told me it was in fact a Sufi song about Oscar, his Sufi teacher.

With me pregnant and working, and James writing and recording, we were in one of the mellowest periods of marriage ever. After a difficult summer, we'd relaxed into a nice year and a half. A good explanation of how I was feeling is expressed in a song I wrote at the time called "I've Got My Mind on My Man."

He's a lotus that opens and closes
I know that he won't always let me in
But I've got my mind on my man again, my mind is on my man
Sometimes he's sleepy, and I don't think he loves me
I worry about his lovin'
Ain't I crazy?

He's a northern baby and a southern child
He's a gentleman lost at the fair
He's a cowboy getting drunk at the Plaza
He has a place in my heart anywhere.

From my diary:

Dec 1st, 1973:
I'm generally euphoric and more in love with James, I don't know how it can keep growing. How much capacity do I have? It's wonderful. I am a lover.

"Mockingbird" had its origins in a car, in the wake of a toasty little beach party, and maybe a glass of rum. We were in the car on the Vineyard, about to make a left turn onto Lambert's Cove, when I said to James, "We should think about a duet we could do."

"Do you know"—a pause for some Jamesian humming—"how about 'Mockingbird'?" It wasn't the better-known version parents sing to their children—the one that begins, "Hush little baby, don't say a word, Momma's gonna buy you a mockingbird . . ." a lullaby I would eventually record on my album *Into White*, but a 1960s novelty song written by Inez and Charlie Foxx. James began singing the song right away, leaving off the introductory "Mock." *Yeah . . . Bird . . . Yeah . . .* It was James who arranged the song, decided who would sing what verse, or note, but the topic of "Mockingbird" didn't come up between us again until I offhandedly mentioned to Richard Perry that James had suggested it would make a good duet. One day, in New York, Richard brought up "Mockingbird"; he thought it was a great idea. As usual, Richard was relentless, whipping James and me into a "Let's get it done right away, it's a hit" mode.

The quality of the musicians living in New York in the late 1970s was so high, it was borderline ridiculous. You could simply call up the choicest musicians in the world, knowing they'd be at any one of a handful of studios, and schedule a time twenty-four to forty-eight hours later. One was Robbie Robertson, another was Mac Rebennack, otherwise known as Dr. John, and the others included drummer Jim Keltner, bassist Klaus Voorman, Jimmy Ryan, Ralph MacDonald, Bobby Keys, and Michael Brecker.

Richard suggested that Mac make the sound of a bird on the organ, while Jimmy, Robbie, Klaus, and Ralph were busy working on keys and tempo, a gumbo of ideas and inspirations from some of the most creative people in the industry. Michael Brecker and Bobby Keys (whom I'd last seen at Ahmet Ertegun's Hollywood party) didn't come in until later in the day, but in the meantime James and I cut the basic track of "Mockingbird" during a single afternoon, and by the time we went home that night, we'd laid down a rough track.

On the line "Everybody, have you heard . . . ," James swapped out *heard* for *hoid*, showcasing his Muddy Waters genes. He would always sing "Mockingbird" live that way, too, never on the first verse, mind you, where I take the lead, but on his own verse. I took it as James's way of out-Uncle-Peter-ing me, since Uncle Peter would often incorporate the spirit of New Orleans or Chicago in his delivery by singing notes with a "black" or "jazz" accent. James and I performed "Mockingbird" live a few times, most memorably, maybe, at the No Nukes Concert at Madison Square Garden in 1979, which to me counts as one of James's most animated performances. When the two of us were onstage together, there was often a healthy, unspoken competition, one that lifted James's energy level up to mine, which, I should add, was always disastrously high, not on purpose but because of my ever-present anxiety levels.

When I accompanied James on tour—and I went on at least some part of every one of them until the late seventies, when it didn't seem fair to drag our small children, Ben and Sally, along with us—"Mockingbird" was always a showstopper. Singing it together, James and I were always flexible, comfortable and sexy in our dancing and patter, eternally loose in our vocal play. James was dry and funny, and whenever I laughed at what he did, and said, it seemed to spur him to even goofier levels of outrageousness. Our two voices would do their call-and-response, dancing, jabbing, flirting, sparring with each other until the moment comes, a minute or so into the song, on the line "I'll *ride* with the tide and go with the flow . . ." when our two voices, hand-holding, land deftly, perfectly on a musical fourth, my grind against his gentle upswing, that note for me, now and forever, James's and my musical hearth and home.

By 1974, we had completed a new wing on the Vineyard house, plus a few new sunlit terraces, only to begin imagining other, future wings, carports, gardens, and—because I was left with too much idle, swimming-pool-construction time on my hands while James was on tour—a swimming pool. When James came home, the pool was already filled with water, its borders surrounded by dirt, mud, and sand. It was completely audacious of me, and there was no excuse for me not walking James through it beforehand, though I could have sworn I had. (Judging by his response, I hadn't told him, but there was no way I would have gone ahead with a decision as monumental as that without clearing it with him first.) That was only one of the liberties I took that made him angry. Another was the circle garden I planted a year later. James was not happy about that, either. Both were bourgeois and selfish gestures on my part, utterly at odds with James's cabin-in-the-woods, no frills, New England sensibility.

Mick told me once that whenever he wished to increase his emotional distance from me, he would remember the time I'd told him I had a Swiss bank account. The only problem was it wasn't true. Back in the early seventies, I wouldn't even have known what a Swiss bank account meant! That doesn't matter. The point is, Mick was simply saying that I skirted around being "bourgeois," and therefore the opposite of what he stood for. Which is another way of saying that at least two important male role models of mine, James and Mick, had "labeled" me. Hadn't Albert Grossman told me I'd be a perfect ten if only I didn't have money? But the irony of it was that my father had been robbed, though I didn't know it at the time, nor did I know that there wasn't much money left in the Simon family coffers. When would this rich-girl image quit dogging me?

James and I had other head-buttings, too, including conflicting ideas about the best color for the trim on our now-expanded, increasingly fanciful cedar-shingled house. By the mid-seventies, thanks to the forty-five-foot-high hexagonal tower James designed, which rose up four levels, it was a very visible structure. James voted for yellow trim so it would look sunny all the time through the windows, whereas I wanted an equally optimistic rosy pink color. We worked out our differences of opinion amicably by counting the trim-worthy surfaces and splitting them in half, with each one of us getting an even amount of paint. In the end, half the trim was yellow, the other half pink.

Both the press and the people who loved us, I knew, imagined our lives on the Vineyard in a glamorous, seaside mist, as a musical Camelot on the edge of the stormy, crashing sea, but our day-to-day life was a lot more pedestrian than that. People sawing and hammering eternally on a house that, it seemed, would never be done, never cross the line of being able to be "lived in." I cooked almost constantly. I got to be friends with a lot of Vineyard hippie girls, especially Kate, Jeannie, and Brent Taylor, James's sister and sisters-in-law, with many of us pregnant at the same time, our aprons billowing white jibs over our swelling stomachs. Kate was having a very successful singing career at the same time.

Mixed in with home and domestic and pre-childbirth matters were the typical worries of two people in a very tough business. James and I would often swap concerns about the state of our careers. One day he would console me, and the next it would be the other way around. This show business stuff, I once wrote in my diary, is for people narcissistic enough to put themselves through hellish reductions for the occasional ego gratification. What's more, the appetite for more attention, more hits, more publicity, more triumph, simply increases. I added, "It's good to have James as a mate—so constantly understanding and comprehending of every career situation. He is so fine. I love every hair on him."

By that November, James and I had moved out of the Murray Hill apartment into a larger place, a four-story brownstone on East Sixty-second Street, between Second and Third Avenues, where we would "live" for the next three years, even though we were spending most of our time in L.A. or the Vineyard. We had the first three stories to ourselves, and we rented out the top floor. New homes mean new faces, new carpenters, but James, I remember, was especially husbandly and sympathetic to me, his newly pregnant wife.

If ever a girl baby didn't want to leave the womb, it was our daughter, Sarah Maria. She was three weeks late, and James and I spent practically all that time with Dustin and Anne Hoffman. Dustin, I remember, had a plan: he would make me laugh so hard it would induce labor. While we waited for *that* to happen, the four of us whiled away the time by playing cards, eating hot Indian food in our brownstone, going to restaurants and shows—including a Peter Cook–Dudley Moore night on Broadway—and listening to Dustin read aloud from *Lenny*, which he was just starting to shoot. Dustin was determined to induce my labor, but as it turned out, the one time I *wasn't* trying—for Dustin's sake—was one night I went to bed on the early side. That night, I recall, the moon was closer to the earth than it had been in twenty-three years. The night was brisk and clear, and I had a sudden thought from out of nowhere: I should clean all the copper in the house. The next morning, at around 6:30 a.m., my water broke. In a panic, James called for Lydia, our housekeeper and cook, telling her there was water everywhere.

Lydia wrapped a couple of towels around my waist as James hightailed it onto Sixty-second Street to hail a cab. I'd had a bag packed all month, and as Lydia placed my winter coat around my shoulders, all I had to do was pick it up and delicately pile inside the cab next to James. It was January 7, 1974, and as we sped to the hospital, it felt to me as though we were driving right into the moon, which was still full, still bright. Beside me, James was doing his best to maintain calm, though he made it a point to keep the towels around me at just the right level to keep in check the possibility of a backseat flood.

But this baby, Sarah, was going to take her sweet time. She had other plans. She would wrap her umbilical cord around her darling little neck, and once we got to the hospital, with the help of Demerol, I would end up pushing for seven hours. James and I had attended a few childbearing classes in tandem, where he learned a few techniques about what would be most helpful during the contraction stage, but they fell away once my contractions started, since no one—no one—had instructed James to sit by my bedside, pretending to be a seagull flying high above the beach in Menemsha. Every time a contraction came through, James, in full seagull form, murmured, "Carly, Carly . . . the wave is coming in gently . . . Carly, go with it now . . . relax . . ." By now it was harder and harder to relax and I'd start shrieking, but James's seagull-voice rose up to meet my volume. "Carly, relax . . . the wave is coming in, it's breaking gently at the shore . . ."

"NO IT AIN'T, BASTARD! IT'S NOT STOPPING!" That was the best response I could come up with.

But my seagull-husband was a champion improviser. "Okay, we'll go to the South Shore, then. Now we're on Lucy Vincent Beach in Chilmark, and there's a pretty big wave coming on. Oh my, I should have brought my seagull hat with me, the waves are strong, the wind's picking up . . ."

The pain was unbearable, though that's hardly an uncommon reaction. James called for the doctor to do something, and the doctor did, ordering me into surgery for a C-section. There followed a cluster of sounds from muffled to metallic and clattering—probes, scissors, shots, towels—as the nurses tried to stay in control. As if from another zone, I heard James's voice, growing more and more faint and birdlike: "Carly, see the seagull? I'm flying over the falls of Niagara . . . it's beautiful . . . you're gonna be fine . . . that's my girl . . ."

Inside the small surgery room, the doctor requested scissors; a mask was placed over my face; nitrous oxide. As I went down for the count, I heard James, singing softly, "Bad, bad Leroy Brown . . . baddest man in the whole damn town . . ." Was he trying to make me laugh? "Badder than old King Kong . . . meaner than a junkyard dog . . ."

And then there was my beautiful, golden, magical daughter in my arms. While waiting for Sally to be born, James had written the entire song "Sarah Maria." Sally's birth meant so much to him, and he was such a wonderful father to her when she was a baby. That night, as I dozed with my beautiful new baby in my arms, James took a taxi over to Trax, the New York nightclub, and sang the song to the audience:

Well, the moon is in the ocean
And the stars are in the sky
And all I can see is my sweet Maria's eyes, oh
Sarah, Sarah Maria.

Sarah Maria and the world at its best.

"I've come home to stop yearning."

---

CHAPTER TWENTY-ONE

heat's up, tea's brewed

There's always that peculiar thing that rescues you, the thing that's so hard to name. If I were to locate and then identify all the hellish things we all have to go through in life in order to uncover one minute of happiness, it would take up a lot of space.

With James, that "thing"—that diversion from the pain of life—lay strongly and squarely in the music that surrounded us, and that he and I sang and played. James's music gave me grace. It gave me inspiration. Witnessing his creativity—his writing, his singing, his playing guitar—was something I never took for granted. Those times we could sing together and make harmony, or join in a melody in a different octave, were like a gift from some other dimension. We watched the Watergate hearings while James wrote "Let It All Fall Down" and the essence of the time, the denouement of a hellhole in history, was pinpointed and clarified and rounded out. Ford installed, song over.

From the moment we met, James and I gave each other tacit permission to write about our own fantasy loves, or even real loves, with no questions asked. Monogamy was our physical ideal, but as far as our work was concerned, it would only take us so far in our imaginations. We both needed muses, fantasies, private realities we wouldn't necessarily share with each other. Even "You're So Vain," one of the most intellectual songs I've ever written, pulses with sexual energy, not that the two are mutually exclusive. Making a cameo in James's song "Mexico" was a sleepy señorita "with the eyes on fire," just as one of the lyrics of my song "Waterfall" is "I saw you and it made no sense at all . . . Now I feel like there's too much caffeine in my blood." As for James's song "Slow Burning Love," who was that about? Not me. Much later, I found out it was about some girl he met in the South, who was that song's spark, its spirit, its engine, its reason for being. In fact, she *had* to be there, to inspire and help James write words, and who was I, who needed the same ignition humming and simmering beneath my own lyrics and melodies, to engage in the hazy jasmine scent of someone else's intrigue? For James, that fantasy part of his brain, centered on women with fresher sexual identities, was partitioned off by mutual agreement, just as he allowed me to write songs in which, if he'd listened to them closely, there appeared lines that could have only been about another old love. We both went so far as to sing backup on each other's *songs* about each other's intrigues.

When Bianca Jagger called up the night before our wedding and James defended me, telling her he knew all about Mick and me, and that he trusted what I'd told him, we were establishing an unspoken barometer, one that permitted both of us to have enough of a private life, or even a secret life, that could serve as food for our music. Without the "gleam in the eye," you simply lack the juice to write lyrics, or a melody, to woo what you're feeling into verses, a bridge, a chorus—in short, a song.

When James wrote "Believe It or Not," did I believe for one moment it was about me? Did I corner him, shine a flashlight into his eyes, interrogate him? No. I learned not to ask. I didn't want to smother him. I didn't want to choke off that thing that made James as great as he was, patting myself on the back, am I not? Some bits of courage were just "smart." From my perspective, fantasy is healthy and necessary, though at the same time, I set guidelines for myself that were inviolable. Cheating, for one. If I had acted on an attraction to a man who wasn't James, I would have risked making my marriage unsafe, and my relationship with my husband was far more important than anyone the Beast might be temporarily eyeing.

In my living room today, beside the fireplace, is the same chair where James used to sit with his guitar, with our black, heavy, oversized Sony cassette tape recorder tracking the sounds of the household and our family. In that chair James composed what would soon become "Secret o' Life," as baby Sally goo-goo-ed and ga-ga-ed in the background. "That is July 5, 1974, Tisbury," James says on one tape, before his voice shifts over to fatherly teasing. "And this is Sarah's tape. Sarah's getting fed right now. That scraping sound you hear is the sound of the spoon in her bowl. Sarah's a very hungry, very greedy little girl . . ."

James was very fluid and unself-conscious about composing, or trying out new lyrics or melodies in front of me. He would always be playing the guitar, whereas when I wasn't working on my own music, I was cooking, or giving the kids their baths, or picking up their toys. Another example of "Great Mom." In general, though, we would trade back and forth, now and again doing informal joint recording sessions together at home. It took me a year or two into our marriage before I could make any musical commentary on what James was composing, but from that point on, I was always pretty open about giving him ideas or comments without feeling annoying about it (I knew from experience that the more brilliant a person is, the touchier he can be, too). In "Secret o' Life," I can take some small credit for the mention of "Einstein" in the lyric "Einstein said he could never understand it all," since James had no specific line in mind at the time. "You use that chord too often," I remember telling James. "Can you maybe play something I'll be surprised by?" I suggested he pin the lyric on either the name of a city or a star or a person, and in the end he came up with *Einstein*.

In return, James was always generous with giving advice. Sometimes I'd ask him for help, and he would always give me pearls, perfect lines. In my song "Boys in the Trees," it was James who gave me either the lyric "Sheets the color of fire" or "Curse my own desire"—I can't remember which. We traded back and forth, James and I, and he never hesitated to help me in the studio. I never played guitar or piano on any of his records, but I did sing backup on "One Man Parade," "Rock 'n' Roll Is Music Now," "Let It All Fall Down," "How Sweet It Is," "A Junkie's Lament," "Shower the People," "B.S.U.R.," and many others, too. James, of course, more than returned the favor with "Mockingbird," "Devoted to You," "Waterfall," "You Belong to Me," and at least twenty other songs.

Then there was the duet we did on James's song "Terra Nova," from his *JT* album. One day, James, no doubt after an afternoon spent browsing in Manny's Music Store on West Forty-eighth Street or the drum store across the street, brought home an accordion-like Indian instrument known as a shruti box. With its charming, dronelike, bovine sound, the instrument is based on a system of bellows, which players can tune as they wish by adjusting various buttons, dials, and slabs of wood.

When the shruti box showed up in our house, I used it just as an accompaniment for my simpler tunes, including a simple melody I played whenever I put Sally to sleep in her automatic swing. One day, as Sally was suspended in her swing, I sang an *ahhh* vowel sound, shading it with a melody simple enough not to stir a dozing child. Five minutes later, I started singing some lyrics: "Out to the west of Lambert's Cove . . . there is a sail out in the sun . . . and I'm on board though very small . . . I've come home to stop yearning . . ." followed by a second verse: "Burn off the haze around the shore . . . Turn off the crazy way I feel . . . I'll stay away from you no more . . . I've come home to stop yearning . . ."

Over the course of that summer and the following one, I kept my eye on Vineyard Sound, off the west of Lambert's Cove, from the top of our house's hexagonal tower—watching the sky and the trees breathing their top branches into its changing colors; glimpsing, just past the trees, the sailboats out in the sun; gazing at the sun as it rose and set. Some nights James and I climbed up to the tower together to look up at the shooting stars. We'd find a perfect night to savor, climb the narrow winding stairs that still lead to the tower, and make love high up in the sky, while Sally slept the night away in her crib two floors below. I liked to imagine myself aboard one of those boats, and in that dream I found a few more words to add to what had begun, simply, as Sally's shruti box chant.

When James and I were in L.A. in 1976, he had finished writing, and was starting to record, the album later known as *JT*. He was singing "Terra

Nova"—a song about his father's sailboat—in our bedroom, putting the finishing touches on the lyrics, as I put on my makeup in the nearby bathroom. Five minutes later we were in the car. Sally was whiny, and in an effort to calm her down, I started singing my shruti box song, "Out to the west of Lambert's Cove." At which point James said, "You know, I think that goes naturally into 'Terra Nova.'"

It was an aha moment of sorts. When James and I got to the studio, naturally we had no shruti box, but it was easy enough to imitate the sounds it made on a synthesizer. Clarence McDonald, the pianist, played the right chords in the right key, and a few minutes later Peter Asher said, "Carly—just start singing it during the outro, when James sings, 'Got to be on my way by now . . .'" Which I did. I sang my lyrics over the drone of the chord, with James joining me, singing a harmony— "I've come home to stop yearning"—on the last line of every verse. We passed through our perfect-fourth harmony, and when we did I literally experienced goose bumps. It was another mystery of the physics of sound, or the ghosts of music, making a natural, or should I say unnatural, reverb—since the lyrics and melody of what James and I were singing overlapped so eerily well. Ultimately, in order to make my part of the song truer to the original source and power of the shruti box, we called my friend Carinthia West, who was staying at our Vineyard house, and asked her to ship the instrument to L.A. She did, and it still had the sound of a musical cow.

Just being around James, on the Vineyard and in New York, during those years, even when we weren't playing music, rarely failed to have a magical effect. When James walked into a room—any room—he transformed it, charging it up with his radiance, his message of "I'm just passing through, but while I'm here, it's the night before Christmas." Thinking about it now, many years later, I can still feel that *Oh-dear-sweet-Jesus, he's here—James is here!* feeling. And that's all there is to it.

And you know who I am
Though I never leave my name or number
I'm locked inside of you
So it doesn't matter

There's always someone haunting someone
Haunting someone.
　—"Haunting," 1978

James and I spent the winter in L.A. renting a house on Rockingham Drive in Brentwood, the very house that O. J. Simpson would buy a year later. Both of us were working on new albums. I must have been on the lookout for omens—Will James and I stay together? Will he be okay? Will *we* be okay?—but the only omen I was ever aware of was that I awoke one morning at 2:50 a.m., noting the time on my watch—Should I put on the oatmeal yet?—and glanced through the bedroom skylight just in time to see a comet streaking down through the dark blue sky. I fell back asleep, not bothering to wake James, as the comet would be long gone, but not before first touching legs with him, my darling husband, who forever kept me on my toes.

As much as motherhood was a diversion from worrying about myself, so was my continued sense of falling in love with James—with his mannerisms, his profundity, his wit, his insights. Any worries I had shrunk in the presence of the love I felt for him, one so strong that it banished any concerns that James, in return, didn't love me as much as he had when we spent our first night together in another city, another apartment, another time.

Although James and I were both glued to Sally, we spent our time in L.A. working on new music, thanks to our beloved babysitter, Patty Kelly, whose presence made it possible for us, James and me, to leave Sally each day and drive half an hour to our respective recording cells in Hollywood. On the days we brought Sally with us, she got quickly used to the heavy bass pulsing through the floorboards, making her blue elephant shake and quiver along to the beat.

Like most new parents, we found it hard to be without her. Still, in the interests of a getaway, one night James and I decided to drive up the coast to Santa Barbara. Sally wasn't even three years old, but James and I hadn't tried for a grown-up honeymoon since her birth, and our night away, at least as I foresaw it, would be devoted to lovemaking. But almost as soon as we pulled out of the driveway, we began remembering her, nostalgically, as though she were a beloved song we couldn't get out of our heads. As we drove north, we suffered together as we discussed her delicious smell, the sound of her giggles, each of us bemused by the other's imitations of her two-year-old voice, expressions, yawns, twitches, stretches, movements— the entire glorious baby package that was *her*.

We arrived at our destination, and once our bags were parked in our sumptuous hotel suite, I went into the bathroom to tidy up. Raising my eyes to a window to the right of the toilet, I let out a sudden scream. The bell-hop, who had lugged our bags to our room, and was no doubt accustomed to guests making their way directly to the bathroom after a long car ride, had found himself a perfect perch from which to peek.

The bellhop was bad enough, but outweighing even a stray peeping employee was . . . Sally. Our little girl. James agreed with me: Why stay? When we told the concierge what had happened, he didn't charge us, and having been settled in our lovers'-lane getaway for less than ten minutes, we returned our unopened luggage to the car and hit the highway back to Brentwood. All the way home, relieved and excited, James and I both talked about how much we missed Sally, more than we could have possibly imagined, and how dazzlingly great—what a homecoming—it would be to see her again.

Parenthood didn't get in the way of James's and my writing, singing, and, in his case, touring. Sally, bless her heart, made our already complicated lives even more complicated, while exaggerating the volatility of our domestic life, with a soupçon of my postpartum hormones thrown into the stew. The sheer theater of the following few years, with its mixture of bad news followed closely by good news, of births and lies, kicked off in the spring of 1976.

May 18th, 1976:
Dear Diary:
Something happened in Knoxville. Maybe our marriage was too
good. Maybe he just had to hurt me out of love. It was most
probably simpler than that. Just drugs and the spirit of the occasion

and the influence of loose southern jackasses. Anyway, James announced to me yesterday that he had to get checked out for clap. I reacted predictably (for me)—very understanding and guarded. The first thing out of my mouth was "You poor darling. It must have been so hard to tell me that. We'll go together to the doctor. You must feel awful. I understand." That was 3:00 p.m., maybe 3:30 latest. Ironically I was just about to tell him that I thought I was pregnant. I was waiting to see his face light up, waiting to kiss him and tell him our boy was on his way (though we didn't know it then that it was a boy).

When I turned around 180 degrees and snapped, it was 8:30 p.m., and I was lying in bed. I went downstairs to break the Whitebook guitar on his head. He caught me in time, and I hit him with my fists as hard as I could, got in my car, and went driving 80 mph around the curvy narrow roads of West Tisbury—returning because I loved him and didn't want him to worry about me behind the wheel in such a state—oh, a state of hate. Blind, convulsive, killer rage—the thought of those other bodies.

James is vomiting in the bathroom. Suitable to this entry. He's really sick. Maybe he was poisoned. With a little more hate, I could have slipped something in his dinner. How I loathe him and the thought of those secrets he has and those memories he'll always keep. Of those Knoxville groupies and their putrid, scented, magnolia bodies. Spit spit spit. I don't want him to touch me again. He did last night— but he was passionate and loved me and I actually felt that he loved me more than ever. But my blood has turned to ice again, and I wonder how he'll melt it.

June 5th, 1976:
Yesterday I found out, via the usual rabbit test, that I really am pregnant. It sort of calmed me down a little—the definite knowl- edge. I will certainly have doubts about my self-image. . . . With two children, you're a dowager, and just too old for rock 'n' roll . . . and then . . . what about Knoxville?

In the times when my head
Was together about you

I was an expert at silence
I enjoyed the blondes in their red jeeps
Stopping you on the streets
Knowing no one could compare with me
In my airy skirts and my cool retreats

You could have told the truth all the time
I was that at ease inside
You never made me cry
And then one night I lied
I got down with a boy in the back woods
I didn't tell you and you didn't see
And that's when jealousy got the dog up in me . . .

But in times when my head was together about you
I was an expert at silence

Now every look you get
Seems like another threat
I pick your pockets almost hoping to find

Something to be hurt about
To prove you unkind
Oh but I still love you baby
Though now I just can't sit still

And though that boy
Meant nothing to me,
I believe I've lost that simple thrill

Of the times
When my head
Was together
About you, and I was an expert at silence
    —"In Times When My Head," 1976

By 1976, James and I had sold our town house on East Sixty-second Street and were scoping out other places to live. Where, though? James and I went so far as to look at houses in Greenwich, Connecticut, though I could never picture him as a southern country squire in an uptight suburb filled with finance people wearing coral-pink pants and docksiders. We began subletting Apartment #2N in a beautiful rent-controlled building at 135 Central Park West called the Langham, a block north of the Dakota, and we ultimately ended up moving just upstairs to a sprawling north-facing rental on the sixth floor of the same building.

Ben was born on the twenty-second of January, 1977. Nine pounds, two ounces. "Carly, Carly, Carly Carly, Carly Carly Carly" . . . it went on and on. Through labor and finally the delivery of our boy, Ben. James with his deliberate calling forth to me and to the boy he had wanted so very much after the sweet girl of his heart, Sally. James had predicted, when we were first falling in love, that we would have a girl first and then a boy. When the shoulders came out first (upside down), Dr. Martens said: "If this is a girl, she's going to be a football player!" Indeed, he was a very big boy.

James had a tape recorder on him, one of those little ones available in the late seventies. The tape currently lurks somewhere in the stash in the Sony archives. On it is James chanting. He was moaning with me, he was giving me songs, on and on, two syllables in a row, for hours. "Carly Carly Carly." It felt like I had never heard my name before. It had such significance coming out of his mouth, such a primal yearning for attachment.

The rhythm of it made me think of one time in the waves at Windy Gates. Before *Jaws* and being afraid in the water. I was eleven. Mommy was on the shore and couldn't hear me. There the grown-ups sat smiling and passing a juice and vodka jug. I had been pulled by the tide way out of my depth, until I was just a small head on the horizon, bobbing up and down. Then, thank God, someone saw me: Jonno (Jonathan Schwartz), our mate, my mother's godchild, our friend, jumped into the waves and swam to me and carried me back to shore. Under a wave and then with a wave and then over a wave again. He stayed with the energy of the current but just subtly enough to lead us against the riptide. We washed up on the beach in one enormous wave, both of us breathless. My mother and Peter and everyone on the beach came running. We were coughing and spitting up water and everyone was congratulating Jonno. The only way to survive that is to go into shock. I withdrew into my heart. I remember the feeling, and I felt it again while giving birth to Ben. The other parts of the body can be dancers, but the heart must be resilient and feed the rest.

With the ever-joyful presence of baby Ben and his older sister, as well as the various great friendships I developed during that time, including with Mia Farrow and Anna Strasberg, two other residents of the building, I remember the Langham as the setting of pretty fun times, mixed as always with the difficult ones. There was a big career change for James, too. I remember one night around that time when producer Russ Titelman and Lenny Waronker, the president of Warner Bros. Records, who had produced James's last two albums, *Gorilla* and *In the Pocket*, flew from L.A. to New York to convince James to re-sign with the label. Peter Asher and Nat Weiss, James's manager and lawyer, were equally eager to sign James to Columbia Records. Lenny Waronker went so far as to offer James Warner Bros. stock (James owned some already, but Lenny upped the amount). That night in our apartment, the overall vibe was *We need an answer now, now, now.* The pressure on James was torturous, and I remember his sky-high anxiety levels, how at one point he lay prostrate on the floor of our bedroom, nearly crying and banging his fists on the floor. By night's end, James had gone with Columbia, and the subsequent album, *JT*, released in 1977, with its handsome, eye-contact cover photo and songs including "Handy Man," "Secret o' Life," and "Your Smiling Face," served as a comeback of sorts for James, not that he needed one.

August 5th, 1977:
Our relationship is far from the idyllic one that the general public reads about. James continues to escape. He can express his angry feelings to me much more readily than his loving ones. He tells me he loves me either in songs (no little measure) or when I am sleeping and he's just turning he will say "I really love you, Carly, I'm sorry

*I'm being a bummer," and I'm too tired to respond. Still, by the end
of every day, I always soften back to my default position of delight
and thankfulness that I'm married to James.*

I toured in 1978 after the release of *Boys in the Trees* (the album). "You
Belong to Me" was a big hit as a single going somewhere very nice on the
charts. I could look it up, but I'm one who doesn't like to remember the
very good or the very bad in positions of popularity. I had a mysterious
response to performing at that time. Sometimes I could sing in front of an
audience without problems and other times I was overtaken by forceful
heart palpitations and felt I was about to die. There seemed to be no rhyme
or reason. Different things would rattle me and I would end up looking for
another reason, another syndrome, another dream, or hire another therapist. James wasn't involved but was bemused. It was really the heyday of
grand group-encounter sessions. (Remember EST?) Everyone was demeaned
and called names, reduced to sub-human turds and then raised again under
the guidance of an enlightened trainer who doled out praise in very small
amounts and had us all in his thrall. We left after a weekend and we were
all still "pigs" but we'd learned to like being "pigs."

I was just one more typical idiot of her time who was trying to replace
religion with New Wave good intentions. Even skeptical Jake was not beyond the infection of his mind with the talk of New Age Sufi-ism. Medita-
tion classes and yoga classes, and reissues of books by retired or ancient
swamis were on everyone's bedside table. The usual arguments about the
after-life and past lives took place at every dinner party. There were those
who could bifurcate and those who could levitate and those who had been
abducted by aliens. I had so many different wise men and women from different sects casting predictions and suggestions, but hardly did two of them
ever agree. Surprisingly, the Beast would let me know when I was going over
the line. With all the contradictions, my faith became somewhat confused
and eventually I stopped collecting pamphlets. It was a grown-up decision,
after years of wandering from agreement to disillusionment. Growth is
wisdom and resulted in a decrease in bitterness. My values became clearer
and more pointed. I had less anger toward James. Also less passion.

As the 1970s came to an end and the eighties began, I had a couple of big hits in "Nobody Does It Better" and "Jesse," which was originally inspired by my son, Ben, and how in an attempt to "baby-train" his sleep patterns, I was advised by all the books to leave him crying alone in the crib for a limited period of time, which was traumatizing for both of us. The song began as "Ben, I won't go to you . . . I won't come and pick you up," or lyrics to that effect, that later turned into "Jesse, I won't cut fresh flowers for you / I won't make the wine cold for you." That all started with leaving my baby boy in his crib to cry things out.

But overall, despite having hits here and there, my albums didn't do as well on the charts as they once had. My assertiveness receded slightly, and I retreated to a more hushed place in my head. I grew quieter and quieter. With James often on the road, my days were mostly overtaken with domestic and maternal affairs—taking Sally for pancake breakfasts at the Black Dog, the little restaurant on the Sound; going shopping for lamps and rugs in Edgartown; picking up food for dinner at Cronig's supermarket. I totally agree with Diane Johnson, who once wrote in *A Shadow Knows*, "I often think that motherhood, in its physical aspects, is like one of those prying disorders such as hay fever or asthma, which receive verbal sympathy but no real consideration, in view of their lack of fatality, and which after years of attrition, can sour and pervert the character beyond all recovery," a quote I identified with strongly enough to put in my diary.

I was very preoccupied with Ben's health. He became sicker and sicker, with constant fevers. We took him to one doctor after another and he spent almost a year on gamma globulin to strengthen his immune system. After Christmas in 1978, we decided to get him to a warmer climate, and took a trip to Tortola. James's mother, Trudy, came with us. One day on a coconut-gathering trip, James badly injured his hand trying to cut the fruit open.

After that, Trudy was concerned with being a mother to James, whereas I had my hands full being a mother to Ben, who kept coming down with one illness after the next. Parallel moms. Nothing worried me so much as the state of Ben's health, and as much as Trudy wanted to tend to James's hand, the underlying problem with James was drugs, in the same way the underlying problem with Ben, we would find out only later, was a dysplastic kidney, which was causing his immune system to break down. In retrospect, my focus should have been 50 percent on Ben, 50 percent on James. Instead, it was 80 percent Ben, 20 percent James.

I wasn't focused on my love for James, nor was he focused on me. He spent our Tortola vacation searching for coconuts, or out sailing with friends. It wasn't that I was blind or insensitive to James's drug use or his sliced hand; I simply had my worried mind full to the brim with Ben's physical condition. It didn't occur to me at the time that James might have had a girlfriend, or that she even had a name.

"Ride with the tide and go with the flow."

"Here we are, like children forever, taking care of one another."
— *"There We Are,"* James Taylor

CHAPTER TWENTY-TWO

showdown

How's Ben?" I asked when I got home one night in the spring of 1980, and was relieved to find out from Lillian, the babysitter, that my three-year-old son didn't have a fever. Still, an hour later, Ben woke up and told me that both his tummy and his back hurt. When I took his temperature, it was skyrocketing: 104. I tried to reach James, but couldn't.

It was a time when things between James and me were unbuckling in slow motion, with the status quo of our world no longer sufficient for either one of us.

I didn't know of any rock 'n' roll guys who didn't cheat on their wives or girlfriends. They'd have sex with someone and the next day have no recollection of who that person was. Did that count as infidelity? Then there were any number of "behind the stalls in dressing rooms" moments. What about those—did *they* count? The rules, it seemed, were foggy, bendable, forever in play. Out of town and out of sight, James would get wasted alongside his "brothers" and end up doing God knows what with God knows whom. Rock 'n' roll aside, men did these things anyway, I told myself, especially when their beauteous wives are transformed suddenly into *mothers*:

milk-spewing, overprotective lionesses, preoccupied with the safety and well-being of their kids, the husbands in turn feeling rejected and becoming resentful small children themselves. Around that time I read Tolstoy's novella *The Kreutzer Sonata*, which tells the story of a man who claims his marriage began to deteriorate when he first had sex with his wife. The man describes sex in the most guilt-ridden terms, as a perversion, an obscenity, a "fall" from a quixotic ideal of purity, and tells how after his wife had children, he began to hate her. It made a huge impression on me.

The down-tempo unraveling of our marriage began when I discovered that James had had a dalliance with one of his backup singers during his 1979 summer tour. A close friend mentioned it to me casually, assuming I must already know, but it came as news to me. It was a discovery that opened a revolving door of mutual deception. As revolving doors go, was this one going to stop and let me out, or keep spinning? I confronted James about it, going so far as to fall onto the rug in despair. "This isn't about you," James said coldly. But if it wasn't about me, who, then, was it about? Did James feel, as I did, that we were not really living, but merely simulating? That something once clear, sharp, generous, infinite, a window view looking out over some forever landscape, was now too hazy to see through?

Smarting with hurt, and feeling unloved and alone, I embarked on my first extramarital relationship with another man. Scott Litt was my engineer, and when I confided in Scott how unvalued and uncared for I felt in my marriage to James, he let me know repeatedly that it was okay for me to flirt with other men, as if that was news. The recording studio had a suggestion box where anyone could leave anonymous notes, and two or three of them, I remember, said, *Dump James*. It was obvious they could have come from no one but Scott. He came to be one of the few men in my life whom I really trust.

In light of Scott's and my relationship, my producer, Mike Mainieri, insisted I had to tell James in the name of honesty. Why I so instantly took his word over my instinct to wait is beyond me. I guess I wanted to hurt James very badly. The following weekend, on the Vineyard, as James and

I sat on a boulder in a field we called "the poison ivy patch," I confessed, and felt tormented doing so. In spite of whatever dalliances James had had over the years, I couldn't bear to break the vow that, when I had made it, felt as religious as any experience I'd ever had. It was then that James confessed that he'd been "seeing a few other women," among them Evey: an Asian dancer who, he told me, was currently living in the fourth-floor walkup apartment on West Seventieth Street he used for rehearsals.

It was an awful conversation, one I didn't want to have. Nor did I wish to spend a second longer with Scott if there was the remotest possibility that James's and my marriage could be on solid footing again. I left the conversation with the conviction that James's "thing" with Evey was temporary, but as time went on, it became clear that Evey wasn't going anywhere, and that James didn't want her to, either. The one time I asked, James had refused to let me meet Evey. "She won't talk to you," he said.

It was a shattering time in my life, especially in my marriage. I still wanted things to work with James. I had married him forever. It wasn't an illusion. Ours would never be an easy marriage to hold together, but it would also be nearly impossible to leave. Then again, beyond precoital love, did exclusivity in love really exist? Hadn't Tolstoy written in *The Kreutzer Sonata* words to the effect that asking that kind of love to survive was like asking a candle flame to keep burning forever?

As the two of us continued treading water, making and missing appointments with couples therapists on the Upper East Side, other issues reared their heads. James and I had gone to an appointment with a doctor—an expert—so many experts!—who told me that if I could remain nursing Ben a little longer, I would produce one extremely healthy child, both emotionally and physically. I'd taken his advice, but my nursing Ben, who was two and a half, made James angry. As James grew unhappier, he pointed fingers at me about even the smallest things. As the conflicts between us simmered, James seemed to slip away from me even more.

Once, at the end of 1979, when I came across a love letter intended for James from an old girlfriend from the 1960s, James seemed nonplussed by her professions of love. "It's not your problem," he said to me. "It's got nothing to do with you." Come again? What a way to erase me completely. Casting around wildly for some solution to our marital problems, I followed a recipe provided by a Spanish witch doctor (signs of my own desperate thinking getting messy), smearing myself with oils and unguents—it was a love spell, designed to restore whatever passion or magic had left our relationship—but when James came into the bedroom that night to be faced by red and black candles, fragrances, and Latin music purring from the sound system, he asked if there was anything medicinally interesting in the vapors.

At the same time, there were moments of love, grace, wonder. James and I sang "You Can Close Your Eyes" together at a concert in Long Island. On the way to the concert, my emotional pendulum had swung back to an ardent belief in our marriage and awe in the combination of James's qualities—genius, craziness, fascination, selfishness, joy. Onstage, when we sang "You Can Close Your Eyes," James's gaze communicated: *You have this. You always will, too, because I will always love you.*

Another day, James and I turned a Robert Burns poem into a song, in two-part harmony. Creating a melody was fun and came easy to us. *"John Anderson my jo, John, when we were first acquent, your locks were like the raven . . . your bonnie brow was brent . . . but now your brow is beld, John, your locks are like the snaw . . . but blessings on your frosty pow, John Anderson, my jo!"* The song had never had a melody before. This was how James and I operated, though—as though we were following each other's spirits around the notes.

That afternoon, as we sang the Robert Burns poem, both of us cried, as we improvised melody and harmony, in part because it was so easy and natural, like breathing, almost inevitable, for us to do. That mixture of music and tears made us realize how ideal things could be if that was all there was.

In the end, it seemed to me that so much about love, no matter what you did or tried, was left to chance. In my diary I wrote, "If I could manage to achieve constant forbearance . . . but when James would return after a make-up vow of repentance, and many apologies, my worries would remain: How long would he stay? Long enough to open new wounds, demand promises, looking good from the outside, claim shared songs and poems, flirt with new ways of expressing our undying love . . . James is visiting the marriage. Always on the verge of moving off. James is always a half-departed man."

The state of our marriage gave me the lyrics to what is perhaps the saddest song I've ever written, "We're So Close," from my album *Spy*, which I wrote one day in 1979 on the Vineyard while James was keeping me waiting for an hour in the car as he pulled his sailboat from the water. By the time he returned to the car, more than anything I wanted to read the lyrics back to him—"We're so close we have a silent language / We don't need words at all . . . He says: We're beyond flowers / He says: We're beyond compliments . . . We're so close we can dispense with love / We don't need love at all"—but something stopped me. What would James have done if I'd read him those lyrics aloud? Most likely nothing. But he would add it to a column in his mind: a long, stern, silent column of recrimination.

As for Evey, I would rather James lived with her and pined for me than the reverse. What had happened to "Devoted to You," the song James and I recorded together in 1978, which appeared on *Boys in the Trees*? The Everly Brothers recorded the most famous version of the song back in 1958, and James and I were both generationally attached to their harmonies, chords, and vocal deliveries. The summer after Ben was born, James and I gravitated to that song as a lullaby we could sing around the apartment. It sounded good soft, just like good Swedish pancakes. I still have a cassette tape of James and me rehearsing the song at home, with Sally, age four, breaking in repeatedly, "No—that's not how it goes! That's not how it goes!" and singing her own version instead, which included mention of a teddy bear's tail.

"Devoted to You" made the most of James's and my voices while also planting emotion in the listener, even if it was just us. Then as now, it's the most natural song imaginable to sing, and in that way it's not unlike James's song "You Can Close Your Eyes," which also made the most of how our two voices sounded in harmony. Somebody told me once that "Devoted to You" was an almost perfect intersection of James's gorgeous cello tone and my own airy alto flute sound, which feels embarrassing to repeat, but it was true.

"I'll never hurt you . . . I'll never lie . . . I'll never be untrue . . ." Our love—and our vows—used to be so clear, so complete, so inevitable, both to us and to our fans. Now, our love seemed providential, in play, its future outside our control.

Ben's fever was still worrisome, and James still hadn't come home. I gave Ben baby aspirin, told him stories, waited, and made a few calls to friends, seeking reassurance. Two hours later, James finally crawled through the door, a Steppenwolf divided cleanly in half between his higher nature and his animal one. I kept my mouth shut. We placed a cold washcloth on Ben's burning forehead, doing our best to cool him while Sally dozed nearby, knowing nothing of this ragged, wretched period James and I were going through, me hoping and praying that sooner rather than later, the four Taylors would be an *us* again. Later that night, after the aspirin took effect, Ben's fever broke, and we were all able to get some driftlike sleep.

But then, the next evening, Ben's fever was down, and James bounced up and told me he had to go pick up a friend. "I'll be right back," he said. He didn't return until eight thirty the following morning.

I sat there in the living room, stone-faced. "Either you're here or you're not," I said wanly.

"All right," James said after a silence. "I'll move out."

"Right now," I said. "And I don't want the kids to see you again . . . I'm calling a lawyer. I want a trial separation."

I was that pissed and exhausted—but that certain of what I was saying, too. What got me was the ease with which James announced that he would move out, since I hadn't expected, or really wanted, him to acquiesce. *Fight for your love. Burn for it. Can't help it. I'm a fool for you. There's nothing you can do to turn me away.*

But I said none of this aloud. I took Sally to school, and when I got back, James was gone.

When I broke down a few hours later, it was a deluge, a big, fat, noisy, teary one. In the middle, the phone rang, and not caring who heard me gulping for air, I answered it. It was Alex, James's older brother, responding quickly and fiercely to the news that James had moved out. In no time at all, Alex mobilized James's mother, and God knows who else, which made me feel good, wanted, and supported, as if the problem were James's and, ultimately, fixable.

"What can I do?" Alex asked before hanging up.

"You can keep us away from each other," I said.

Trudy Taylor called several times that day. "Everybody's got problems," she said at one point, adding that in her opinion, James should dry out somewhere, like the Betty Ford Clinic. Nervous about offending her, I suggested that James's father, Ike, was the only person who could possibly get through to James on this topic. That day, I was snooping in James's pants pockets, where I found a note from Evey. Written on sky-blue stationery, it was a hippie dancer's version of a poem, and in it she called James "Jamie"—his childhood name—and spelled *love* "luv," ending with the line, "As they say down on the ranch, 'You're my kinda guy.' No one's gonna tell us what to do!"

That afternoon, as Ben, Sally, and I were playing with a doll-sized Japanese tea set on the floor of Sally's bedroom, keys jangled and the front door opened. It was James. He had come back. For the rest of the day, he said nothing about moving out, which frankly came as a relief to me, as it spared me from the reality of something too alien to grasp. Before dinner, I told him I was planning to visit my sister Joey, who was in an East Side hospital, having had back surgery—could he and I meet for dinner afterward? He replied that he'd be "delighted" to have some fun with Ben and Sally until I came back. He spoke quickly, his energy twinkly. Maybe he realized that here—home—was where he belonged, as he tightly hugged Ben and Sally, who, not surprisingly, had many things to show their daddy.

The hospital was on the other side of town, but somehow I managed the round trip in under forty-five minutes, taking my emotional temperature every time the taxi paused at a red light. Was I still angry at James? Of course I was, maybe even livid. At the same time, I was aware of a never-ending current of hope. Facts were facts: James was a dad babysitting his two kids—on the same day that I told him I never wanted him to see Sally and Ben again. Right. The warp speed of my inconsistency stunned me, the chain-link fence of sarcasm, panic, fury, blindness, withering despair, and now, optimism . . .

Back inside the building on Central Park West, I discovered I had left home without my apartment keys. I rang the loud kitchen bell. No answer. For five minutes, I kept it up, calling out, "James! James!" Just before I went back downstairs to find a pay phone so I could call our home number, I heard Ben's little voice calling out to me. He sounded scared, and in my mind I could see through the front door with X-ray eyes, see my little boy straining on his tiptoes as tall as he could.

"I can't open the door!" he cried.

I did my best to keep my voice calm. "Where's Daddy?"

"A-sweep," came Ben's voice.

"Daddy's asleep? What did you say, Ben? Asleep?"

"Yef, Daddy's a-sweep."

The mutability of both our moods during that period was immense, a pendulum that rocked back and forth, sometimes several times a day. Insecurity. Protectiveness. Frustration. Love. Loathing. One day I would beg James to forget our differences, and the next day I would apologize. He would forgive me, and then it was his turn to apologize. Two days would pass, and I would turn cold, only to touch up against James's own frost. One day he told me, "I love you," and when I told him not to go to Evey, he promised he wouldn't. "Not a chance," he said. Two nights later, I told James that it seemed as though he and Evey were happy together and that he should pursue her seriously, but I was just baiting him, hoping he'd swear his undying love to me and to our family. Another day, another night, another mood, as we inflicted hurts on each other both accidental and intentional.

New York teems with accomplices to human wiles and passions and urges: doormen who look the other way and let the wrong people upstairs, bank tellers who cash phony checks, florists who write neat cursive notes to concubines. Mine was a locksmith on Columbus Avenue, who, in exchange for an autograph for his aunt Gloria, I'd convinced to make me a set of duplicate keys to James's coke-'n'-whiskey abode on West Seventieth Street, which I had never visited. Yes, it was sneaky, but it wasn't nefarious, corrupt, or dangerous, and I had long accepted a certain degree of stealth as part of my necessary defensive armor. I wouldn't use the keys just yet, tucking them deep into my wallet's change purse before walking home six blocks south and one block east to our apartment on Central Park West. I don't know what I was waiting for, but I'd know when the time was right.

When I opened the back door, James was sitting in the kitchen, wearing a black, hooded terrycloth robe and devouring Italian sausages. It was morning. The apartment was thick with the small of sausage fat, mingling uneasily with expensive, scented Christmas candles.

"Good morning, baby!" I said enthusiastically.

"Hello, sweet thing." James, otherwise occupied, didn't look up. He was busy burning a piece of bent-out-of-shape metal clothes hanger, and melting both ends of a length of heavy nylon rope. James was always having inventive encounters with tinfoil, carbon-stained spoons, and other makeshift ingredients. Whatever he was concocting this morning, the explanation was bound to be eccentric, maybe even incomprehensible, so I didn't ask. Unless pressed, James rarely offered up an answer anyway, so I simply stood there, taking in the clutter on the table and the miasmic wafts of cigarette smoke, sausages, and green French candles.

"When did you get up?" I said at last.

"Oh, 'bout an hour ago." A pause. "Your brother Peter called. He has tickets to some sports game, and wants to take the kids. There may have been another call, I think I wrote it down."

My body tensed under all the uncertainty of the past twenty-four hours. All those pink slips of message paper filled with phone messages, all the grocery bags scribbled with set lists, all the pieces of paper towel with James's handwriting on them: a fledgling lyric, decodable, maybe, as a message meant for me—or was it a message for her? *Were James and I going to break apart—yes or no?*

"Listen, darling," I said now, "I'm planning on going to an Amnesty meeting this afternoon if you'll be around." My friend Rose Styron was a founder and board member of Amnesty International USA, and Carinthia West and Mia Farrow were joining us. The General Electric repairman was also coming to fix the dishwasher motor: Would James let him in, and also tip him?

No answer. Just the dim electricity of underground thoughts.

New smells now conjoined with the old ones. James had burned the ends of more rope and was now tinkering around with some electrical cords. In a way I loved it. It was so *him*.

Inside the bathroom, I washed my face and, just to add insult to the already phantasmagoric collection of apartment smells, put on cologne. Reaching into my pocket, I fingered the outline of the keys the autograph-seeking locksmith had made me. What would happen if and when I took the plunge of interfering with James's extracurricular love affair?

I returned to the kitchen, and James asked me if it was okay if Ben and Sally went off to the basketball game with Peter. "Absolutely," I said, "I'll call him."

Someone told me once that we are capable of loving only four people in our lives. Another person told me that human beings can love an infinite number of people. I'm more comfortable with the infinite-number theory, the crucial difference being the number of people I feel I can love *well*.

I loved James in a way that couldn't possibly be deeper or more sure. I loved him in the same way my fingers snap when the rhythm of a song syncs perfectly with my brain's own cellular clatter. I loved James not despite his broken-down spirit, but because of it. I loved James in his pain even when the last thing he seemed to need was someone to love him. When I thought ahead, into our shared future, I had an image of myself filling up the flesh and wrinkles of my aging skin with a smile so sunny and warm that even if James didn't see it, he would be healed. Did it seem completely out of the question that he and I would continue churning our butter for years and years in some thatched-roof cottage on a flowery Alpine slope? It didn't matter if I hated him simultaneously.

James and I spent the next hour acting as if nothing were out of the ordinary, small talk sprinkled with the usual "darlings," and when we passed each other in the hallway, a polite tennis volley of "Excuse me's." I was amazed, as ever, by how many potentially life-altering thoughts can take place under the patina of small talk. Inside, I was thinking: Keys. Tonight. What shall I wear? How will I behave in front of her?

This wasn't how my father had loved my mother. It wasn't what kept Daddy, in the end, from demanding that Ronny leave our house, vacate that third-floor room with its secret door, and insist that his wife respect, honor, love, and obey him in sickness and in health. Mommy did none of those things at a time when Daddy needed her the most. Why didn't my father stand up for himself? Why didn't he take care of himself? Why didn't he *act*? Why was I putting up with so many things, in almost exactly the same way my father had? Daddy must have accepted his life as it was, as I did sometimes, too: successful on the surface, and perhaps the surface was the only thing that really counted. When faced with a life gone off its tracks, Daddy kept going, kept walking around the house, showing up at work, letting himself get progressively blinder until he was left with only the faintest peripheral vision. That way, he wouldn't have to share a real glance with Mommy, the adulteress, while the much younger rival was stealing her away. No, he was polite as a lake.

That was precisely what I would *not* do.

Dinner that night in our apartment was quiet but tense. Sally, almost six, and Ben, almost three, were both tired from the basketball game they had attended, and Ben was rubbing his eyes.

James and I sat, occasionally purring gentle names at each other, though passing the bread was about as romantic as things got.

"Baby," I said at one point, "look at Sally's new dress. Do you know that she made it?"

"I honestly did not know that, sweet pea. Sal, is this dress for a certain occasion?"

Sally told him that she and a few classmates had written a play at school, and that a couple of kids had made costumes, and that Mommy—me—had told her I could wear it at dinner.

Ben jumped in, from his high chair: "I spilled ketchup on it."

"Why did you do that, Ben?" James said.

"It's okay, darling," I said. "I got it off. Or almost."

That night I spent a good forty minutes putting the kids to bed. They both slept in Ben's bed, big, roomy, and crowded with stuffed animals, each child holding one of my arms as I told them stories in the dark. I waited until their breathing was even, turned on their night-lights, left the door open a few inches so they could have the benefit of the dim hall light—and then slipped away.

I had no idea what James was planning for that evening. If he planned on going out somewhere, I would stay home with Sal and Ben. Because of his steady uptake of whatever he was drinking, I suspected James would probably crash early.

I made my way down the long hall, from Ben's bedroom into the den. James was on the couch, watching TV, still wearing his hooded black terry-cloth robe. He'd bought it the first week we were in love, dashing to Bloomingdale's with a shopping list including gifts for his parents and all his siblings. He ended up buying everyone the same robe, though Trudy got a version in regal, maternal blue. Eight years later, James looked rumpled, his mustache shadowing his top lip, his hair long, dirty, sexy, and stringy, bare legs extended, strong, squarish bare feet crossed. Guitars surrounded him, three acoustic and one electric; he was making inroads on a new song. A cigarette burned from between two fingers, though no ashtray was in sight.

James seemed transfixed by what he was watching—a VCR tape called *Animals Are Beautiful People* that I could have sworn had been playing all day. I would have done anything to curl up beside him to watch crocodiles nuzzle, orangutans kiss, leopards copulate. I would have done anything to return with him to Bermuda, to frolic in the bathtub there, to imitate Uncle Peter's dance. Instead, I stood in the gap of the double sliding French doors and announced, in a clear, unemotional voice:

"I'm going to your other apartment to meet Evey."

James must not have taken me seriously. If he had turned toward me, he would have had to acknowledge what I'd just said. He didn't.

And he had no idea that I had an extra set of keys.

Five minutes later, I'd washed my face, my hair was loose and messy, reaching to the middle of my back. If James came in, it would look to him, and to anyone else who cared, as if I was simply getting ready for bed, that I'd changed my mind, that my announcement had been nothing more than some daft comment. My heart began pounding. I switched on the radio and called Lucy, telling her my plans. Our conversation lasted for half an hour or more. She, Reasonable Lulu, tried to argue me out of going, but to no avail. "You know who he is," she said. "He's not going to change tonight. You just have to get through this awful period." Staring at myself in the mirror during our whole phone conversation, I opened up my makeup kit. On the radio, Chrissie Hynde sang "Brass in Pocket," a song I loved and immediately castigated myself for not having written.

I was wearing jeans and a lightweight tan leather shirt. In the hallway outside the dressing closet, I slipped my bare feet into rubber fur-lined boots. They made no noise on the carpet, or on the hallway that led to the tile in the kitchen. I put on my full-length black leather coat and very quietly exited the apartment. By now it was well after midnight.

Why was I planning to face down my husband's mistress in their West Seventieth Street love nest? Because I wanted Evey to see that I was not a character in a story James was telling her, not some phantom abstraction, but a real person, and a nice person, too. I wanted her to respect James's and my marriage, our children, our life together. As I left our building, I slipped into a Gothic night. Looking up at the barbicans and the turrets of the Dakota, the half-moon slid white and ghostly between tar-stained, vaporous clouds, which softened the hard lines of the building's architecture.

The temperature was in the low forties, and the weatherman had predicted a "chance of precipitation." I followed the point of the moon, heading in a southwesterly direction. I'd blazed similar trails countless times. This was my neighborhood. Now it was probably close to 2 a.m. on a weekday morning.

As I made my way down that first very long block between Central Park West and Columbus Avenue, I forced myself to go slowly, my heart still pounding, as my brain sifted through possibilities of how I would confront this bizarre unknown. The streets, naturally, were empty, the avenue itself bleak looking and exposed, jittery neon shut down for the night, storefronts armored with metal gates. I noticed that Charivari, an upscale boutique on the corner of Seventy-second and Columbus, had new mannequins in its windows, imports from Madison Avenue, wigless, with hard, white, pouty-lipped faces, shoulders ringed in fake fur. Two of them looked in my general direction and said: "You're one of us. You stare into the night just as we do, c'mon darling. Look down, that's it. Look fierce in your eyes. Only the face you put on is important. Why can my legs do just about anything? That's what mannequins do. Women yearn to be like us. Men find us erotic."

I wondered whether James had even noticed I was gone. What antelope was being ravaged by what tiger on *Animals Are Beautiful People*? Was James blinking, or were his facial muscles in a relaxed hold? When James was writing a song, guitar in hand, head bowed down, in a trance almost, he often uttered the most delicate, profound things. I've never seen anyone reveal himself so mysteriously, yet approachably, at the same time. Oblique and vague, touchable and remote, the flashes of his dream world opening his listeners' eyes to the lonely spinning galaxy he believed was his true home.

On Seventy-first Street and Columbus, I passed by Victor's Café, a Cuban joint that had been there for decades. Through the windows a waiter was pouring sangria into waiting glasses, and I heard dull, scattered sounds of laughter. Tucking my thick brown cashmere sweater inside my coat, I pulled up the collar, like elephant ears, around my long neck. It was a gesture, but for whom? The few stragglers inside Victor's looked friendly enough, and I decided to join the fray. I knew I had a Valium in my coat pocket—why hadn't I taken it earlier? I dug around for it, found it, placed it righteously under my tongue so that the little fragments of powdery "chill" would dissolve.

I took a seat in the back, keeping my coat on, and when the waiter came around, ordered a single glass. He took my order with a smile of recognition: Didn't I remember him? Juan? Well, of course I did. "You come in here with your *oosban*," Juan said, glad I knew him in the same way he seemed to know me. Juan was wearing pure patches of black and white, a starched shirt under a rumpled black waiter's jacket. A mustache. Short black curly hair. Noticeably kind eyes, whose darkness covered most of the surrounding white, eyes that looked that night both like a full moon in eclipse and as though they were on the verge of tears.

Juan asked me where I was going on such a cold night. I had to think for a moment. "I'm out for a spin with some good thoughts," I said at last.

He saw right through my lie. "You *oosban* and you ev a fight, you can tell Juan." When I demurred he repeated, "You can tell Juan. *Ee* come in with the Japanese girl. She no good. She try to spleet you"—and he made a gesture with his hand of a string, or a rope, snapping, breaking in two. "C'mon, you ev a nice glass of red wine from where my mother leev in Cuba."

That was when I told him that my own grandmother, Chibie, had lived in Cuba, raised there by a foster family who had shipped her off to England to a convent. I wished I knew more about her, I went on. Then, overcome with the relief of having a friendly, familiar person in front of me, I blurted out suddenly, "Please—tell me something true, Juan, something to believe. And I will."

Whether it was the sangria, or the Valium, or the night, I could feel my eyes well up as Juan spoke in a gentle voice. It was *love* that leads all, he told me. It was love that knows what babies need. *Love*, he emphasized, knows *all*. God tells all men to know love, tells men to open their hearts, to be on the lookout for the secrets of the night. As for that Japanese woman, he went on—"She try to take your *oosban* away. Stay to love. Don't let it get away from your side. Go home now and love eem. Love eem over everybody else but God. Love is good," he concluded, "and God is love."

I gave Juan a hug, leaving behind a big bill before I took my leave. But rather than going home to tell James how much I loved him—which, I might add, I desperately wanted to—I resumed my trek south. It was too late to turn back, though I was newly equipped with a profound realization: I would not "visit" my marriage, as if it were a second or third house, or a pair of flip-flops I slipped my feet into now and again. No: James's and my marriage was a religion, holding the two of us strongly together. Then and always, our marriage was the definition of *home*. "Love eem over everybody else . . . over every other."

The building on West Seventieth was discreet and dark-bricked, of the Edwardian type popular on that and neighboring blocks. The key fit easily into the downstairs lock. The door to the building opened in, and my head flooded with *You can do it, you can do it*. Mommy's words to a stutterer. Once I was inside the lobby, I immediately heard wails coming from several flights above. James's apartment, I knew, was on the fourth floor: 4F. Was the wailing I heard coming from Evey? I'm turning around now. No, I'm not.

There was no elevator, just a staircase with a faded, ancient carpet runner, its drab color acquired from countless shoe soles traipsing up and down through the years like barges on the Cuyahoga River. The banister was oak, solidly built, the steps lacking much if any squeak, which disappointed me slightly: Wouldn't a squeak have added some much-needed apprehension? In the same way I wrote songs, I was turning the "I" that was me into a third-person "her": the dramatized film-noir wife in the movie that had become her life, the one whose director seemed to have quit.

I continued up the stairs, the hallways a dim, early-morning blur of high-hung sconces and dark wooden doors. With each step I advanced, the wailing sound grew more eerie. From the second or maybe third floor, I heard, very dimly, the second movement of Mozart's clarinet quintet, the one Benny Goodman played back in '56, that Jackie Robinson talked about with him. James must have told Evey how much he admired the piece, and in turn, I fantasized that she'd promptly run out to Tower Records to buy it. She was now playing it to comfort herself, or maybe it had even incited her wailing.

By the time I reached the fourth-floor landing, I was breathing hard. Then came a shock: even though I hadn't knocked, or made any noise, a door suddenly burst open. She, Evey, had known, somehow, that someone was outside in the hall. Swami. Buffalo Girl. Psychic. Bitch. Enemy. Had James called to forewarn her?

"I'm Carly," I said.

"Well . . . you're not any friend of mine," she replied.

"I know. But still. I'm Carly."

She stood there, hair in her eyes, which were wide with what I interpreted as terror and angst. The woman before me, Evey, was tiny and muscular. She wore a black leotard, dance pants, and small black dance slippers—size four, I guessed. Her torso was beautifully molded, and her hands were white, perfect, not a single mark on them, only a band on the fourth finger, the fingers of a child-ghost. My hands, by contrast, were large, unrefined, a peasant's hands; wishing I hadn't removed my gloves, I automatically concealed them in my coat pockets, shoving my shoulder bag to one side. My self-confidence was on trial, and my hands, poor things, had already failed. I quietly thanked God for the Valium and the sangria.

Sniffling, snuffling, and breathing, as if to herself, "Oh, my Jamie," to my surprise Evey indicated with one hand that I should come inside.

Come inside? Take off my coat? I didn't understand. Was Evey merely being polite? No: she was, in fact, asserting ownership of James's apartment. The place—a loft, actually—was pristine, sparsely furnished, with a futon on the floor.

"Evey, it is you, right? Just to be sure."

This irritated her. "Very funny."

Removing my coat, I took a seat on the futon, my hands folded. Evey, who had turned off Mozart's clarinet quintet, burped loudly. It might have been an imperious belch or a sign of respect, a Japanese tradition of welcoming visitors. I spoke first:

"I want you to see that I'm not such a monster."

"Oh, yes you are," she said.

She trying to take your oosban.

"I'm trying hard here," I said. "Can you help me a little? I want us to be the best we can both be." What I was trying to say, I went on, was that I wasn't her adversary. I wasn't a conniving, manipulative product of a moody, unhappy husband's imagination. I was a real person, married to a real man, James.

"No, you're not," she replied in her broken English. "Jamie doesn't love you. Don't you know that? He calls you a JAP—and he told me you buy big Mercedes convertible, and drive around California trying to be a movie star, but you're not pretty enough." She continued in this vein: Jamie had told her that I'd built a swimming pool because I couldn't bear to step on any seaweed or any rocks beneath my feet "where real people go swimming."

Jamie had also told her I disliked the feeling of sand, and that if any got in the house, I would take a bottle of spray cleaner out from under the sink and spray out all the sand as if it was some dangerous fungus. Hmm, not a bad idea. "Jamie tells me about you and the mosquitoes and the spiders and how you scream," she went on. "He says you spend all day shopping and buying fur coats and that you are dressing up your children just like you. He tells me you nurse your little boy still and that he will grow up to be a fairy." Evey's voice rose. "And don't think I don't know the difference between 'fairy tale' and 'fairy.'" Pausing, she scoured her brain for other sins. "He said you don't really sing well and that you spend all day getting bikini waxes so you look good for all your rich boyfriends who send planes for you all over the world. He says you won't even notice when he is out of your house because you're so in love with your diamonds and your fancy shoes and you try them on in front of your mirror. You are party girl. You are a bitch. A city girl, a lazy playgirl. What did he call you? Yes—a swash-buckler. That's it."

She stopped there, the stampede of words over, short of breath. Was she goading me into responding? Was this all part of a strategy? I had prepared nothing in return, and now I wished I had. I felt speechless, mortified. I knew there was—or was there?—practically no credibility in Evey's gar-bled version of James's depictions, but it didn't altogether matter, since no matter which way you looked at it, the litany of faults I seemed to have com-mitted in James's eyes was bad news.

All of a sudden, Evey began wailing again, this time the sounds coming from her throat more operatic and staccato. I froze. I couldn't walk out now. I couldn't just leave, erase what I'd just heard from my consciousness. What was I supposed to do with it? Where was I supposed to go? I remem-ber wishing she hadn't turned off the Mozart; the clarinet would have soft-ened the whole picture. Evey stood in front of me now, both hands in her pockets, drawing a graceful circle on the floor with her small, demure foot, a strange gesture, as if she were casting some kind of spell or trance. I had to raise my voice to hear myself over her howling.

"I know you want to believe everything James has told you," I said as clearly as I could, "but you have to see it can't all be true. He would never have loved me in the first place if I was all those things. He just said them to justify his actions to you."

Evey fired back: "He said once you were sexy and fun and now you ruined it all with your greediness and your furniture and your manicures."

Ha—finally something good! This, I knew, was horseshit. I could feel the Beast, my ally now, stirring inside me, this time in a good mood, reminding me that James had actually complimented me more than once on my lack of hand and foot grooming. "Thank God you don't do those things to your hands and feet that almost every other female I know does. Your feet are beautiful."

"I need to use the bathroom," I said. Evey didn't bother to follow me with her eyes, staring instead at one of the walls, blankly, like one of the Charivari mannequins glancing sightlessly west, in the direction of Riverside Park, the Hudson River, and beyond that, New Jersey. What a sight she was. Lost.

The bathroom was tiny, airless, the sink counter made of some kind of plastic painted to resemble marble. Scattered on its surface was Evey's small assemblage of accoutrements designed to embellish her already perfect features: an eye pencil, Pond's cold cream, Seba-Nil astringent, cotton balls bound with a loop of string, a toothbrush in a glass. A single razor. What did she do with a single razor blade? Picking it up, I had a sudden, violent impulse to cut myself. My thoughts were fast, flurrying: No, I can't cut myself. I would just wind up dead on the floor, with no one feeling remotely sorry for me but instead, furious that I'd left behind two babies. That's the one thing that ends when you have children—you can no longer seriously entertain those thoughts of ending it all.

"What do you use a razor blade for?"

No reply. Why was I talking to Evey from the bathroom?

At last Evey spoke, her voice deliberate. "Jamie and I have the same trines in our charts. We dig each other. You don't get him."

Trine—a word with which most likely some astrological nuncio had armed her. So that was what it was all about: she and "Jamie" were destined to be together all thanks to their *trines*.

I sat down on the closed toilet seat, mulling my options. How would I emerge from this situation? Short of getting physical, I had very few options. It hit me suddenly: Why would I ever want to hurt another person? Why would I ever want to hurt Evey? Once when my brother Peter was seven years old, I remember pushing him, and as a result, he accidentally toppled down the stairs in our house in Riverdale. As he hit the floor at the bottom, I saw his face and body go into spasm. He screamed, I screamed, and the adults came running, followed by explanations, apologies, tears, and punishments. I never hit Peter again. I felt hopeless, oddly dispirited that one of my weapons had been removed. I'd never be able to hurt anyone again and feel okay about it. And that included Evey.

Standing there, I glanced at myself in the mirror over the sink. The overhead lighting did strange things to my features, and for a moment it was hard to recognize who I was exactly. Something from deep inside me seemed to be overtaking my features, my expression, a transition I'd seen only in special-effects movies. The person before me wasn't a character, or a monster, in a movie. No, it was just me, my own reflection. Whatever was coming through at this moment was something I'd been afraid of my whole life, but in its emerging outline I wasn't afraid of it at all. I didn't have to squint to see it. No, it was purely, completely mine, filling me with something that felt, uncannily, like awe. I could control what I was seeing, but I no longer had to. It was in command. It had no competitors. It might not stick around permanently, it might come and go, and even vanish for long stretches of time, but I knew now, for certain, that it was there. In the light of the mirror, I didn't look pretty, for sure—nor was that the point—but I did look fierce. In truth, I was staring the Beast in the eye. I held its gaze and I thought, Cool, God is in me.

I wasn't exactly being a pacifist. Nor was I being a coward. Instead, I was where I'd found myself many times in my life—somewhere between those poles—the difference being that tonight I had defined what I felt in a way I never had before: I felt unshackled, strong, finally freed. . . . Our marriage was the only god I knew, my only religion. Religion was my home. "Over everybody else. One over everybody else."

My next thought, as I needlessly flushed the toilet, was: Poor Evey. She's not my problem.

I came out of the bathroom and without a single word put on my coat. I held out my hand to Evey: Shake? Instead, she looked down at the floor: "Evey," I said, "I'm really glad I came here tonight. I'm sure it didn't make you happy, but I want you to know that I will tell James that I saw you." I tried not to sound pompous, or insincere, and considering the context, felt as though I'd succeeded in being decent.

When our eyes connected for a split second, I smiled broadly. Evey didn't smile back, nor had I expected her to. I didn't need her to.

On the way home, the Charivari mannequins glanced past me, disjointed and erotic, but did they really have any choice? I felt strangely settled, weirdly satisfied. Back on Central Park West and Seventy-third Street, I let myself into the apartment, turned off some lights, and checked in on Sally and Ben. Ben was clutching a couple of uncuddly battery-operated mechanical dogs, a gift to James from a Japanese promoter, whose hard metal bodies weren't exactly what most children would want to cuddle in the moments before sleep. Quietly, softly, I lifted his arm, my goal being to set the dogs on his bedside table, but as I was lifting it, Ben called out in his sleep, quite loudly, "Where are the dogs?" I couldn't help but laugh. Even in his sleep, that boy was funny. I leaned down to kiss his head, replacing the hard-bodied dogs back in their proper spot under his arm. Ben's room was stuffy—the damn heaters were loud and clanking, and always left the rooms either too hot or too cold—and I opened his windows a few inches.

When I went into our bedroom, I saw that James had lit a candle. Was there a message in that? I didn't know, but it didn't matter. I felt good. James was asleep, and I lay down on the bed beside him. "I love you so much, my darling man," I said, feeling a forgiveness much, much larger than myself.

Of course my husband didn't hear me. He was dreaming, no doubt, about his own fascinating rhythms and moods, his comedy, his codas, his craziness, the sawing, hammering, musical, lyrical circus that was his life. Somewhere in the soft gulf between dreams and sleep, maybe he could intuit the love I had for him, and love me back in return. I undressed, put my hair up in a hasty ponytail, and got under the covers. This was destiny. That's what destiny is: *This.*

One of us slipped last night and said "Darling"
There in the middle of the night
Between dreams and sleep
Did you say it, or did I?
I don't know
But it interrupted the war
That's the way these cold wars are
I love you, we said
Or one of us did
And the other agreed from the heart

One of us slipped last night and said "sorry"
There in the middle of the madness
Between the dark and the light
Who cares if all the doors had been closed
And no love had entered for days
Cold wars like these go up in a blaze
"I love you," we said, or one of us did
And the other agreed from the heart

Through the haze of the dream
The truth could come through
You can see that I'm still open to you
"I love you,
I love you," we said, from the heart
　　—"From the Heart," 1980

Destiny—Tranquillo.

On stage at the Stanley Theater in Pittsburgh, 1981.

CHAPTER TWENTY-THREE

sheets the color of fire

A year later, James and I were—somehow—still together—and I was in Pittsburgh, as part of a fourteen-show tour with my band. I was at an all-time low weight. I was looking shrivelled, scared, and anyone aware of the serious bundle of nerves I was should never have allowed me to leave home, much less perform.

The previous six months had been incredibly challenging, starting on the day when a physician informed James and me that Ben had been born with a "dysplastic kidney," which, in layman's terms, meant his kidney had been busy recycling urine back inside his one-, two-, and three-year-old body. His whole life, Ben had been worrisomely sick far more often than was usual, and it wasn't until his grandfather, Ike, urged us to make an appointment with a kidney specialist that we found out Ben had a congenital problem that surgery would fortunately be able to rectify. We set a date for the operation in early June.

When Ben finally came out of surgery, the relief was enormous. Six months later, in a daze of sleep problems, stress-related weight loss, adult acne, worry, and nerves, I was pressured to go ahead with rehearsals for my upcoming tour, trying to connect with my band, forcing a smile onto my stuttering lips. After all, I kept telling myself, it's only fourteen shows. I continued to pour my really heavy emotions—my nerves, my utterly lost feelings—onto the shoulders of my sweet lover, Scott Litt, in the same way James still had Evey or maybe even someone else entirely.

I'd been writing songs, too, some of them about James. Far more painful than writing about shadowy crushes was writing about my own husband. My method was often mildly passive-aggressive, in the hopes James might pick up or learn something about how I felt, that way bypassing an actual conversation likely to end up in an argument. Or sometimes my lyrics were direct, hopeful. In 1980 I remember writing the song "James" when he was asleep on the couch, totally wasted on one thing or another. "Your voice is like the water / when I lift the shell I can hear you pouring out your heart to me / James, the beauty of your voice fills me with sadness / James . . ."

Warner Bros. had invested a lot of money into backing my tour. My manager, Arlyne, strongly believed that it would be good for me to get my mind off the two crazy, empty shells my homes in New York and Martha's Vineyard had become, as well as off James. I was consoled by the fact that my children were in good hands. Sally was in elementary school, and well taken care of at home, plus I would be gone no more than a few nights a week. Ben, now fully recovered from his surgery, would either stay in New York or travel with me, depending on how near the venue was.

As I began rehearsals, I felt oddly detached and disembodied, a stranger to my own image and self. I had a hard time reading people's feelings for me or mine for them. Despite the revelation in the mirror at Evey's, all of a sudden, it seemed, I knew nothing about myself, including what I should wear, and why, or how to wear my hair, which, at the time, looked just wrong, like a hayfield shorn by an anxious, fluttering scythe. Internally, banging around inside the cage of my frazzled brain, I felt equally lopsided, as if my entire being had now tuned to the wrong note, one that had been further distorted by the high-pitched EQ of an early 1970s heavy-metal guitar, the words on repeat: *Ben. Sally. Ben. Ben. Sally. Sally. James, oh lord, my darling James: I need you. I can't go on without you. I want our marriage back. I want the day we were born back.*

Backstage at the Stanley Theatre in Pittsburgh, everything was well appointed. There were flowers everywhere, in ultrabright colors of yellow, orange, red, and even bright blue, the latter no doubt genetically modified to assume the rich, regal hues befitting a star. I felt less like a star than a gangster's girlfriend receiving a withering bunch of those unnatural, food-dyed azure flowers. They depressed me right away. Worse, Arlyne wasn't around that night. No doubt she was fed up with me—I'd been nothing but drama for her, and Arlyne, like most people, had other drama to deal with—or maybe she intuited that I would fail and embarrass us both. But Lucy, my wonderful sister, had insisted on flying to Pittsburgh and attending the concert in person. She understood how much I was struggling. She got it.

It was the first time Lucy had ever shown up at one of my solo concerts, not that there'd been that many over the years, just a few short tours' worth and various public appearances with James. Of course, in our early years, the two of us had performed and traveled here and there as the Simon Sisters. When I broke out on my own, I missed Lucy terribly. Ever since we were children, Lucy was always my boss, the sister I knew would always take care of me. Now, tonight, she had come to Pittsburgh. Had she known, somehow, that she would have to take care of me? Did she have any inkling of how dire the situation was? I doubt it. Even I didn't realize it yet.

My solo act had begun one April night in 1971 at the Troubadour in Los Angeles. That night kicked off my career. I was all of a sudden on the "A-list," being compared to Janis Joplin, Carole King, Joni Mitchell, even Julie Christie. I'd joined a new club, was given a new ladder to climb, the scene not much different from high school popularity games. In truth, each and every group to which you are assigned is illusory; the ground perpetually shifts, and new groups pop up all the time. Fame is manic and terrifying, especially when your identity and status become gradually and exclusively dependent on others' opinions, jealousies, and rivalries. Show business is no place for any normal person, as you develop an overwhelming need to retain the highest possible position on the world's popularity rosters, your fear of slipping a notch gradually overshadowing talent, art, creativity, empathy, and, hardest to lose, love.

Countless times over those years I'd come face to face with the Beast, which understood, intuitively, that for any one wish to come true, ten would never be granted. Whenever I was gratified by a good review, a flattering remark, or a compliment on my dress, I knew I could look forward to the next time a magazine voted me the Worst-Dressed Woman of the Year. At Evey's, I thought I'd put the Beast to bed, but that night in Pittsburgh it returned.

Whenever James and I sang or appeared in public together, we ignited almost unimaginable amounts of excitement. I could credit our individual charisma, but as a couple, we were somehow much more than the sum of our two parts. Even as our marriage went through its agonies, James and I were still able to convey a profound, jointly held illumination. In response, the public projected something back that enveloped both of us in a radiance that neither one of us ever understood. Except that I remember that right after our wedding, I'd felt emotionally protected for life. Signing my name *Carly Simon Taylor* and thinking, Well, that's just about the perfect place to be. For me marriage was a perfect island, one created for the two of us to live on. Outside our marriage, in public, we were a unit, singing songs on-stage that promised a warm, positive, loving future not just for us but for everyone. Music's two symbolic parental figures—still solid, still intact, still looking good, still making music. It seemed the two of us were living out an empty version of the lyrics of our 1972 cowritten song, "Forever My Love."

I'm looking forward to looking back
From further on down the track
Together in fact
Forever my love

People still write to me today, with genuine compassion, claiming they were there "that night in Pittsburgh," and their empathy never ceases to touch me. That night my energy was focused exclusively on maintaining my sanity. I also felt exceedingly nervous, even more than usual. The paradox, one I've confronted repeatedly over the course of my performing life, was that performing was an opportunity to detach from myself, to dive into the love of the ten thousand people in the audience, and ten thousand more waiting for the second show afterward. If only I could lose myself in the beat of the music. The more I needed the bliss of losing myself, the more losing myself felt as though I'd *lost* myself completely between drowning and bad dreams.

After sound check, I retired to my dressing room and changed into a light pink pantsuit made of thin, shimmering satin. It clung to my bones, making my knees look like two matching medical reflex hammers. Nor did I realize before the show just how physically weak I was. An hour before I took the stage, I called home and spoke to Ben, Sally, and James, my three night-lights whose shine, I knew, would never fade, at least not until their stars led me back home. I needed that reality so badly—like hanging on to Santa with all my might.

If I didn't conquer this fear, I remember thinking, I would soon find myself confined to my home, and *only* my home, and as the years went on, sequestered in my bedroom, and finally, simply, alone in my bed with a quilt over my head.

My opening act, a local Pittsburgh band, played for forty-five minutes. I heard the sounds of applause from out front and took one last appraising look in the mirrored wall, the fake blue flowers reflecting back at me. I looked pretty damn swank in my pink satin pantsuit. Although my bones were sticking out, overall I was feeling pretty okay. The Valium I'd taken earlier kicked in, and there was no reason to believe my Pittsburgh show would be anything out of the ordinary.

Did things fall apart because of the accumulated stresses of the past year? Ben? James? Over the years I've wondered: Did I fall apart that night because Lucy was in the audience, and I still felt guilty, so many years later, performing solo, as the headlining act, without my older sister by my side? I have no answers.

When I first appeared, the audience was giddy in a familiar way, but why wasn't their energy and enthusiasm making me giddy in response? The set list opened with "Come Upstairs," an up-tempo song of mine from my recent album of the same name, whose instrumental beginning sounds like a group of whirling dervishes. The song would have been vital, fun, and fresh, if only . . . if only I could reverse all the things that started to go so horribly wrong.

When I began to play the tambourine for an eight-bar intro, my body started moving in some wild gyration, like James Brown, like Mick, like a dervish. I started to sense the first of several thudding heart palpitations, like giant steps across the arid landscape that was my chest. Turning my back to the audience, I found myself facing Mike Mainieri, my musical and social director, who saw trouble on my face—or, more likely, sheer panic.

I was bent at the waist, trying to pretend I was moving along to the music, my arms seemingly groping for something, a bird-of-paradise effect that I'm afraid looked more like a wind-up monkey having a seizure. Four bars too late, and edging upstage toward the band instead of toward the audience, I began to sing "Come Upstairs," a heart palpitation stopping me every few words, at which point I'd gaze back beseechingly at Mike, as if he had an automatic defibrillator on hand, silently begging him to scoop me up and get me into a straitjacket. I could hear the sirens now. Why? Why? Why?

By the time "Come Upstairs" ended, I had sung at most a third of the song, and was trying to comfort the audience by blaming the microphone for whatever was going wrong.

The bigger point was that I'd lost my cool. It's a good thing audiences spend most of the opening number distracted by the visuals, yet in this case the only visual they got was the thrilling spectacle of my hunched back. "The Right Thing to Do" was up next, a well-worn slipper of a song I should have settled into easily. It was a song I'd written in 1972 during the short flight from the Vineyard to New York, with James asleep in the seat beside me, breathing softly, looking so beautiful, so loved.

That night, though, I couldn't even seem to settle into a song I'd performed countless times. With my adrenaline still flooding me, I felt a fresh wave of dread and thirty seconds later, I stopped midsong, frozen and embarrassed, and turned my back again to the audience.

Based on the strange, halting applause at the end of the song, the audience was starting to get alarmed. By now, I was convinced that unless I left the stage right that second I would really die, with poor Lucy given the unenviable task of pronouncing the official time and cause of my death: hysteria, mixed with ventricular fibrillation, Miss Simon leaving behind her darling brave blond children, Sally and Ben, and her on-again, off-again husband, James. . . . Again bending over at the waist, I tried to steady my breath, make it less frighteningly erratic. It didn't work. That's when I stood up straight. This is your moment, I remember thinking. You can either run away from it, or live through it.

Facing the audience, I blurted out, "I'm having an anxiety attack, I guess. What's happening is what I'm always afraid might happen." I told the audience that it would help me immeasurably if they would be willing to come onstage with me. "If you want to sing, please do, but just . . . I don't want there to be any separation between me and you."

At least a hundred audience members took my words seriously, clustering up front, with the guards standing sentry ultimately allowing about fifty people to join a stage already populated by musicians, amps, wires, and scrims. It felt almost as though having invited my neighbors over for a spontaneous glass of holiday eggnog, the entire block had shown up, and now had little to do other than circle a shaking, frozen singer whom some liked, others possibly revered. Most took seats on the edge of the stage, as though I were a living, barely breathing funeral pyre, a woman in flames flailing, disintegrating, atomizing.

Somewhere inside me, a small voice ordered me to sing "De Bat," one of the songs off *Boys in the Trees*, which was about bringing Sally home in my arms one night. That will make you lose yourself, I told myself.

Good idea, wrong night. Still, I began singing and was able to animate the images, impersonating, or trying to, the bodies of the bat and the cat.

As I waited for my heart to resume its normal beat, I could only hope that "De Bat" was just what the doctor ordered and could get me back on track. Oh, how different it would have all been if I could have had the dispassion to survey the scene onstage from a great height, or even as a member of the audience. My brain began the following argument with itself, a sequence of unrhyming lyrics:

"Hey, I'm doing okay. I'm getting through this."

"No, you're not, did you just feel that? That was a palpitation. You're not going to live much longer."

"No—you can control it."

"No, Carly, this is hardwired. The phobic process is a loop that feeds on itself. You're doomed. You always have been. You always will be." The back-and-forth monologue alerted my adrenal glands. With my adrenaline in free-flow release, my heart palpitations now went into overdrive. Then there was this: I was also hemorrhaging from between my legs. What began as a near-imperceptible slow drip turned gradually into a single hot stream. My bed was burning, the sheets on fire.

What was happening to me? By now my sister Lucy had made her way onstage and was sitting beside me, along with a dozen or so audience members. They sat there, rubbing my feet and ankles. "Carl, you're doing great," I remember Lucy saying, and I couldn't help wishing that she would grab the mic and finish the rest of the show for me.

One fan said, "I love that song," and sang "De Bat" along with me.

A second one said, "I get anxiety attacks too."

A third one said, "Can we stay up on the stage with you, even if you don't get better?"

The fourth one had this to say: "You have blood on your pants."

I began to address the audience in their seats—"I'm just going to run into the bathroom for a second, and I'll be right back"—but excited to be part of a "happening," most were yelling so loudly they could hardly hear me when I said it. Handing my guitar to Lucy, I started exiting the stage, whereupon the audience began to boo.

After such an extraordinary show of support, why would they boo me?

I was mistaken. What resembled booing was instead *Don't go! Don't go!* After a moment's hesitation, I reversed course and Lucy gazed back at me strangely. "It's okay, I have to stay," I told her.

"Are you all right?" Lucy said, though I sensed she was concealing deeper concerns. "It sounds great." I ran to the bathroom, splashed cold water on my face, and was back on stage in a flash. The audience was thrilled and glad that they'd helped.

I started to sing something, anything, followed by "You're So Vain" and "Anticipation." I was holding my legs tightly together. I still had little idea what was happening, but my chest palpitations were easing up, which in turn allowed me to focus on a Kegel exercise, squeezing tightly to keep the blood flow to a minimum. By now, I'd reached a point of complete indifference as to whether I lived or died. I kept looking over at Mike, who was nodding up and down in an exaggerated way as if conveying to the audience—and me—that everything was going to be all right.

Once I'd finished singing "Anticipation," the audience gave me a standing ovation. Some fans were even standing in their seats, or flocking the aisles, hoping to trade places with the fifty or so fans onstage. By necessity, the guards seemed less vigilant than usual in keeping the peace, but as it turned out, they were at precisely the right height and distance to see where the blood had soaked into my pants.

Soon enough, it became clear where everybody should focus his or her gaze. Things were made official when one college-age boy, who'd been patting my leg as if consoling an injured, scared child, or animal, took away his hand. All at once, everyone in the band and the audience could see that his hand and my two pant legs were saturated with blood. I won't go into any more detail. I will say, though, that if you can recall a night as strange as that, it serves as an excellent gauge by which to compare the other highs and lows of your life.

I could make out Lucy's voice faintly: "We have to get you backstage."

"She's bleeding!!!" someone called out, sounding alarmed. By now I was beyond shock, as Lucy, always and forever the boss, engineered a pathway and led me offstage behind the curtain, followed by Mike.

I took a Valium. I took a shower. I took my pulse. I put on a pair of jeans and a T-shirt, and within five minutes I was back onstage, moving like a hero in a sports movie, resuming my concert. The audience rose to its feet as my arms found my guitar. When I sang "Legend in Your Own Time," ten thousand people stood and remained standing for the next twenty minutes I remained onstage.

As I said good night, the ovations were long and numbing. I really wanted to believe and take in the cheers and applause, but instead I was overcome by annihilating shame. As I was leaving the stage, I thought about the Beast and gave it a silent nod. I knew it was up to something but didn't know what it was yet. I fell onto the couch in my dressing room and blacked out.

For obvious reasons, the night's second show was canceled. Lucy insisted on it. I was just too weak to perform. We canceled the six or seven remaining tour dates. Unfortunately, the insurance companies didn't pony up the full amount to refund the losses, which infuriated the promoters, and even though I had a hit song, "Jesse," at the time, the album, *Come Upstairs*, didn't sell very well.

As ever, music was the only thing that could bring me back to life. But before returning to the studio, at my family's insistence, I checked into a general hospital. I now weighed even less than I did before the Pittsburgh concert. Doctors assessed my blood, glands, heart, and brain, advising me to remain under professional care until I was eating regularly again. The awful pressure of Ben's sickness and operation, and of James's and my splintering marriage, followed by the calamity that was Pittsburgh, was more than I could take. So I stayed on in the hospital for another month, and by the time I was released, James was already in another relationship, this time with Kathryn Walker, an actress who would later become his second wife. Scott visited me often, and James came too, once bearing a very large bouquet of blue irises. I placed myself into the mental frame of mind that I wanted James to be with Kathryn, that he'd be better off with her than with me, and that I also wanted our relationship to be put out of its misery—though that feeling lasted for only a day or so. Still, I continued to see Scott; and the next few weeks were a blur of me gaining weight while fighting off various lawsuits from promoters who had never heard of the contractual phrase *act of God*, or if they had, were doing their best to declare themselves atheists.

Pittsburgh was just the most recent, horrific example of the condition I've suffered from for as long as I can remember: depression and the other side of its tricky coin, anxiety. It began with my childhood "worry lump," the term my mother gave it, her hope being that my lump could somehow become a lifelong trusted pal and companion. In the 1950s and '60s, no one ever spoke of "depression." When I was young, I didn't know that my father had his own version of that same lump—depression and anxiety—though I must have intuited it when I hoped that my incessant, superstitious, compulsive knocking would keep him alive. When my anxiety attacks looped around each other to the point where I couldn't tell what was nerves, what was my fear of stuttering, what was shyness, what was not wanting to sleep at anyone's house, what was *anything*, I began convincing myself I was becoming just like Daddy. My Dear Daddy, who lived in a time when it was much too soon to speak easily about "depression."

For me the connection between depression and anxiety is complicated. Depression is a low-grade energy, sending me into a dark place where only the darkest thoughts are invited to live. Then, seemingly without warning, it flips over into anxiety, at which point I'm likely to take a sedative, retreat into a quiet room, or try out another one of the many strategies I've done my best to master over the years. With anxiety you know exactly what's next: You're going to feel crazy. You're going to have to lie down. You're going to snap your own wrists with the rubber bands you keep handy. Then my anxiety gives way, again, to depression, its funnel of brown, single-minded thoughts telling me I don't look good, I can't keep a man, I'm uninteresting, I can't read or even sit through a movie. I remember two acutely zestless years when I never cried, never sang around the house, didn't laugh, and had no appetite for food or much of anything. Clearly that was not the answer, either.

Looking back, I realize that during our marriage, James looked as though he was more depressed—though not more anxious—than I was, self-medicating his condition with a wide assortment of specialist-ordered (and newly invented) antidepressants, as well as alcohol and other inebriants. I distracted myself from my own anxiety by diverting him using peppy words my own mother might have used, like "How 'bout a nice brisk walk on the beach?" If we did go, James wouldn't even bother to glance at the water. Back then, not understanding the disease of depression as well as I do today, I would also ply him with food, music, or lovemaking. Those were the times I was boldest about singing, playing guitar, and even writing music in front of him, in an effort to bring him back into the harmony and blend of life. In an effort to make James laugh, I would talk in various accents, make up poems, and sometimes—when a lucky star shone down from above—James would shoot me a sideways glance of appreciation. He would fake getting unstuck from his depression, and either chase me around the apartment or tickle me. Amazing how very much alike we were. Just exchanging masks.

James told me once I had a very low tolerance for any kind of pain, particularly the psychic variety, and he was right. Antidepressants and other medications have helped me, off and on, over the years. When they're working, I laugh and sing songs around the house, but when I'm depressed, it's another thing entirely. Home helps me. Family helps me. My children help me. Which is why the end of James's and my marriage, when it came, was such a blow to my sense of wholeness. I never imagined that our concepts of the meaning of divorce would be so different, that we would truly stop being a family, and that it would be so devastating to me. When a marriage ends you don't always get to choose what remains.

James: He walked straight—looking neither right nor left. 1980.

It turned out to be a vase after all.

CHAPTER TWENTY-FOUR

strip, bitch

A nd yet, things were reluctant to the end.
About a year or so after James and I were officially separated, he
came to the apartment we'd once shared on Central Park West, where I continued to live with Ben and Sally.

It was right before dinner. James was dropping off the kids, who had
just finished doing their homework at his new apartment on West End
Avenue. It was unusual that he came up with them, as he usually left
them in the lobby. James entered the kitchen, wearing his heavy, faux-fur-
collared coat. He was still the tall apparition of the man I loved. He mentioned in passing that a cab was waiting for him downstairs, and that he
was en route to the Village for dinner.

During this period, relations between us were confused, sharp sometimes,
heated in hate, our visits and phone calls whirling with eloquent insults, a
lion and a lioness in winter. "Angry man, hungry woman," as James himself
once wrote. Other times, we were civil. With a cab waiting downstairs, I assumed he would simply turn around and reboard the elevator. But instead,
once the kids were settled in their bedrooms, James took a seat in one of the

kitchen chairs, facing me. That night I was wearing a suede, leopard-print wraparound dress as I leaned against the counter. Behind me, the dishwasher was on its dry cycle, the steam emanating from its borders possibly making my own edges blurry and tempting—for a poor old southern baby in his cups (James was either drunk or stoned, or both) I could very well have been a sight for sore eyes. Two feet away from me, tipped over slightly at the waist, his left elbow propped on his left knee, James gazed at kitchen tiles he once knew well, a lit Camel between the thumb and index finger of his right hand. The laces of one of his large boots had come untied. He still had on his coat.

Tension: there was certainly *that* in that room. Steam was coming through my dress. The angled distance between James and me was jagged, irregular somehow. A scream was going to happen; a song was about to start; something was about to blow. After exhaling smoke, James's lips remained half-open, as if he'd gotten distracted and forgotten to close them. Any minute, I assumed, he'd stand up, give me a gentlemanly nod, open the kitchen door, and leave, with nary an insult, at least not tonight.

Instead he glanced up. He was taking me in. Usually I could decipher James's legion of expressions. Tonight, though, I couldn't. He snapped ash onto the floor, then flashed me two or three milliseconds of his faintly bloodshot baby blues. I noticed he was sweating.

"Strip, bitch."

James hadn't moved; his posture remained the same as he exhaled perfectly concentric rings of smoke. Waiting to see if I'd take his bait, he didn't blink; I glanced up, and for a few seconds he just observed me. Looking up at the ceiling to halt our eye contact, I took fast, furious inventory. A few more seconds passed. From the kids' perspective, it wasn't out of the question that Mother and Father would vanish behind a closed door, where conceivably they might be having a conversation, maybe even a quarrel. They might be talking about school schedules, pickups and drop-offs. They might be taking out their calendars and coordinating vacation times. It wasn't so unlikely a scenario. Not all that long ago, after all, the bedroom where I now slept alone used to be "our" bedroom.

Underneath the too-bright overhead kitchen lights, neither of us had the time or the inclination to do anything but erase all judgment and be from a family of earlier hominids. I don't remember how we got to the bedroom and how I silently locked the door.

Time had gone by, but there was nothing uncoordinated or awkward about what we did. We were hardly new lovers; it had just felt like ages since he or I had inhabited the same nervous system. We were silent but blatant. With the front of his body to my back, he pressed himself into me. I noticed that James's long, aristocratic fingers were stained with nicotine. Mostly I noticed that he wasn't wearing a wedding ring. There was a hesitation. But that familiar weight, like that of some sleek animal, grafted onto me. Later I knew he'd say he was sorry, that he hadn't meant to, that it didn't mean anything, but in those moments I was in heaven that lust had toppled him. I felt I was Orpheus leading Eurydice out of the underworld, not daring to look back until we had at least reached the upper air.

But unlike the myth, and despite the gender roles being reversed, I never looked back, and James still disappeared.

Three years later, in 1984, at a dinner party on the Upper East Side, I was introduced to the then-CEO of Simon & Schuster, Richard Snyder, and his wife, Simon & Schuster president and publisher Joni Evans. Dick and Joni were a certified New York power couple who did everything they could to match and even exceed their reputations. When dinner was over, Dick turned to me and announced that I *must* bring Sally and Ben down to the publisher's new offices on Forty-eighth Street and Sixth Avenue. "Have you ever been there?" he asked, and when I told him I hadn't, he proposed that I stop by the following afternoon. My answer, I think, surprised him:

"If you really mean it, I'll be there," I said, adding that Sally and Ben got out of school at three forty-five, and would four fifteen work for him? Dick smiled, did a little shuffle in his pointy shoes, mock bowed, and said, "Okay, yes, Carly Simon, I'd be delighted. Just ask the receptionist to show you to my office."

The next day, I held the hands of Ben, seven, and Sally, ten, as we piled out of the taxi and made our way into Simon & Schuster's dark, cavernous lobby. I'd never given my kids all that much background about their grandfather, Dick Simon, how he'd once been the reigning king of publishing, how, with his tremendous talent, innovativeness, and vision, he'd created from nothing a company that has since become part of a giant media conglomerate. Ben and Sally seemed to remember only that Daddy had crossed paths with Albert Einstein—and wasn't Einstein the same person who discovered America?—being far more interested that Daddy's hairline had started receding when he was in his mid-twenties, and did that mean that I, their mommy, would go bald someday, too?

The three of us took the elevator up to a high floor. It was hard not to remember another elevator ride I'd taken in another building, in another decade, to meet up with Daddy alone in his exile on the twenty-ninth floor. But that was twenty-five years ago. In contrast to the old Rockefeller Center elevator, this new and improved one was smooth, faceless, frictionless. It made a delicate *ping* as it came to a stop at Simon & Schuster's executive floors. When the doors opened, I was momentarily jolted, frozen almost in my tracks. My eyes fixed immediately on the names etched on frosted-glass double doors: SIMON & SCHUSTER. That same moment, as Sally's gaze met mine, I sensed she'd just come to a new, slow-dawning awareness of who her grandfather had been.

As we waited for Dick Snyder, the three of us sat on navy blue leather seats arrayed around an ultramodern, magazine-strewn table. Ben, wearing his Lawrence of Arabia headdress, immediately began sketching an action figure on a notepad. Sally began making a cat's cradle. Still fidgety, she began to unwrap a piece of gum before my eyes threw her a gentle *Not the right time.*

At that time, I was in a career downswing in the volatile, up-and-down weather pattern that was show business. When you're hot you're hot, when you're not you're not, and I was no longer as good as I'd been once at maintaining my indifference. Married to James, I'd been moated off by the Camelot status of our marriage. People loved us, hated us, feared us, denigrated us, and circled us with their jealousy and desire and longing. They opened doors for us when we wanted them opened (which was practically never), anxious to find their way somehow inside this tall, strapping, lanky duo. A near-mystical allure of power had protected, surrounded, and trailed behind us for years, but with James and me no longer two against the world, I was in temporary stasis.

Naturally, I wanted to be on top again—to feel connected, wanted, admired. Knowing the fakery of show business all too well, I should have been above status seeking, but I wasn't. At the end of the day, the illusion of glamour and fame is as potent and insidious as any other drug. You're suckered into thinking you desire something you know very well is shoddy, phony, and fleeting. The problem is, it also makes you feel good, gives you a voice and an identity, fools you into believing you belong to a higher tier of people who are more fun, more sparkly, more worthwhile to be around. Most of all, showbiz makes you feel wanted, but with my marriage over and my career in a lull, I felt doubly unwelcome.

Thirty minutes passed. Then forty-five. Michael Korda, Simon & Schuster's editor in chief, appeared in the hallway, and we chatted for a while before Korda was called into a meeting. As I kept on waiting for Dick Snyder, I told my children stories about how brilliant and risk-taking their grandfather had been. Like mercury, which made Daddy, by definition, *mercurial*, an adjective that joined the word-of-the-day grammar list on our fridge, which that week alone included *defenestration* (the act of throwing someone or something out a window), *lucubration* (laborious, intensive study by lamplight), and *pusillanimous* (cowardly). Daddy wasn't only brilliant and charismatic, I told Ben and Sally, but his reputation for grooming and tending his writers was legendary. He never used false praise, either. He genuinely *meant* it when he greeted one of his stable of authors with an enthusiastic grin or a generous pat or clap on the back.

The longer I sat there, the tenser I got, my wallflower instincts receding, replaced by anger. Dick Snyder was an hour and a half late. I was beginning to feel affronted and disrespected. My reasons for coming here were simple: to show Sally and Ben the company my father had founded at the impossibly young age of twenty-five, in the hope they'd be as proud of Daddy as I was. Just then a receptionist shepherded us from the reception area into another large room, this one bereft of objects other than a streamlined modern desk the size of a lap pool. With a Diet Coke can before him, Dick Snyder stood up and sauntered over no farther than the front of his desk, looking down his Pinocchio-pointy nose at us.

I introduced Ben and Sally, adding, as an aside, that Ben's middle name was "Simon." At this, Dick Snyder deigned to make eye contact and even shook Ben's small, sturdy hand. Retreating behind his desk, he seemed finally to notice Sally, too. He spat a little cough into one hand before murmuring, "Sally, you said, yes—nice of you to come," and indicating we should all sit, make ourselves at home.

"Either of you kids top students?" he asked Ben and Sally. "You want to come here and work some day?" Both kids responded politely, with "ums," Ben even adding, "Yes, sir, I'd say so." Simon & Schuster was a pretty darn nice place to work, Snyder said. He took one last slug of his Diet Coke and pulverized it in one hand. Pulling his arm back, he fired it into the wastebasket across the room. He made the shot with practiced ease. A hard man in a soft profession. Along with Sally, I couldn't have cared less, but Ben was obviously impressed. Then, with the confidence of any number of white boys in pin-striped suits, Dick Snyder gazed down at Ben and Sally, leveling one final, booming admonition: *"Well, if your grandfather had been smart, this could have been yours."*

Was history repeating itself? Was my own life, like Daddy's, a gleaming surface under which the most degenerate forces simmered and fumed? Had I spent my life trying to save my father, to avenge the losses he suffered, while also doing everything possible never, ever to end up like him?

Like everyone, I had losses of my own, starting with minor and ending with big. The biggest loss of all over the past twenty years has been the togetherness of our family. Some core things stay the same. My stammer still comes and goes, unpredictably, as does my stage fright. I still believe wildly, wholeheartedly, in the power of love. I might add that losses aren't entirely negative, either. Just as night follows day, sadness follows joy, and the underworld sometimes takes aim at innocence, a lifelong nemesis like my stammering turned out to be the very thing that made my music crucial to me in the first place.

How does a person—me, or anyone else?—move ahead, push forward through life? The answer is that none of us does, not entirely. I have simply found a way of loving through whatever absences or dejections have fallen like tree branches in my path. I move forward by incorporating whoever or whatever is missing or vanished into my very being, my body, my breath. The psychologists call this introjection, but I call it surviving. I lost Daddy, and incorporated him inside me. I lost my marriage, and James became a part of how I look at life. I let go of Orpheus, not realizing, perhaps, that I just had to get to know him before I could become him.

The shack, 1970, Martha's Vineyard.
"I've lived in all the houses he's built
The one in the air
The one underground
The one on the water
The one in the sand."
—"We're So Close," 1979

Hidden Star Hill, 2015.

epilogue

I used to have a whole other life. Very little has changed in the surroundings where I live today on Martha's Vineyard. I live in the same house, even sleep in the same bed, where James and I once slept. It's been years since this was our house together, and I still haven't taken down his fishing rod from where he placed it above the sliding doors in the living room. In fact, the living room is pretty much the same as when he and I lived here. The Plexiglas that James nailed into the window frames is still there keeping out the cold. It stays far too warm in the summer, for as original as his idea was, it makes opening the windows a major event. Still, I never wanted to change anything in the living room because it was the part of the house he built before we met. Before I came into the life of this house so many Thanksgivings ago and the two of us began adding bathroom doors, closets, odd-shaped windows, towers, eaves, catwalks, and circular staircases.

Everyone says the house is uniquely beautiful, like a Russian cathedral, a fairy tale castle. Only James and I knew it was a folly: a testament to our romantic brainstorming. We pretended to be practical. He gave in to me, I gave in to him. He said the bathroom for the children should be small and neat, functional, like a ship's head. When it was finally completed, it looked more like a bathroom for the criminally insane, with a door that opened *in*, taking up most of what was already a cramped space lined with dull, gray tile. It sported a miniature toilet which the children outgrew almost immediately. The toilet remains, and now you have to crouch down to the size of a small child to use it. It should have been padded, that bathroom. You can't help knocking yourself silly even when brushing your hair in the mirror: an elbow collides with a cabinet, a knee with a drawer.

Then there was the matter of the kitchen. I wanted a large family kitchen that I could go bustling about in, feeling all earthy with flour powdering down my long apron. With the builders hired to recognize our dream, we built that kitchen, the only problem being that we forgot to extend the plumbing beyond two feet of one corner of the room before all the walls were plastered and painted. The finished effect was not unlike the bathroom for the criminally insane, though this was the "kitchen for the cook confined to a wheelchair." You didn't have to move more than a few inches to get from the sink to the stove to the refrigerator, but you had to make sure the dishwasher door was closed in order to open the refrigerator.

James and I were like two maniacs posted at the gates of domesticity, feverishly going about preventing anything really comfortable from happening. I wanted a circular garden, he wanted a forty-five-foot hexagonal tower. I wanted a cobblestone driveway, he wanted individual houses for the pig, the tractor, and the dog. I wanted a pool, James wanted a pond and a windmill.

So we spent lavishly and lived with carpenters, landscapers, painters, and sawdust for most of our summers together as Sally and Ben, three years apart, were growing up. When the most ambitious addition—the flying bridge over the courtyard leading to the kids' rooms—was completed, James and I gradually moved farther and farther apart and finally resigned from building any future life together. Still, and with many alterations over the years, I live in this flamboyant white elephant, and as I go around its many curvy steps and corners, as I move through new times and claim new and further spaces, I add up past and present and this house becomes more and more a home that steers its own course and knows its masters, the echoes of its songs, the barks of its dogs. Every reconciliation of a roofline adds to its personality, the latest overflow of books calling for a new shelf (and I'm home alone with a hammer), every flowerbed that takes off, *finally*, changes the shape of the lawn, every touch-up of a wall that has required a coat of paint, the new speaker in the tower, the hammock on the deck, the brick walkway to the guest cottage, the curved door to my bedroom getting three coats of warm-toned varnish. Ben's fire pit down the road, the sheep shed, the deepening cracks in the beams. Each room is my life. This sky, this hot summer eve, is a new room. This is a home where I am so much more welcome than in the first twenty years, when I didn't quite understand what a home could or might be.

I am not the type of person to let go of my past easily. My memory is too good. That's why it doesn't seem to make much difference if I take down James's fishing rod or not. Leaving things as they were is a relief. It takes less energy to glimpse that fishing rod than to conjure it up. Fact is, I am still partly living in the imagination of the man who made the life I lead in this damnably difficult, audaciously original house. But how to erase him? I wouldn't know just who to erase. Everyone identifies with being two people. One who he very naturally allows himself to be, the one who surrounds his soul. The other, the one he pretends to be, has gotten into his system and is fixed in place like a mask. He is the visiting man. The vanishing man. Always on the verge of moving away. If I were trying to erase all traces of James, then I could never look at Ben, so similar to his father in many ways; brilliant and charming, with a sweetness beneath the cutting edge of a wit, already devastating, even as a child of five. And Sally, the golden, beautiful daughter of her father's dreams, the Sarah Maria of his song.

Recently, in one of the compartments in the guitar closet, I found a little assemblage of James's. Guitar strings, bits of twine, two or three burned-out matches, a pair of grandpa glasses with one lens missing, and a Polaroid snapshot of me. Except for the picture, it was a fairly typical pile of James's. Probably the detritus of a pocket that got too full. He emptied his pockets almost at random, anywhere he happened to be, when they became too crammed. Their contents now reveal to me the pain he was in. Not so much the individual items, but more how the piles themselves were so unrelated to each other. James was never like those men who empty their pockets each day onto the same bureau top until their wives come along to sweep or tidy everything up. No, James's assemblages would materialize on top of the fridge, beside a bed, at rest on a window ledge. What I once saw as a sort of hectic masculine jubilee, I now see as something terribly poignant. Maybe he wanted me to make some sense out of these offerings, to decipher a puzzle piece in the bigger jigsaw.

The Polaroid I recognized as one James took the year after we got married, the summer we went to Vienna. I was sitting across from him outdoors at the hotel café, eating Sacher torte and drinking café au lait, my pregnancy making me ravenous: Sally on her way. "Come to me my melon-bellied baby," James would sing, looking to see if he could detect the minute progress every day of our ripening fruit. I never liked it when James took the camera from me. He'd take too long to focus or frame, and I got self-conscious waiting for the snap. He put that Polaroid snapshot in our scrapbook, and then one day it was no longer there. He must have removed it like a kidnapper with no obvious motive.

It always amazes me that we can look right past something that finally smacks us in the face. That blind spot. How could I for years have overlooked the chaos—the spidery string-ends and ash-clumps James accumulated; little bits of hope he thought he could piece together. But damn, if it didn't move me something fierce to see that old Polaroid of me in the pile. Me wearing that attempted mirror grin, unsure without the mirror. Why did he add *that* to his pile of pain? That clutter and confusion. The tribulations of our remorse. He never really criticized me, he just grew cold. The heartbeat went out of our house, the rhythm went out of our romance, but so what? In life that happens, doesn't it? You just have to remember to breathe. But our breathing became irregular and strained, and instead of managing a peaceful farmyard, we found that we had corralled a wild animal. When it broke loose, it jumped the fence and got out the gate.

When we made our parting official, neither of us thought we could stay in this house. But Sally and Ben had attachments that went beyond the ends of the land here in these hills and valleys and wooded trails, pools and ponds and circle gardens, trees where they began to climb and collect the apples in August.

I tried to create a new bedroom out of the space Kate had been using as her bedroom when I first arrived in December 1971. In the following years, it had turned into a playroom. Moving to the new wing seemed to make good sense. The room was like a great big barn, with a peaked roof, a hexagonal bright red stained-glass window and a circular staircase leading to the loft where James and I slept for at least the first two years. This was the same room where James recorded his album *One Man Dog*, with my favorite song of his, "Don't Let Me Be Lonely Tonight." The band and gear lay just a few feet below the bed. All those Orpheus-like men making that jazz, those beats, the melodies, and words, just underneath my head. It wasn't all that different from Daddy playing the piano below the floorboards of Joey's and my bedroom in Stamford. Times, periods, decades that feel like no more than a few seconds ago in the appalling span of years.

Out of that music room I tried to make myself a new bedroom. Something a little more feminine, with my old dolls playing house with Sally's new ones. Attempting to create a soft-toned ambience, I treated the hexagonal window to new violet-colored glass and installed flowered chintz to frame the French doors. I brought in a lilac-colored carpet, wicker lamps, and a brass bed with a deep purple embossed velvet bedspread.

This all fit as uniquely as a powdered, sweet-scented seventeenth-century courtesan's wig on the head of a stable boy. The experiment failed, and I let the guests have it, moving back down the long bridge over the courtyard to the old bedroom, which still leads up two flights to the top of the tower. A different division of the museum. This is the very tower where the kids and their friends wandered around nooks, angles, and dark-stained beams, up the two staircases to that peak of six angular glass windows that fracture six spaces of our sky. Now just as we did when the trees were all still short and spiky, we come to its zenith to watch shooting stars zipper through the blackness. The shack is still a work in progress.

Since our divorce in 1983, James and I both have lives that we work at in our own ways. Many relationships have come and gone, with most remaining solidly entrenched in the glad, grateful part of my memory. Over the years, I've learned something that has made my life easier, more honest and satisfying: I've stopped trying to stop loving. If the rules decree that you are allowed to love only if that love is reciprocated, then whoever made up those rules is cutting an important part of their authenticity away. The commonly accepted belief that once you begin a new life, or move on, you must stop loving someone, has nothing to do with your own private heart. That heart might have been broken, but brokenness doesn't stop it from loving. It has nothing to do with masochism, and it's not a conscious decision either. How can you not love a person whose genes are in the two people, your children, you love most in the world?

Looking back, I made lots of mistakes. I remember and have made peace with each one, just as I forgive James for anything he may have done or not done. I replace any unhappy, hurtful memories with those of music and joy and the perfect fourths and the shared genes and this house on the hill and the things scattered around the house that remind me that we are all ever *only* stewards of something larger than ourselves. I am deeply lucky to have continued to build a family home on this land.

The Vineyard will always be home for me. Even on charcoal-colored, dismal days, what do you do when where you live is home? How can I possibly pretend anyplace else would come close to looking or feeling the same? I've always especially loved the trees here in the middle of the forest. Some have grown extremely tall, and are home to thousands of birds that nestle and hide in high branches, singing songs I try to learn and communicate back to them. Whether they think I'm a bird myself is in question, but either way we have a close relationship. The Vineyard and Hidden Star Hill in particular are part of my family's history and rootedness, from fainting at the fair as a baby, the smell of the honeysuckle on the path to the North Road, to meeting Davy Gude, Jamie Taylor eating half of my vanilla pop, running down the splinter-happy steps away from Nick, living and loving and writing songs in this house. So many of them. Maybe a hundred songs. Some of them anyone might be proud of.

Orpheus, that lifelong boy, comes and goes, darting from star to twig to beam, landing lightly, taking up no space at all, as is his habit, with his bony, delicate ways, his starry beauty, his hands absorbed in melodies forged from skin and bone and strings. Sometimes he shows up with a rustle, a little jump, so graceful and soft I can barely believe there's anyone in the orchard. Other times he heaves a single brown leg over an outstretched branch and settles in for a while, until the days and the notes in my head jumble together long enough to find one song, or ten songs, or twenty. Then he's gone again, his speed dreams lighting the way, pouring himself through the warm night like my old childhood friends, Mr. Hicks, Meany, and Ha Ha Ginsberg. He's not the only one. On this property, especially in the summer, there are still boys in the trees—Ben, or my grandson, or the thick-trousered man who's kind enough to saw off the top branches of the nearby wisteria that winds itself up the perfectly well-established oak. Together the two tangle, to veil the view of the stars from my bedroom window. But I don't wait for Orpheus to come anymore. What would be the sense in that? Wait long enough for anyone to show up and you forget that all the things you ever longed for, all those impossible gods, were inside you the whole time. Give me a sound, give me an ocean, maybe even a large pond. Give me just enough forgetfulness as my opium. I can't think of a nicer state of mind in which to begin anew.

Give me a sound, give me an ocean . . .

ACKNOWLEDGMENTS

A special thank-you to Ken Burns.

In my memoir I have focused in on my childhood and my early life. Let's say age five until thirty-five. In reading and re-reading my old diaries and letters, I discovered certain patterns having to do with love, family, lies, and commitments. As I came out of childhood and into becoming a responsible adult, I looked to my parents and siblings as role models, wanting to find the truth, and to see who I was in this family of mine and in the greater world at large. But as my parents drifted further and further onto their own paths, still pretending it was the "same" path, I watched them leave what once was a healthy place to raise a family, and begin the lie that closed in on all of us. The way it closed in on me and made me so preoccupied with my "lack of," so unsure of my strengths, is the subject of this book.

Just as fascinating was how what went on revealed to me a "new" way of looking at stories. I had experienced the truth, but didn't know it at the time. In re-reading these diaries, I saw so many roads out, so many possible courses of action. One nurse, one teacher might have made all the difference. What if they had read the signs differently and steered me in a new direction? Revisiting that most vulnerable time in my life when I was trying to understand more than I was prepared to understand, I was helped immeasurably by my agent, Betsy Lerner, who read every single diary and assured me there *was* something of value in the material. She continued to be unsparingly "there" and not only edited me at first, bringing things into focus, but also acted as the great defender.

She also introduced me to the editor who brought his talents to this large, overwhelming table and formed a circle outside of which he wouldn't let me step unguided. He, Peter Smith, is one of the best writers I have ever read or talked to, and it was intimidating to live up to his intellectual expectations. He made me, as any good teacher will do, better than before, by which I mean, more honest, more explicit, more literate. In addition, he and I laughed at my life. Doing more of that is one of my goals.

Before the actual writing came the research. I read letters and sleuthed out my father's fallout with Simon & Schuster, and the keenly destructive forces that came together in a perfect triangle to smoke him out. If there had been nothing else to prove it, one of Daddy's last ventures said it all. My father came up with the title, *The Man in the Gray Flannel Suit*, and with typical savvy, he cross-promoted it with another one of his books, *The Organization Man*. It was the beginning of Big Business, and Daddy knew it. As one company was consuming another and bosses were busy one-upping bosses, my father's partners were acting out their own version of *King Lear*, with lawyers on the sideline lying to get in on the take—a gruesome and confusing sight for me, a young girl who saw nothing but the shadowy outline.

I want to thank Evan Brier and acknowledge his excellent book *A Novel Marketplace*, which helped explain more than I had ever known about what went on at Simon & Schuster in the late 1950s. In addition, Evan also went to the archives at Columbia University in New York—my father's alma mater and also where his papers ended up after his death in 1960—to take photos of the most important documents, which added crucial detail to the story of Daddy's demoralizing professional demise.

Speaking of Daddy, all the photos in the first part of the book were taken by my father, who, in addition to his other talents, was a brilliant photographer. Most of the others were taken by my brother, Peter Simon. Peter's quality and sense of style came naturally to him, as photography closely bound him and my father. Peter took over the darkrooms in Stamford and Riverdale, with their chemicals and giant vats. Growing up, my sisters and I spent hours watching the images emerge from the limp pieces of white paper Peter had just dipped in the solution. (In the tradition of men in hats with pom-poms on them!) Thank you, Peter, for taking up the baton so brilliantly and sharing your negatives with me.

Thank you to Meghan La Roque, my personal assistant, who not only knows where all the keys are but knows where the *keys* to the keys are. Meghan is generous and smart and has the kind of mind most people wish they had—not forgetting things and keeping what she remembers in strict order of importance. She makes everything work when it really shouldn't and takes as good care of the sheep as she does of all things digital.

To Larry Ciancia, my manager at the time we brought this book home. He is a great friend of the family and has been essential to my years of writing.

At Flatiron Books, I want to thank the president and publisher, Bob Miller, whom I have known since I was still living within the timespan of this book. I don't think I'm lying when I say I remember conversations between him and my mother at our kitchen table in Riverdale. Bob had been after me to write a book for as long as I can remember, and when the time came, he introduced me to Colin Dickerman, Flatiron's editorial director. When Bob and Colin visited Hidden Star Hill to work on the book, Bob mentioned that he played guitar—lefty, too. It just so happened I had some strings, and he was able to restring the ones he needed. For most of the weekend, Colin and I could hear Bob Miller playing the blues from an adjacent room. Colin is funny and deep and smart, and we got to know each other at a fast pace, which proved the worth of what we worked on together, because I don't think either of us thought we were compromising. Thank you, Colin, for understanding why I made every phone call to you after it was a little too late to change the placement of a comma.

Also at Flatiron, I want to recognize James Melia, Liz Keenan, Marlena Bittner, Karen Horton, and my copy editor Greg Villepique.

And then there are those special people on my team who have contributed immensely, organized in no particular order: Jonathan Lyons, Berta Baghjajian, Susan Kamil, Mali Hunter, Claudia McGinnis, Andy Ward, Frank Filipetti, Diane Hirschhorn, Deb White, Martha Sherrill, Danielle Ambrose, Arlyne Rothberg, and Bob Levine.

Of course, there are the people who have read some of the book and re-marked on things deeper than typos. In order of picking them out of a hat: Jessica Hoffman Davis (as conspicuously important to my life as she is to this book, also a great editor and friend), Herman Wouk, Carol Craven, Trish Kubal, Carinthia West, Jenny Blackton, David Seidler, Pam Frank, Tamara Weiss (my longtime friend and mother to my godsons Jules and Noah. She is my foremost tracker), Mia Farrow, Kenneth Cole, Jimmy Ryan, Terence Blacker, Jim Hart, and Rose Styron.

And finally, thanks go to my family and roommates in this housing complex:

Richard Koehler, my mate.

Ben and Sally Taylor, both of you, my funny and dear-hearted children. You assured me that writing about your father was a reasonable and brave thing to do. Naturally for me, this was the most sensitive issue.

My sisters, Lucy and Joey, who heard things they might have preferred to forget. In contrast, other memories described herein provoked howling laughter.

My brother, Peter, the outstanding photographer and gentle soul.

Dean Bragonier, Bodhi Bragonier, and the entire extended Simon and Taylor families.

Special thanks and love to Jim Hart.

I would especially like to thank all the trees that produced the wood that was needed to make the paper used for the many drafts of this book. If any tree is personally and unduly affected, I will send a young girl up to the top branch of a "Sister tree" and have her sing this song (in nine languages):

I'm home again in my old narrow bed
Where I grew tall and my feet hung over the end
The low beam room with the window looking out
On the soft summer garden
Where the boys grew in the trees

Here I grew guilty
And no one was at fault
Frightened by the power
In every innocent thought
And the silent understanding passing down
From daughter to daughter
Let the boys grow in the trees

Do you go to them
Or do you let them come to you
Do you stand in back
Afraid that you'll intrude
Deny yourself and hope someone will see
And live like a flower
While the boys grow in the trees

Last night I slept in sheets the color of fire
Tonight I lie alone again
And I curse my own desire
Sentenced first to burn and then to freeze
And watch by the window
Where the boys grew in the trees

For more information, please visit www.CarlySimon.com.
Look for Carly Simon's *Songs from the Trees (A Musical Memoir Collection)*
on CD/Digital.

Made in the
USA
Monee, IL